Playing for Time Theatre Company

Playing for Time Theatre Company
Perspectives from the Prison

Edited by
Annie McKean and Kate Massey-Chase

intellect Bristol, UK / Chicago, USA

First published in the UK in 2019 by
Intellect, The Mill, Parnall Road, Fishponds, Bristol, BS16 3JG, UK

First published in the USA in 2019 by
Intellect, The University of Chicago Press, 1427 E. 60th Street,
Chicago, IL 60637, USA

A catalogue record for this book is available from the
British Library.

Copy-editor: MPS Technologies
Cover designer: Alex Szumlas
Production manager: Tim Mitchell
Typesetting: Contentra Technologies
Cover photograph: Pa Ubu and Dogpile,
Ubu the King, 2007, © Toby Farrow (Hide the Shark).

Print ISBN: 978-1-78320-951-4
ePDF ISBN: 978-1-78320-953-8
ePUB ISBN: 978-1-78320-952-1

Printed and bound by TJ International, UK.

Contents

Acknowledgements

Thanks to all the people who were kind enough to read draft chapters: Dr Helen Grime, Dr Stevie Simkin, Richard Daniels, Paul Clough (who also sorted out Chapter 9 graphics), Kerryn Davies, Maggie McKean and George Platts. From early on, Kate Massey-Chase read my chapters and those of the other contributors and through this process has become my co-editor and most invaluable support.

My thanks go to the charitable trusts and foundations who supported the work including The European Social Fund, The Hampshire Crime Prevention Panel, Winchester City Council, T-Mobile, The Ernest Cook Trust, J. Paul Getty Jr. Charitable Trust and Arts Council England. HMP Winchester also made significant financial contributions to the work, as did the University of Winchester. The Vice Chancellor of the university, Joy Carter, was unwavering in her support of the productions. Heartfelt thanks also go to the university theatre technicians, particularly David Buss. Thanks are also due to the volunteers outside the university who have supported the shows, including Sandy Taylor, Sarah Litton and Helen Bliault. Rosa Martinez provided invaluable insights into the work during her research project on the 2006 show. Thanks also to Anna Herrmann, from Clean Break Theatre Company, and Michael Moody, previous director of Pimlico Opera, for their support.

Special thanks go to Laura Jones and Steve Manley, from LaunchPad Productions for their fabulous documentaries, Toby Farrow (Hide the Shark, toby@hidetheshark.com) who became the official photographer for the Playing for Time shows in 2006, and our team of directors and co-directors: Kerryn Davies, Bethan Clark, Brian Woolland, Marianne Sharp, Natalie Brett, Nick Cooke, Martin Constantine, Kate Massey-Chase, Tom Timms and Leigh Johnstone. Also thanks to project managers Steve Manley and Gina Theodotou.

I would like to thank the staff of HMP Winchester, the many prison officers at West Hill who were wholehearted in their support and the teams of governors who had the vision to see that supporting this kind of work with prisoners could make a difference. Particular thanks go to HMP Winchester Security Manager, Mark Watts, Heads of Learning and Skills, Russell Trent and Jo Bird, the prison music tutor, Bryan Robinson, and musical director and composer from 2006, Richard Daniels.

Thanks also go to the undergraduate students who took part in the projects and who worked tirelessly for nine weeks and more; they were the core and foundation of this work. Without their support and commitment we could never have achieved what we did.

Particular thanks go to my partner, George Platts, who patiently supported me on the journey of putting together this book about Playing for Time Theatre Company and who sat through a daily litany of ups and downs during the nine weeks of each of the eleven projects.

Preface

'It's nice to feel sort of human, like normal people...'

These are the words spoken by Prisoner L., one of the many participants who have made theatre with Playing for Time Theatre Company in its eleven-year history of working in HMP Winchester. He is talking about how taking part in the company's 2006 production of Joan Littlewood's *Oh What a Lovely War* makes him feel. This play was chosen by the company specifically due to its focus on themes related to the context of war and because some of the participating prisoners were ex-armed forces personnel. Prisoner L. continues, 'No, I'm not kidding, sometimes we're treated like animals, you know what I mean? And sometimes, you know, when we're out and doing the drama and that and talking to the students, you just forget about where you are. It's really good' (Chapter 1, p. 29).

Between January and September 2016, there were 324 recorded deaths in prison, the highest figure since records began. A third of these deaths were self-inflicted and rates of self-harm are also the highest on record, with 36,440 incidents recorded that year, between January and June. Within that time frame, there were also 2462 serious prisoner on prisoner assaults, and the Tornado Team (an elite team of prison officers sent in to prisons to bring riots under control) responded to over 400 incidents between January and September of the same year. This is more than in the whole of the previous year. The United Kingdom's prison system is overcrowded, with nearly one quarter of the prison population sharing cells designed for fewer occupants than they house, and with one in three of those who are serving sentences in local prisons spending less than two hours a day out of their cells. It is hardly surprising that Prisoner L. feels that the system treats him like an animal.

Those of us who are involved in making performances in prisons and young offender institutions know first-hand the positive effects the arts can have on our participants and the quality of their lives. As advocates for socially inclusive drama, we know that the arts can develop a range of soft skills and that producing a play demands hard work, technical skill and collaboration. We know that arts projects have concrete goals, develop concentration, discipline, teamwork, self-esteem, listening, self-awareness, empathy, control and can be the gateway to continued education. They can build responsibility and positive relationships. More than that, we know, or at least believe, that *everyone* should have the opportunity to participate in and create art. This book tells the story of how Playing for Time has invited inmates to explore, create, play and 'feel sort of human' for over a decade. It describes the challenges, compromises, joys, frustrations, the failures and the successes of working in secure settings.

Writing a preface for a book that is as significant as this one is a daunting task. Annie McKean has worked for over a decade making theatre with the prisoners of HMP Winchester, inviting them to 'feel … like normal people', in an abnormal world. This book tells the story of this work, which I was lucky enough to be invited to see in 2003 and 2013. It is a remarkable book that documents, analyses and critiques a sustained theatre practice within one institution over an eleven-year period. That alone makes it an extraordinary addition to the current literature on prison theatre. In her introduction, Annie states that the 'heart of this book is the prisoner experience'. I would say that Annie, her vision and her practice are the heart of this book, and that prisoner experience is at the centre of her work.

Over the years, I have repeatedly heard about Playing for Time Theatre Company from students who had worked with Annie; each talked of her energy, skill, enthusiasm and commitment to the field of applied theatre, particularly to the work in HMP Winchester. Many of them have come to the MA in Applied Theatre that I convene because of their work with Annie and the desire it has created in them to continue the work they started with her. Creating theatre in secure settings is not easy: practically and emotionally it is hard work. The directing and facilitating are a joy, but the regulations, environment and systems all work against artistry and creative risk-taking. Having worked within the criminal justice system as a trainee teacher, I found it to be both overwhelming and demoralising; now, working with students in prisons, I still find it a tremendous challenge. Annie has been a source of inspiration to me over the last decade. Her rigorous interrogation of the work, its ethics and its value to both inmates and students, as well her inventiveness and perspicacity, have been illuminating to me and my practice. I could not have been prouder when she asked me to write this preface, and I am overjoyed that this book is now going to print so those not lucky enough to experience her work first-hand can now benefit from her knowledge and wisdom.

Dr Selina Busby
Principal Lecturer, Course Leader MA Applied Theatre, Course Leader PG Cert Applied Theatre with Young People – Royal Central School of Speech and Drama, University of London.

Introduction

Annie McKean with Kate Massey-Chase

Playing for Time Theatre Company productions.

Date of production	Play	Playwright
2003	*Refuge*	Dawn Garrigan (unpublished)*
2005	*Our Country's Good*	Timberlake Wertenbaker
2006	*Oh What a Lovely War*	Joan Littlewood's Theatre Workshop
2007	*Ubu the King*	Alfred Jarry trans. Kenneth McLeish
2008	*Stand or Fall*	Brian Woolland*
2009	*The Convict's Opera*	Stephen Jeffreys
2010	*The Government Inspector*	Nikolai Gogol
2011	*Soul Traders*	Philip Glassborow (unpublished)*
2012	*The Accidental Impostor*	Adapted from *Accidental Death of an Anarchist* (Dario Fo) by Bethan Clark
2013	*Our Country's Good*	Timberlake Wertenbaker
2014	*The Fight in the Dog*	Rib Davis (unpublished)*

*Professional playwrights were commissioned to write plays for Playing for Time in 2003, 2008, 2011 and 2014. Arts Council England funding for new writing was key to this process. Other plays were chosen for their content and relevance to the participating prisoners.

Introduction: Setting the scene

> You are in a one-way tunnel and when you are let out you go back to what you did
> years ago because that's the only thing you know.
> (anonymous female prisoner in HMP Winchester 2002)

The intention of this publication is to reflect upon over a decade's worth of theatre
productions in HMP Winchester. Eleven plays were staged by Playing for Time Theatre
Company between 2003 and 2014. They were framed within accredited programmes of
education that focused on literacy and transferable skills. This book is a collection of writing
about these theatre projects, with contributions from a variety of people involved in the
work. The interdisciplinary nature of the contributors – coming from diverse fields and
backgrounds – is central to both the book and the theatre company's intention of bringing
together a multiplicity of perspectives. The contributors have not attempted to offer a
comprehensive account of the politics of crime and punishment, nor to deconstruct the
failings and deficiencies of the current criminal justice system in the United Kingdom.
However, a number of recurring themes weave their way through this collection. Augmented
by participants' testimony, the threads of a variety of arguments related to arts projects in
prisons challenge current thinking about what works in terms of rehabilitation and the
particular contribution the arts might make.

> The arts make us feel connected to one another and less isolated.
> Through the arts we share an emotion and that sharing connects us with each other and
> we realise we all feel the same emotions. The arts are our last hope.
> (Miller 2003: 6)

The arts may be our last hope; they may be one piece of a complex jigsaw of personal and
social support. In this book, we hope to show how even when we are losing hope, the arts
might be a light in what felt like a one-way tunnel, guiding us down a new path or inspiring
us to go on.

The context: HMP Winchester, UK

Between 2003 and 2014 there were repeated changes to the regimes and management in the prison. At the time of writing, the prison complex in Winchester comprises a Category B prison holding male prisoners on remand and adult young offenders, who were moved to the prison in 2013 after the closure of HMP Reading. The main Victorian remand prison holds 561 men. Within the site is a newer building, West Hill, which is a Category C prison and The Hearn, a 40-bed Category D prison holding a total of 129 prisoners. The 'certified normal accommodation' of the three prisons is 469, a figure which reveals the state of overcrowding of these prisons which have a total population of 690 male prisoners (Her Majesty's Inspectorate of Prisons 2017: 7).

In England and Wales prisons are categorised according to the sentence and the severity of the crime a prisoner is convicted of:

> Category A prisoners are those that would pose the most threat to the public, the police or national security should they escape. Security conditions in Category A prisons are designed to make escape impossible for these prisoners. Category B prisoners do not need to be held in the highest security conditions but, for Category B prisoners, the potential for escape should be made very difficult. Category C prisoners cannot be trusted in open conditions but are considered to be prisoners who are unlikely to make a determined escape attempt. Category D prisoners can be trusted in open conditions.
>
> (Offenders' Families Helpline 2017)

Prisoners who have not been sentenced or who are held on remand (awaiting trial) are generally housed in a Category B prison unless they have been provisionally categorised as Category A. Categories will be reviewed and changed depending on length of sentence. Category A prisoners will not have their first category review until two years after their initial categorisation; if a prisoner is judged as low-risk or less likely to make an escape attempt, then they may be moved to a lower category prison.

In 2014, HMP Winchester was reclassified as a Resettlement prison; this means that prisoners coming to the end of a sentence who come from the area will be moved to Winchester for at least the last three months of their sentence. Resettlement involves prison staff and outside agencies working together to find prisoners accommodation, training and work. Writing this at the end of 2017, the prison system in England and Wales appears to be in a state of crisis. The idea that 'prison works' has informed sentencing policies over the last twenty years, resulting in a doubling of the prison population to 84,737. In January 2017, the number of men serving custodial sentences was 80,870 and the number of women was 3,867 (Official Statistics 2016). Drug use in prisons in the United Kingdom is at epidemic levels and violence and self-harm have increased exponentially. A government White Paper, *Prison Safety and Reform*, published on 3 November 2016, outlined the UK Government's proposals for future legislation. Proposals include more autonomy and devolved powers for prison governors, strengthening the role of prison inspections and improved safety levels in prisons. The White Paper proposals are set against a backdrop of cuts to prison budgets, which have been made year-on-year with a consequent decrease in the number of prison officers. In November 2016, the UK Government promised an increase of 2,500 frontline prison staff in addition to the extra 400 staff that has been promised to the ten least safe prisons in the country; HMP Winchester is one of those ten prisons. Even with these staff increases the service will still have 4,500 fewer officers than in 2010 (Travis 2016).

Although the government White Paper proposes reform, none of this is particularly radical. For example, there seems to be no political will to close down prisons and impose non-custodial sentences for all but the most violent offenders. Most of the focus is on making existing prisons safer places for staff and prisoners. There is some new thinking in terms of education and training, with prison governors being put in charge of commissioning education provision and deciding on the priorities for education and training. The ways in which prisoners can be supported upon release from prison are also highlighted. In terms of education, proposals within the White Paper are focused on the development of functional skills (Maths and English) and training programmes, designed to equip prisoners with a skills-base and accreditation for future employment. However, a recently published report on prison education notes the following:

> The provision of art, drama and music courses is not a core part of current OLASS[1] arrangements. Where they do operate, and where there have been one-off projects or performances with visiting arts companies, they are often the first thing that prisoners, staff and Governors tell me about. The arts are one route towards engaging prisoners when they have had negative experience of traditional classroom subjects, or struggle with self-esteem and communication. They can be the first step towards building confidence for more formal learning.
>
> (Coates 2016: 29)

In July 2017, Her Majesty's Inspectorate of Prisons published a report on the workings of the Inspectorate system. Under the section entitled 'Men's Prison Expectations', a set of guidelines focus on the delivery of creative activities with the expectation that these will promote learning and boost employability, improve health and well-being and enable prisoners to reflect on their lives and social responsibilities. It is interesting to note that the same section that relates to 'Women's Prison Expectations' has not been updated since 2014 and contains no references to creative activities.

In view of the parlous state of the prison estate, it is therefore timely to consider what kinds of interventions can make a difference and whether it is possible to see the arts as part of education and training provision, designed to support processes of rehabilitation. The 'what works' debate underpins questions about how prisoners' lives can be turned around, particularly in view of the current high rates of reoffending (Craig, Dixon and Gannon

2013; McGuire 1999). 'Currently, almost half of all prisoners are reconvicted within a year of release. The cost of reoffending by former prisoners is estimated to be up to £15 billion a year' (Ministry of Justice 2016: 5).

Desisting from a life of crime

Understanding the process of desistance is central to assessing the impact of the arts on patterns of offending behaviour. Desistance is generally understood as a process involving change that will lead from an offending lifestyle to one of non-offending. This process is often seen as having two stages. The first, primary desistance, where an offender stops offending and the second, secondary desistance, where the offender is able to make changes to their life, which support and maintain a continuing, non-offending lifestyle (Maruna 2001).

When assessing offenders' attempts to desist from patterns of offending behaviour, criminologists often cite changes in levels of offenders' maturity, an increase in their ability to form positive relationships and changes in the ways in which they narrate their own history as indicative of their trajectory away from offending. These shifts in identity construction require the development of a skill set that includes self-expression, reflectivity, empathy and imagination (Albertson 2015: 278). In Chapter 1, I reflect on the ways in which experience of the creative arts often provides prisoners with opportunities to develop and practise these skills. Such projects also allow prisoners to create a narrative that is constructed around an exploration of potential and success rather than one focused on past failures. Experiencing the arts provides participants with the opportunity to explore alternative selves where identity is not defined and constructed through a history of offending activities. Expanding on this, in Chapter 6, Massey-Chase also considers how theatre and storytelling can impact on a prisoner's sense of self and identity. The possibilities for personal and social development are a constant theme throughout this book, as are the ways in which participating in theatre projects allows prisoners to 'form positive identities, build new narratives and build positive relationships with peers, staff and family' (Bilby, Caulfield and Ridley 2013: 6).

Playing for Time Theatre Company

Playing for Time Theatre Company – so named by the women prisoners who took part in the first Playing for Time show – was based at the University of Winchester. Over the eleven years of staging theatre productions in HMP Winchester several thousand members of the general public and prisoners' family members and friends came into the prison to see the shows. In Chapter 2, I outline the model of practice that was developed by the company for delivering theatre projects in West Hill, HMP Winchester. The story of its inception is outlined briefly below.

Between 1999 and 2002, I ran drama workshops in HMP Winchester's male Category B prison and West Hill, at that time a women's Category C prison. During these workshops, I observed the impact that the work had on male and female prisoners. I also became aware of the differences in the experience of women in prison to those of male prisoners and the different criminogenic factors that resulted in women's offending behaviour. In 2001–02, I conducted semi-structured interviews with women prisoners. It was as a result of the interviews and observations of work in the men's and women's prisons that the first theatre project was conceived. I found myself deeply moved by the ways in which the women I interviewed talked about their experiences of the criminal justice system, the waste of lives, the impact of a mother's custodial sentence on their children, and the injustice of sentencing women with mental health issues and those whose lives had been characterised by abuse in childhood and/or as adults.

In the words of some of the female prisoners, taken from the interviews:

Your life stands still here.

It's awful to lock a mother away. The children, they don't understand. They feel rejected because suddenly 'Mummy's gone' and they don't understand why. They're not just punishing the mothers, they're punishing the children too.

I have never felt safe in prison. I felt safer on the street because I can run. If I am in danger I can run. In here I feel trapped. I just want to walk in the woods.

You get out, you've lost everything. Where do you start? Where do you go for help? You don't know where to turn.

This first play, *Refuge* by Dawn Garrigan, was staged with female prisoners in April 2003. In Chapter 3, I offer a close reading of the development of the only show staged with women prisoners and in Chapter 4, Thompson writes about the historical background and research undertaken for the play. In 2004, West Hill was closed to female prisoners due to overcrowding in the male prison estate in the South East of England.

From 2005 onwards, the University of Winchester worked in partnership with HMP Winchester for a further ten years, staging annual theatre productions with male prisoners and undergraduate students working together. Because only one of the Playing for Time shows was staged with female prisoners, there is more emphasis throughout this book on writing about the male prisoner experience, as ten of eleven shows we staged in West Hill, HMP Winchester, were with men. Working with male prisoners was very different to working with the women. Sometimes the men we worked with found it difficult to open up and reflect on their lives, unlike most of the women who were passionate about using the play to communicate their experiences to an audience. However, the framework of drama and theatre work often enabled many of the men we worked with to talk about and reflect on their lives. Working with male prisoners convinced me, as it had with women prisoners, that prison was not the right place for most of them. I remain convinced to this day that only the most violent offenders should serve a custodial sentence and that those with significant mental health issues, social problems and a lack of education and training should have a different kind of experience other than that of incarceration within the prison system. There are those who should be removed from society, for a period of time, for their own safety and that of others but the current prison system with its low levels of staffing and lack of specialist staff is not the place for those who need treatment and care from highly trained staff in fit-for-purpose facilities. I am transparent about this belief here, as it has informed both the delivery of the work and the writing of this book.

Most of the participating male prisoners were coming to the end of their sentence; some were serving life sentences and others serving shorter sentences. We worked with prisoners who had committed crimes ranging from petty to violent. Prisoners arriving at West Hill are risk assessed for education, work and training programmes. Our theatre projects were framed within programmes of accreditation and so prisoners who were recruited to take part in the theatre projects were assessed for their suitability to take part in education activities. Over the years we have found that participating in arts projects has provided access to education for people in prison who had previously found it neither accessible nor engaging. The ways in which creative writing helped prisoners process their experience of taking part in a play and supported an exit strategy are discussed by Boucher in Chapter 10. Chapter 11 is a detailed reflection, part of a programme of accreditation, in diary form, by Scott, a prisoner, in response to his participation in the 2013 production of *Our Country's Good*.

In Chapter 5, Woolland examines the ways in which staging theatre in the context of a prison reanimates debates about the power of theatre, the anxiety that it has provoked in the past and the tensions such work creates. It sits uneasily between the contradictions inherent in a system that addresses the rehabilitation agenda whilst remaining essentially punitive. Another analysis of theatre practice and process is offered by Sharp in Chapter 8, who critiques the effect of context, in relation to the performance in a prison of *Our Country's Good* by Timberlake Wertenbaker, a play that explores the dichotomy between punishment and rehabilitation. Rehearsal processes and ensemble practices are also examined in some detail in this chapter.

We have always seen this work as a small part of the jigsaw of activities that might lead a prisoner to seek self-determination and abstinence from a life of crime. I believe that prisoners' responses to the work will depend on where they are in their journey to constructing a different, non-criminal identity. At the most basic level, prisoners will find that time passes more quickly and enjoyably as they socialise with others, particularly the staff and student teams who work with them and engage in activities that are not prison focused. Working in a safe and creative space, with people who will not judge them in relation to their past behaviour, means that some participating prisoners have been able to articulate their experience of the impact of the work, including the acquisition of transferable skills. In the future, these skills may be used to gain agency and control over their lives (Albertson

2015: 282). It is possible, as evidenced by one of the members of Over the Wall Theatre Company in Chapter 12, that experience of a theatre project might provide a catalyst for change and a turning point in a person's life.

Due to a lack of longitudinal research, we can only evidence the changes that have been observed during the projects (and, to a small extent, retrospectively – see Chapter 12 by Mackie). However Henry, writing in Chapter 9, offers positive results from a small scale quantitative research study conducted during the 2010 production. Prisoners have often stated that they have had enough of their previous lifestyle and that taking part in a theatre production has prompted them to consider what changes they may want to make to their lives and reimagine their futures. Chapter 12 offers hope for long-term change, secondary desistance, as ex-prisoners and others who have suffered disadvantage in their lives reflect on how a sustained experience of taking part in drama has supported their efforts to maintain a non-offending lifestyle, or one that is not dependent on substance abuse.

In 11 years of staging theatre productions in HMP Winchester, there is much to say about the complexities of each show including the prisoners' engagement with the work, the aesthetics of each piece, rehearsal processes and much more. It is beyond the scope of this book to afford every show the detail it deserves. Some productions get more attention in this book, yet the case studies they provide are relevant to many of the productions we have staged and highlight issues that transcend particular projects.

Playing for Time in context

Playing for Time's work sits within this country's vibrant and varied canon of prison theatre, which itself sits within the broader national picture of arts in criminal justice contexts. The National Criminal Justice Arts Alliance, the leading national network supporting the arts in criminal justice, has nearly 800 members (NCJAA 2017), and its website is a key resource for locating evidence of the efficacy of arts in criminal justice work and to connect with the varied organisations carrying it out. Different prison theatre companies across the United Kingdom have different approaches, priorities and artistic styles. Geese Theatre (UK) is one of the most well-known prison theatre companies, based in Birmingham and established in the United Kingdom by Clark Baim in 1987, after he had worked extensively with the original Geese Theatre (USA), a touring company established in 1980 by John Bergman (Geese 2017). Like Theatre in Prisons and Probation (TiPP) Centre, their intentions are explicitly rehabilitative; Balfour describes Geese as 'a company specialising in the use of theatre to focus on an individual's responsibility for their offending behaviour' (2009: 349). Indeed, *The Geese Theatre Handbook* identifies social learning theory, cognitive-behavioural theory and role theory as the theoretical frameworks that inform their work (Baim et al. 2002). Geese are also famous for their use of theatrical metaphor and mask work, which not only carries a distinctive aesthetic, but is also crucial to their theory base.

In 'recent literature relating to the arts in the criminal justice sector there is an explicit move away from cognitive-behavioural approaches towards engaging with offenders on a more affective or imaginative level' (Hughes 2005: 58), as theatre practice that is overly instrumental is seen as reductive and 'risks sacrificing the very aspects of the work that make it uniquely valuable' (Davey, Day and Balfour 2015: 800). This mirrors the theoretical turns in broader applied theatre discourse; see, for example, the move from effect to affect, led by Thompson (2009), and the concern for the aesthetic.

Alongside its other prison theatre work, which it describes as having a 'strong, simple, beautiful aesthetic', Synergy Theatre Project, in London, is committed to producing new plays: 'both professional commissions and work by prisoners/ex-prisoners to put unheard voices into the mainstream', running multiple playwriting courses and script writing competitions (Synergy 2017). Other companies have different priorities and models of practice. Safe Ground uses drama to explore family relationships, for example with its programmes 'Family Man' and 'Fathers Inside', whereas Clean Break Theatre Company works with women with experience of the criminal justice system or at risk of offending, through their education programme and the staging of new plays.

There are a number of key texts about prison theatre (Thompson 1998; Balfour 2004; Shailor 2010; McAvinchey 2011; Scott-Douglas, Palfrey and Fernie 2011; Trounstine 2001). Davey, Day and Balfour's exploration of 'the potential for re-positioning theatre practice in criminal justice settings within emerging alternative frameworks such as criminological theories of desistance from crime' (2015: 799) makes the case for the literature in this field to intersect with other discourses. Although this book does not position Playing for Time's work within a single framework – Hughes's review of the research literature, practice and theory on arts in the criminal justice system gives a helpful breakdown of the key theoretical frameworks in prison theatre practice and the main models of practice (2005: 52–55) – we hope that the multiple perspectives found in this book illustrate our commitment to providing a space for the multiplicity of voices and perspectives at the heart of our projects. This case study of Playing for Time's work thus provides an original contribution to the field, due to its extended focus on the evolution of this unique theatre company, its distinct model of practice and the multiple perspectives on the work provided by the range of authors in this collection.

Learning from the learners…

Although most of the names of the participants in the eleven Playing for Time theatre productions do not appear in this book, I will never forget a single one of the men and women who took part. We are lucky in having photographic and film records of the work. We also have the programmes from the shows where the participants were asked to write a biography for the programme prior to the performances. Bravely stepping into a place of some vulnerability, they offered up thoughts about whether or not they had experience of drama or theatre before taking part in the shows, their experience so far and the difference that participating in the work had made to them.

> The reason I wanted to do this project is because it is something I have never done before and wanted to challenge myself. I wanted to bring myself out of my comfort zone, I am so pleased I have taken up this project and proud of what I have achieved so far. Whilst doing this project I have gained confidence, motivation and creativity. I have enjoyed the singing, the acting and the overall journey of the project. From doing this project I really feel I can take the skills I have learnt and use them in the future in the outside world.
>
> (Prisoner L., programme 2014)

> I felt the drama course was an opportunity to do something new and offered something constructive to which I could apply and push myself. It reaffirmed that change from within is possible and shows that when people have confidence in you, encourage and give you responsibility, then you develop confidence in yourself. It shows how individual contributions interlink and when channelled and directed towards a common objective can achieve something in which everyone can be proud. We may not become actors when we get released but we proved to ourselves that we could tap into our creativity, concentrate, take direction and contribute suggestions, all imperative life skills that can be transposed and applied to situations in the outside world. For me it is this aspect of the drama project that has made it a positive, innovative approach to supplementing the rehabilitation process.
>
> (Vinnie, programme 2008)

We have met people who have endured unbearable cruelty and abuse, whose lives have been characterised by social exclusion, poverty and deprivation. However, their stoicism and humour has often transcended their histories and the negativity of the prison environment. We have worked with very few 'career criminals'; the people we met tended to exist at the very margins of society. Hearing people's stories constantly reinforces the fact that inequality is deeply embedded in our society. In the main, those of us working on these projects have come from relatively secure family backgrounds and we have been able to thrive in the education system and the world of work. This is vastly different to most of the people we met through undertaking these projects. In Chapter 7, I explore the undergraduate student experience, which was layered with the insights they gained through taking part in the projects, as they compared their lives with what they had learnt from working with the prisoners.

We believe that prison theatre projects should place participants at the centre of the work, particularly when they have been made partners in the process. The names of the participants in the on-campus drama group (see Chapter 12), have been used with their permission; however, in the rest of the book, apart from Scott, Vinnie, and Richie whose names we have used with their permission, prisoners' names have been anonymised in order to protect their identity. They are subsequently referred to as Prisoner (letter of the alphabet); this is done for clarity (a term such as Participant would have resonated more closely with our ethos, yet could have caused confusion with the student participants), although we recognise that foregrounding this aspect of their identity sits in opposition with the ethos of our work. We thus use this term reluctantly, for want of a better option, and hope readers of this book will understand our decision. The prisoners' and ex-prisoners' voices are not at the end of this book because they are the least important, quite the contrary: we think the last word should go to them.

The prisoner experience is at the heart of this book. As I discuss in Chapter 2, once the house lights were dimmed, the stage lights came up and the music began, the prisoners were the ones responsible for what happened next. Our projects offered them agency and autonomy. The prisoners were the subjects and not the objects for the duration of every performance. After each performance they were given a brief period of time to mingle with the audience, receive praise and talk about the work, to their friends, families and people they had never met before. It was at this point that they were able to celebrate, with the audience (made up of the prisoners' and students' friends and family, and members of the general public), their strengths, talents and achievements, and to be seen as artists in their own right. It is difficult to quantify the impact that this experience had on the participating prisoners, but their voices, heard throughout this book, attest to the impact the work had on them, not least the way they viewed themselves as a result of the experience.

References

Albertson, K. (2015), 'Creativity, self-exploration and change: Creative arts-based activities' contribution to desistance narratives', *The Howard Journal*, 54:3, pp. 277–91.

Baim, C., Brookes S. and Mountford, S. (2002), *The Geese Theatre Handbook*, Winchester: Waterside Press.

Balfour, M. (ed.) (2004), *Theatre in Prison: Theory and Practice*, Bristol: Intellect.

Balfour, M. (2009), 'The politics of intention: Looking for a theatre of little changes', *Research in Drama Education: The Journal of Applied Theatre and Performance*, 14:3, pp. 347–359.

Bilby, C., Caulfield, L. and Ridley, R. (2013), *Re-imagining Futures: Exploring Arts Interventions and the Process of Desistance*, London: Arts Alliance, http://artsevidence.org.uk/media/uploads/re-imagining-futures-research-report-final.pdf. Accessed 16 February 2017.

Coates, S. (2016), *Unlocking Potential: A Review of Education in Prison*, London: Her Majesty's Stationery Office.

Craig, L., Dixon, L. and Gannon, T. (eds) (2013), *What Works in Offender Rehabilitation: An Evidence-Based Approach to Assessment and Treatment*, Chichester: Wiley-Blackwell.

Davey, L., Day, A. and Balfour, M. (2015), 'Performing desistance: How might theories of desistance from crime help us understand the possibilities of prison theatre?', *International Journal of Offender Therapy and Comparative Criminology*, 59:8, pp. 798–809.

Geese Theatre Company (2017), 'Our history', http://www.geese.co.uk/about/our-history/. Accessed 1 October 2017.

Her Majesty's Inspectorate of Prisons (2016), Report on an Announced Inspection of HMP Winchester, https://www.justiceinspectorates.gov.uk/hmiprisons/wp-content/uploads/sites/4/2016/11/HMP-Winchester-Web-2016.pdf. Accessed 21 September 2017.

Her Majesty's Inspectorate of Prisons (2017), 'Home/Our expectations', http://www.justice inspectorates.gov.uk/hmiprisons/our-expectations/prison-expectations/. Accessed 3 November 2017.

Hughes, J. (2005), 'Doing the arts justice: A review of research literature, practice and theory', http://webarchive.nationalarchives.gov.uk/+/http:/www.culture.gov.uk/NR/rdonlyres/D4B445EE-4BCC-4F6C-A87A-C55A0D45D205/0/Doingartsjusticefinal.pdf. Accessed 8 October 2017.

Jackson, A. (2007), *Theatre, Education and the Making of Meanings: Art or Instrument?* Manchester: Manchester University Press.

Maruna, S. (2001), *Making Good: How Ex-Convicts Reform and Rebuild Their Lives*, Washington, DC: American Psychological Association.

McAvinchey, C. (2011), *Theatre & Prison*, London: Palgrave Macmillan.

McGuire, J. (ed.) (1999), *What Works: Reducing Re-offending: Guidelines from Research and Practice*, Chichester: Wiley-Blackwell.

Miller, A. (2003), *Drama in Schools Arts Council England* 2nd ed., London: Sayer.

Ministry of Justice (2016), *Prison Safety and Reform*, London: Her Majesty's Stationery Office, https://www.gov.uk/government/uploads/system/uploads/attachment_data/file/565014/cm-9350-prison-safety-and-reform-_web_.pdf. Accessed 16 February 2016.

NCJAA (2017), 'National Criminal Justice Arts Alliance', https://www.artsincriminaljustice.org.uk. Accessed 17 October 2017.

Offenders' Families Helpline (2017), http://www.offendersfamilieshelpline.org/. Accessed 3 November 2017.

Official Statistics (2016), 'Population bulletin: Weekly 30 December 2016', https://www.gov.uk/government/statistics/prison-population-figures-2016. Accessed 16 February 2017.

Scott-Douglas, A., Palfrey, S. and Fernie, E. (2011), *Shakespeare Inside: The Bard Behind Bars*, New York: Bloomsbury Continuum.

Shailor, J. (ed.) (2010), *Performing New Lives: Prison Theatre*, London: Jessica Kingsley.

Synergy (2017), 'Artistic policy', http://www.synergytheatreproject.co.uk/artistic-policy/. Accessed 17 October 2017.

Thompson, J. (1998), *Prison Theatre: Practices and Perspectives*, London: Jessica Kingsley.

—— (2009), *Performance Affects: Applied Theatre and the End of Effect*, London: Palgrave MacMillan.

Travis, A. (2016), 'Ken Clarke: Prison changes won't work until sentencing is reformed', *The Guardian*, 3 November, https://www.theguardian.com/society/2016/nov/03/ken-clarke-prison-reforms-sentencing-liz-truss. Accessed 16 February 2017.

Trounstine, J. (2001), *Shakespeare Behind Bars: The Power of Drama in a Women's Prison*, New York: St. Martin's Press.

Note

1 Offender Learning and Skills Service: The Skills Funding Agency manages the Offenders' Learning and Skills Service (OLASS) to integrate offender education with mainstream academic and vocational provision. OLASS allows offenders in custody to receive education and training.

Chapter 1

Transformation and Challenge in Insecure Worlds: The Arts in Secure Institutions

Annie McKean

T his chapter examines how the arts, and theatre in particular, have something to offer those who find themselves serving a custodial sentence and explores the ways in which theatre can offer opportunities for self-reflexivity and potential change. Notions of transformation are central to the chapter but are highly contested and difficult to evidence (Nicholson 2005: 12). However, this chapter offers perspectives on change that are supported by comments made by prisoners who participated in the work. This is important as personal narratives are increasingly being seen as credible evidence in research contexts even though they do not fit the quantitative research paradigm (Maruna 2001). The chapter also examines the ways in which arts projects are mediated by the complex variables present when working in a secure environment. These include the barriers created by institutional power and the politics of punishment. In addition to discussing the ways in which the arts can enable prisoners to transcend the difficulties they face, the ways in which their backgrounds can inhibit full participation in the work are also considered. Finally, the challenge of evaluating the efficacy of this kind of work is framed within the context of problems that prisoners face upon release.

Dancing between the shards

In 2006, Playing for Time Theatre Company staged a production of Joan Littlewood's music theatre piece, *Oh What a Lovely War*. I had many dreams after the project was over. The most striking and final dream was one in which the production team, students and prisoners were in a black box studio. We were all wearing black tops and trousers and had bare feet. The floor was lit from above. Covering the floor, with spaces in between, were large chunks of broken coloured glass with razor sharp edges, the kind of glass that Victorian bottles were made from. The lights from above coloured and refracted the glass creating splinters and shafts of light. We were rehearsing a movement sequence that meant we had to step carefully between the pieces of glass so as not to cut our feet. The movement piece was beautiful and was rehearsed in complete silence: a state rarely achieved no matter how many times the director asked for it. This dream, rich with metaphors for our work and my feelings about the process, highlights the deep emotional resonances these projects can have.

For me, writing about eleven years of theatre work in one prison, this dream is important in its symbolism. I am reflecting on experiences that are often beautiful, uplifting and exhilarating but also fraught with contradictions and difficulty. The sense of precariousness and insecurity of working in a secure environment is ever-present. We are working with people whose lives are largely invisible to the rest of society and whose stories remain behind locked doors. Many of them are in prison because of lives characterised by social, cultural and economic deprivation and early childhood experiences. Some of them have histories of substance abuse and personality traits that make them seek thrills and excitement rather than routine and responsibility (Maruna 2001: 11). This is often the case for younger men in the prison population. Additionally, prisoners are likely to come from deprived areas with limited opportunities for employment. The people we have worked with, on the whole, had low levels of literacy and often had mental health issues. In 2012, a Ministry of Justice study analysed the backgrounds of a sample of 3,849 prisoners sentenced to short and long sentences. Of the prisoners sampled, 24 per cent had been in care at some point in their childhood, 29 per cent had experienced abuse, 41 per cent had observed domestic violence, 59 per cent of prisoners stated that they had regularly played truant from school and 60 per cent had been suspended or temporarily excluded or expelled. The study found that prisoners with these kinds of issues were more likely to be reconvicted than those without (Williams, Papadopoulou and Booth 2012: i–ii). However, a deficit model that is predicated on people's issues and problems does not do these participants justice; they have potential that can be unlocked by allowing them to engage in activities that enable them to perceive themselves differently and to find some kind of transcendence from their lived reality.

The arts and change

There is a vast body of research and literature that examines a variety of approaches to the vexed question of imprisonment and rehabilitation. During the time that I started to run drama workshops in HMP Winchester, key questions related to offender management were encompassed by concepts of what works and what does not work in terms of programmes designed to prevent reoffending (McGuire 2013). These included interventions framed within models of punishment – sometimes characterised as 'short, sharp shock' approaches to prison regimes, which were favoured by the Conservative Government in the United Kingdom in the 1980s. The 1990s saw a shift back to interventions that were focused on addressing individual's patterns of offending behaviour, including psychodynamic practices and behavioural and cognitive-behavioural treatment programmes (Hollin 2001: 3–15). Some cognitive-behavioural programmes utilise recognised drama methodologies such as role play and the enactment and critiquing of various scenarios. For example, Geese Theatre Company work in a number of contexts within the criminal justice system and deliver drama programmes that are focused on addressing patterns of offending behaviour. Their work is underpinned by social learning theory, cognitive-behavioural theory and role theory (Baim, Brookes and Mountford 2002).

The prison service in England and Wales currently delivers a number of cognitive skills training programmes, including one based on Reasoning and Rehabilitation

(R&R), a Canadian programme developed in 1988 by Ross, Fabiano and Ewles (Palmer 2003: 159). One such programme is the Enhanced Thinking Skills (ETS) programme, which is targeted at medium risk, male and female, adult offenders (Palmer 2003: 164); this programme was delivered in HMP Winchester until quite recently. The cognitive-behavioural approach of the programme targets social-cognitive deficits and comprises twenty two-hour sessions. The Playing for Time model of practice and an ETS programme are worlds apart in their approaches; ETS focuses directly on prisoners' experiences of the criminal justice system and patterns of offending behaviour and addresses perceived deficits in social cognition. Our work does not start with a deficit model; it begins with an exploration of the individual and the group's strengths and abilities and aims to support, develop and extend these within the parameters of the project. However, the work will inevitably challenge deficits in prisoner behaviour and perception of their self and others because it is essential for the development of team and ensemble work that pro-social behaviour and values are encouraged.

Palmer, in an analysis of the ways in which cognitive-behavioural theory can be used as a framework to analyse criminal behaviour, suggests that there is evidence to suggest that people who offend are more likely than non-offenders to have a variety of social-cognitive deficits (2003: 17). These include:

- self-control/impulsivity;
- concrete vs. abstract reasoning;
- social perspective-taking and empathy;
- social problem-solving.

(2003: 18)

Instant, as opposed to delayed, gratification is linked to lack of self-control. It is difficult for prisoners who have not experienced drama before to comprehend why they are being asked to do what they have to do in order to achieve the end result. Gratification is necessarily delayed and prisoners have to overcome moments in the process where they cannot see the point of what they are being asked to do, even though activities are always framed within a rationale that is shared with them. Prisoners have to overcome the impulse to give up when things get difficult or when rehearsal processes are frustrating. In order to function effectively as a team they have to control feelings of anger and also learn to tolerate differences in others.

The understanding of narrative structures and characters' motivations in a play requires complex levels of abstract reasoning. Concrete thinking patterns are revealed when some prisoners are unable to create improvisations in which symbol, metaphor and non-naturalistic forms are explored. Instead, they devise action-orientated sequences that reference behaviours, often violent, which are close to their own experiences. Getting beneath the surface of actions and considering their cause and effect is important in terms of developing reflective thinking skills. Working within the context of a play allows prisoners to examine causal relationships; they are asked to consider why characters in a play behave as they do and the impact the behaviour has on others, and to contemplate other decisions they could have made and the possible outcomes. Additionally, being able to see situations and events from other people's points of view is central to an understanding of character and motivation. Empathy is important in social perspective-taking, and the analogy of 'putting ourselves in someone else's shoes' in order to see the world from a perspective different to our own is embodied by drama strategies such as 'hot-seating', which deepen exploration and understanding of the thoughts and feelings of a character in a play.

Drama is essentially a social activity, and social interaction is essential to the development of social perspective-taking. Interaction with the staff and student teams, coupled with analysis and engagement with themes and characters in plays, is fertile ground for explorations of self and others. Work in the arts provides a context where the prisoner can utilise their pre-existing skills and knowledge, for example, 'performing' in court, but redirect it to create a very different kind of experience. Theatre gives someone the chance to channel energy that has previously gone into anti-social/criminal activities into pro-social behaviour and pro-social activities.

The arts and identity

The lives of people serving custodial sentences are sometimes characterised by a lack of opportunities and experiences that might help them constantly review and revisit their construction of self. If these interactions are limited to a particular social group, such as those operating within a criminal subculture, then an individual's perspective on life will be necessarily shaped by those encounters. In a criminal context, people may see themselves in roles such as the 'thief' or the 'addict', but they also have other roles in life such as that of the 'good friend', 'loving parent' or 'supportive relative' (Maruna 2001: 89). It is possible that taking part in a play with high levels of achievement can be another role that a prisoner can append to their repertoire of roles; this being one with many positive and pro-social measures that can be internalised and revisited after the event.

Taking part in a play gives participants the opportunity to re-imagine a different kind of identity. In order to do this they have to believe in themselves and the characters they are playing in order for the audience to suspend their disbelief and invest in the fictitious world of the play. As Shailor comments, the opportunity to take part in theatre 'creates a dual consciousness: one is both oneself, and not oneself; a character, and not that character' (2011: 22). This consciousness could be experienced as liminal space: the space between performance and reality. Brazilian theatre practitioner, Augusto Boal, calls this space 'aesthetic space' (1995: 20–23) and refers to the concept of 'metaxis', which is discussed further in Chapter 6 by Massey-Chase. The founder of psychodrama, Albert Moreno, calls it 'the locus nascendi [...] the place of birth and re-birth' (Feldhendler in Schutzman and Cohen-Cruz 1994: 96). It is a therapeutic, transitional space in which dreams and fantasies can collide with reality, stimulating thoughts about different possibilities: a space between the subjective and the objective experience, between the real and the imaginary.

In 2011, Prisoner L. commented on the process of taking on a role and playing a character:

> I've been cast as Danny Frowst and I can relate to him because he's got conflicts, you know. It's about doing right from wrong and as a prisoner that's something you can really relate to, so I saw a lot of similarities there ... it's an achievement, not everyone in jail can sort of get, you know. I came to jail and didn't expect to achieve much but it helps you explore aspects of yourself perhaps you didn't know existed and just sort of discover the talent I didn't even know I had.
>
> (Jones and Manley 2011)

He was clearly aware of being himself and of not being himself. The process of taking on a role and playing a character, of being oneself and not being oneself, of playing with multiple identities, creates opportunities for reflection and evaluation. Prisoners can discuss how like or unlike the character they are playing they are. They can critique the choices and motivation of the character in terms of what they think they might do themselves in that situation. Theatre develops and nurtures self-awareness and allows participants to reflect on what makes them human and what they have in common with others (Shailor 2011: 22).

Working in the arts, like a number of activities undertaken in prisons, gives people an emotional and experiential escape from the constraints of life in a secure institution. A theatre project offers participants a safe place to engage in work, which can give them temporary respite from the routine of the prison regime. This kind of experience can transcend the constraints of prisoners' backgrounds, such as cultural and generational differences, and their history. Through undertaking the work they can find freedom – in the present moment, in artistic expression, creativity and self-discovery. Prisoners can gain a sense of renewed hope in themselves and their future. When interviewed by the Resettlement Team (Tribal[1]) in the prison in 2011, members of the *Soul Traders* (Glassborow 2011) cast said that they greatly enjoyed the experience and articulated important indicators of personal development and change. They all felt they had gained confidence, found courage they didn't know they possessed, discovered skills they didn't know they had and learnt a great deal about themselves. They seemed to *like* themselves more; this strong sense of change should not be underestimated or undervalued.

The experience of taking part in a theatre project also allows a prisoner to see that other opportunities might be open to them. Prisoners answering the question 'what do you think will remain with you in the future?' in 2011 said that it was the realisation that they could achieve more than they ever thought possible. They also said that they felt they were more capable of trying out new experiences having undertaken something that they might otherwise never have done before. Taking part in theatre work can encourage participants to cross boundaries that constrain and limit the ways in which they construct their sense of self and identity. In the same feedback session a prisoner said:

I did a bit of scripting. Didn't know I could do that, it made me really proud.

(Anon., Tribal feedback session 2011)

When reflecting on the work, prisoners often say that taking part took them out of their comfort zone; they then go on to say that they would never have done anything like this on the outside. They do not necessarily want to carry on taking part in plays, but they are able to make the connection that success achieved on a theatre project can give them the impetus to try out new and different things upon release. However, as Thompson points out, this is only possible if the society prisoners are returned to can 'accept them and build new networks for them' (2003: 101).

Institutional power

The act of staging a play in a prison is an action that in itself disrupts the sense of a contained, controlled environment by opening up a rich, creative space within an institution that is paradoxically both rigid and yet highly transitional for those who occupy it. For the duration of five performances over three days, prisoners become subjects rather than objects within the system. For 70 minutes, the prison gym becomes a space where the prisoners are in charge and in control. The success of each performance rests entirely in their hands once the house lights have gone down. Power and control is handed over to them instead of being in the hands of the officers and managers who run that institution.

Vinnie, who was in two Playing for Time productions, reflected on this process saying:

When people put their confidence in you and give you that responsibility I think we all proved we can rise to the occasion and as daunting as it is, it's just a matter of keep slogging away at things.

(Jones and Manley 2008)

Prisoners are contained, observed, categorised and restricted in numerous ways and struggle to maintain a sense of self and identity whilst dealing with regimes that are often dehumanising and disempowering. Once they are incarcerated, they experience disempowerment through a loss of autonomy and the ability to make decisions. Women are particularly affected by the loss of personal freedom and responsibility. For example, women who have previously had multiple responsibilities, such as home, childcare and work, are immediately deprived of the ability to make key decisions in these areas.

Theatre in prisons can give back to the group and individuals a sense of self-determination through engagement with the work. For example, during the workshop and rehearsal period all participants are encouraged to give feedback, make changes to scripts and offer constructive feedback on scenes in rehearsals. Programmes of accreditation that support work on these projects have comprised units of work on theatre practice, including directing, and so prisoners have had opportunities to direct scenes. In these small ways, people can begin to take responsibility for the work and have control over outcomes. This in turn can lead to a sense of agency as prisoners can feel that their work and input are valued.

Taking part in a theatre project in a prison can go some way towards alleviating the sense of isolation that prisoners can experience and the stresses of institutional life (Matarasso 1997: 74). As Prisoner P. said about working on *Oh What a Lovely War*:

> They [the student and staff team] bring a bit of normality into your life, because these places [prisons] are not normal.
>
> (Jones and Manley 2006)

However, the very act of preparing for and taking part in a performance is a stark contrast to how things usually operate within a prison regime. Staff within the system have to balance the punishment of a prisoner, a custodial sentence and loss of liberty, with the need to create regimes where the focus can be on rehabilitation and desistance from crime. The punishment/ rehabilitation dichotomy is problematic because in between these terms sit notions of retribution. This leads to contradictions within a system that is punitive but which also purports to treat people with humanity. Crewe describes a form of 'neo-paternalism' within the system characterised by 'a welfarist concern with rehabilitation and decency, a neo-liberal emphasis on responsibility and self-regulation, and an authoritarian impulse of control and compliance' (2009: 10). Arts work in secure institutions sits uneasily within these complex and conflicting ideologies.

Challenges to the politics of punishment

As stated earlier, our projects are different to interventions that directly address offending behaviour, such as drama work within a cognitive-behavioural framework or dramatherapy. Playing for Time's theatre work is founded in the conviction that engagement with theatre facilitates a subconscious and conscious process, which edges between the cracks of self-perception and may allow people to reconsider who they are and what they have done.

> A lot of people in prison have got problems opening up emotionally .... [P]roblems are exacerbated by being in prison because it's not an emotional environment. You don't want to open yourself up to anyone because there's too many characters about that would take advantage of you, so I think it's good because it allows people to express themselves emotionally and maybe find something in themselves they didn't think was there.
>
> (Prisoner G., in Jones and Manley 2011)

Theatre is a self-reflexive activity, can provide an emotional outlet and encourages participants to draw on their inner resources. It requires one to work within a particular set of disciplines. The act of creating theatre could be the first stage of self-analysis and a challenge to the hardened 'front' prisoner Prisoner G. identified.

The work of Playing for Time Theatre Company has an educational focus, which can have a normative effect on the participants. Balfour comments on the ways in which theatre can impact on prisoners who engage with the work:

> [Theatre] goes beyond the basic perception of art as entertainment, leisure or even education [...]. It can be fashioned into a tool designed to re-educate, re-socialize, and 'rehabilitate' people.
>
> (2004: 2)

The work requires the development of personal and transferable skills that are of a pro-social nature, such as communication skills, group work, self-presentation and literacy, and can be rehabilitative. These skills are, of course, important, but the problem here is that by focusing on these, a practitioner can become part of a system and only work to a prison agenda. It also buys into the deficit model, rather than a strength-based approach or asset model.

After a number of years of working in the prison I have noticed a process of internalising oppressive structures and have felt, at times, that we have become incorporated into the system whilst at the same time attempting to assert the need to resist these structures. Prison officers have commented on improved behaviour in some prisoners for at least the duration of the project. We have been prompted to address the question of whether it is part of our role as theatre-makers to make people more compliant in a repressive system. We may feel conflicted if this is a by-product, yet if prisoners feel happier in themselves because they are engaged in creative and social activities that make them feel validated, then their behaviour with other people may very well be affected, and they may behave in a way that aligns them with the needs of the institution. In terms of our own practice as a theatre company working in one prison, remaining an outsider, or a 'visiting' practitioner, can be advantageous because the relationship that can be developed with prisoners is one of *complicité* and creativity rather than one predicated on containment. As Kershaw points out, the radical nature of the freedom and space that theatre creates is thrown into relief by an oppressive system (2004: 36). The rehearsal room creates a particular working environment, another world to escape into. Prisoner M., one of the women prisoners, said of the experience of working in the rehearsal room and performing the play *Refuge*, '[w]hen we are here I am no longer in prison, you know ... in my mind I am free' (Pack 2004). This statement reflects why some prison officers are mistrustful of this work, because ultimately it may be regarded as a threat to the politics of punishment.

Building relationships

The development of relationships in prisons is fraught with difficulties and contradictions, as the forming of working relationships within an arts project with prisoners can be a challenge to the status quo. The staff and student team are not aware of the nature of the offences committed by the prisoners; this is important because it means that the participants are not judged, categorised or labelled according to the crimes they have committed. Prisoners are made aware of the fact that students work as volunteers on projects and this, combined with a supportive rather than a judgemental approach, has a strong impact. As Prisoner H. commented below:

> Respect for them [the students] really for just giving us all the benefit of the doubt because I didn't think it would be that easy for them to do.
>
> (Jones and Manley 2006)

Taking part in a play in a prison and building new relationships with each other, the staff and the students, can give participants back some of what they may have lost regarding their sense of self and identity; there may be moments throughout the project when they can transcend the label that the system uses to categorise them.

In prisons there are limited opportunities for prisoners to talk to people who are not employed within the institution. Playing for Time theatre projects involve a staff and student team who have time, within the rehearsal process, to talk and interact with the participating prisoners. Prisoner T. who took part in *Oh What a Lovely War* reflected on the role the students played in the work:

> The students are a breath of fresh air, you know, and it's nice to talk to them about things which ain't parole, tag, the screws… it's just nice to talk about other things.
>
> (Jones and Manley 2006)

Prisoner S., in the same show, said:

> Being able to talk to people, that was the main thing, because even on the out I wouldn't talk to a lot of people.
>
> (Jones and Manley 2006)

At the same time, maintaining professional working boundaries is essential within the parameters of the work. Staff working on projects attend two half-day courses in the prison: 'Security Awareness' and 'Conditioning & Manipulation'. Before staff and students go into the prison for the first time they attend a security briefing given by the prison's security manager. Everyone is warned that personal information must not be disclosed to prisoners; however, it is hard not to talk to prisoners about things that connect people. Talking to a prisoner about their family can be a way into gaining insights about their lives, but staff and students have to filter reciprocal information with care so as not to divulge something that could put them or someone else at risk.

Arts projects, in particular, create an environment in which sharing and reciprocity are integral to the development of effective working relationships. This in itself is potentially threatening and resistant to the prison's other agenda of containment and punishment. We walk a fine line in terms of understanding the very real need to co-operate with, and adhere to, the security policies of the prison and the equally deep need to create a working space for the projects that take the participants beyond the walls of the gymnasium (where most of the rehearsals take place). Failure to observe boundaries not only has risks in the moment, but could also lead to future work being curtailed. In Chapter 10, Boucher problematises the ways in which relationships are developed during the projects and are then terminated when a project is completed.

What's in a name?

The name Playing for Time Theatre Company was chosen in 2003 by women prisoners in West Hill. This name encompasses the two worlds that we fuse through our work: the idea of play and playfulness, which is integral to drama-based work, and the prisoners' experience of incarceration or 'doing time'. With Playing for Time, 'doing time' is inherently active and, hopefully, proactive. When engaged in theatre work, participants are constantly playing in different ways and this helps to pass the time in prison. As stated on the Playing for Time website:

> It is possible that a positive experience of arts work in prison might contribute towards attitudinal change and can be part of the jigsaw of work undertaken in prisons to combat recidivism. Arts projects encourage prisoners to value pro-social behaviour and enable them to flourish within an environment of praise and validation which is part and parcel of the rehearsal space and the final performances.

Acting with authenticity

Sometimes casting has mirrored aspects of a prisoner's offending behaviour. For example, in 2009, a career criminal was cast in the role of Peachum in Steven Jeffreys' play *The Convict's Opera*. Playing this role generated discussion between the prisoner playing Peachum and members of the staff team about the merits of crime and whether it really does pay. Of course, it's fun to play a villain and in some plays the villain does not face retribution. As Woolland explores in Chapter 5, questions have been raised in the past as to whether the portrayal of 'rogues' and 'villains' on stage validates the behaviours of these characters. The role of Peachum offered the prisoner playing the part the opportunity to examine the stereotype of the career criminal and to debate whether he might want to find a way out of that role in the future. In his case there was no indication that he did. Yet a fictitious frame does offer a prisoner a safe distance from which to explore aspects of their own life and to potentially imagine a different kind of future.

Some plays have elements that resonate more profoundly than others in the performance space in a prison. For example, the roles of criminals or convicts who are being transported, as featured in *Our Country's Good* by Timberlake Wertenbaker and *The Convict's Opera* by Stephen Jeffreys, are more powerful when performed in a prison theatre setting than on the stage of a theatre on the outside, as prisoners bring an authenticity to these roles that even the most highly trained actor is unable to achieve. Jeffreys, on seeing the production of his play, said that the prisoner who played Peachum was more powerful and convincing than the professional actor in the 2008–09 Out of Joint production of the play. Perhaps this was because he had lived the life of the criminal gang leader and was able to relate to the ways in which the character manipulates people around him for his own profit.

Plays that focus either directly or indirectly on prisoners' experiences have a particular resonance as they enable them to enter into a dialogue about the nature and function of crime and punishment at different periods of history and to use these reflections to consider how they fit into these patterns. Additionally, it is important for people to play parts outside of their experience, as allowing them to do so gives them opportunities to explore different identities and alternative experiences to their own. *Our Country's Good* enables this, as it provides the opportunity for doubling roles, so that prisoners can play both convicts and characters from within the officer class. *The Convict's Opera* and *Our Country's Good* are plays that also allow prisoners to play bullying and controlling authority figures. Playing these characters generates discussion about the nature of power and control within the criminal justice system and beyond. Prisoners have plenty of material to draw on from their immediate context when building character studies for these kinds of roles.

Experiencing and overcoming barriers

Taking part in a theatre production has often been a playful experience for the participants. At times it has been joyous and exhilarating and given them a sense of self, humanity and temporary respite from repressive regimes. Reflecting on the experience of taking part in *Oh What a Lovely War*, Prisoner L. said:

> It's nice to feel sort of human, like normal people. No, I'm not kidding, sometimes we're treated like animals, you know what I mean? And sometimes you know, when we're out and doing the drama and that and talking to the students you just forget about where you are. It's really good.
>
> (Jones and Manley 2006)

However, for some participants, this has not always been the case. There have been several years when groups of prisoners or individuals have been unable to commit fully to the processes they volunteered to engage in. Some prisoners have not been able to commit to the work, or to take it seriously, and have actively prevented others from doing so. Peer pressure is very strong in these contexts, and there may be moments when a participant is about to give something a chance but they are prevented from doing so by someone else who is not ready to do so themselves. Rarely has a prisoner's behaviour resulted in them being withdrawn from a project, and on those occasions it is a decision that is not taken lightly and involves consultation with prison staff. There has been tension at times between the need for the experience to be a positive one for the majority of prisoners and the necessity to deal with an individual whose behaviour is destructive to the process.

For example, in 2012, the prisoner playing the lead role in *The Accidental Impostor*[2] would not leave his cell after the lunch break on most days. Various strategies were tried; the staff team and prison officers spent time talking to him, trying to get to the bottom of what his problems were. In the end, despite repeated promises to do things differently, he maintained this pattern, and it was with reluctance that he was asked to leave the project. His continual absences were proving detrimental to the other participants and the process of rehearsing the play. There is always a sense of failure when this happens, and this feeling was exacerbated during the prisoner matinee when he spoke all his character's words at the same time as his replacement was performing, and also sang along with the cast's songs. He was moved to another prison shortly after this and so it was not possible to talk to him afterwards to try to find out what had been going on. I personally felt a deep sense of disappointment that we had not been able to convince him that he had remarkable talent and stage presence and could have achieved a first-class performance.

The experience with this prisoner also challenged my view that with a sensitive and holistic approach to encouraging people to take part, everyone we worked with was capable of surprising themselves and achieving a good, if not excellent, standard of work. No doubt this view would be seen by many as naïve given the nature of social and psychological damage that is evident in many serving prisoners. The arts cannot be a panacea for all problems experienced by people in secure institutions, particularly when the institution does not have a counselling and psychology service, which could and should support multi-agency interventions. As theatre practitioners, we only access a small selection of the multiple narratives of the lives of the people we work with. We can speculate on the reasons why this prisoner behaved as he did: perhaps the impact of addiction, low self-esteem, self-sabotage – a complex mix of reasons he himself might not be able to identify. It is frustrating that we were unable to work through the causes of his behaviour with him, as those most difficult to work with can be those who have the most to gain. Had the prison been staffed with psychologists and counsellors who could have supported the work, the outcome may have been different.

Our first production in 2003 provides another example of how one prisoner's construction of self affected their commitment to the project, although this time with a more positive outcome. After the final performance of *Refuge* by Dawn Garrigan, a prisoner told me that she had thought of doing the first performance and then letting her student mentor play her part for the final four performances. When I asked her why she had had these thoughts she told me that she had never finished anything in her life. She was aware that she constantly let people down, but this was what she was used to because of her experiences of other people letting her down. She said that she felt a great sense of achievement in having completed the project, not least because the play told stories about experiences similar to her own.

Other barriers that can prevent engagement with the work include issues outside the rehearsal room, such as events that happen on the wings between prisoners, relationships with prison staff and frustrations over institutional practices. Prisoners experience myriad setbacks, such as cancelled visits, difficulties in trying to contact lawyers, anxieties about where they will live upon release and whether they will ever get a job. Healthcare is a major issue, with difficulties in accessing medical and dental treatment and delays in getting correct medication. Prisoners' lives are measured out by milestones, characterised by delay: loss of paperwork, withdrawal of privileges[3] and inconsistencies in the system, which create a constant state of anxiety. This is often channelled into negative behaviour, such as refusing to participate in warm-ups or disrupting rehearsals through a lack of commitment to the process. Issues concerning sentence planning, courses and trainings that are part of this plan, parole, release on temporary licence or getting a tag[4] all serve to prey on prisoners' minds. It is therefore not surprising that this can result in a lack of focus and poor behaviour. Some prisoners have been in institutions for most of their lives and are lacking in self-belief; they can see little hope for a better life in the future. In these circumstances it is often not until the end of the first performance that they fully realise what they have been able to achieve and how their behaviour affected their engagement with the work.

After the first public performance of Rib Davis' play *The Fight in the Dog* in 2014, a prisoner came up to me and said: 'I am sorry, I have been an arsehole for eight weeks'. He repeated this apology during the debriefing session with the whole team, at the end of the project. This young man, with a history of violent offences, appeared to have been touched by the experience; however, throughout the process leading up to the performances his behaviour was constantly disruptive. His mistrust of authority and his need to sustain his reputation as both a 'hard man' and a 'jester' on the wings made engagement with the work difficult. There were a number of prisoners in the 2014 project who were constantly pushing the boundaries. Another young man who had spent most of his life in institutions was continually testing the limits of what kind of behaviour would be accepted. I had the feeling that he wanted the team to sack him so that his world view of people always giving up on him and letting him down could be perpetuated. His probation officer said he was the most damaged person she had ever worked with.

In 2006, rehearsing and staging *Oh What a Lovely War* in West Hill, HMP Winchester, it often felt that we were 'at war' with elements within the prison. As mentioned previously, the group of men recruited to the project were challenging to work with. The whole team used to leave at the end of each day exhausted with the effort of trying to encourage the men to commit to the rehearsal process. One prisoner displayed extremely uncooperative and aggressive behaviour for the first two weeks of rehearsals. At the beginning of the third week he seemed very different. When I asked him how he was feeling, he said he had just got past the worst effects of going 'cold turkey'. No one in the prison staff team had thought to tell us that he was detoxing (from heroin) and that he had not been receiving any medical treatment to support him through this difficult process. This has happened on subsequent projects. From the outset, some prison officers were resentful. One officer berated me for working on a play which '[…] made fun of people who fought in wars […].' I am not sure if he ever saw the play and whether it made him change his mind about what he thought it was about.

Dancing between dreams

At times, doing this work, it has felt as though the shards of glass in my dream were the prisoners, damaged beyond repair, the flotsam and jetsam of a society that consigns them to the rubbish dump. The glass in the dream was Victorian bottle glass – the main Category B prison was built in 1846. It is typical of Victorian prison architecture from that time. At the time of delivering the project in 2006 there seemed to be much that was 'broken' about the system. Having lived in London for a number of years, I also associate this kind of glass with glass that is found by River Thames treasure hunters or 'mudlarks'. The glass is buried in the silt and clay and can only be found at low tide. The nature of London clay means that it is not easily penetrated by water or oxygen thus preserving all that becomes buried in it. There is potential locked up in prisons, but it requires carefully crafted approaches to uncover and display the talent that is that 'treasure'.

Conclusion: Evaluating the impact of the work

I was dreading getting out because I thought I've got nothing to do… it's made me feel I can do stuff, I can do more if I put my mind to it, so yeah, it's left me with a more positive outlook on my future really and it's made me more determined not to come back, to do something with my life than just waste it like I have been for the last 6 or so years. It's about time I made a change and this has opened my eyes to make that change.

(Prisoner I., in Jones and Manley 2011)

I believe that this work can effect small changes in a prisoner's perceptions of him or herself. It would require longitudinal studies to substantiate claims that the work leads to total desistance from crime. The issue of evaluation and evidence is discussed further by Henry in Chapter 9, where the use of quantitative and qualitative research methodologies is examined in relation to the difficulties of evidencing change. Insights that prisoners gain whilst engaging in work can seem random, but collectively they add up to a powerful argument for the power and efficacy of the work. The experience can offer flashes of self-awareness that have not been gained elsewhere, like the one gleaned by Prisoner I. when he apologised for forgetting his lines during rehearsals of *The Convict's Opera* in 2009:

I am sorry I keep forgetting my lines. It has taken doing this play to make me realise that a lifetime dropping acid has affected my memory.

(Prisoner I., in group feedback session during rehearsals in 2009)

The aim of assessing the long-term impact of the project on individual prisoners is a goal that is not easily accomplished, even using the most sophisticated and well-funded research design. It is also a goal that requires investigation of more than one arts intervention as well as other interventions in prisons. Once prisoners return to society, it is virtually impossible for long-term impact research to separate and analytically weigh the different factors that interact in their former lives; no one lives in a vacuum. Evaluating the relative importance of one intervention over another is very difficult. There are so many variables at play in the complex dynamics of the reality of these individuals' lives. The ways in which prisoners upon release are able to manage hope for potential change with complex social determinants and variables are deeply problematic. Thompson reminds artists that it is not enough to accept '[…] a rhetoric of pure social agency or a positivist position of complete determinism' (1998: 207). Somehow, concepts of agency need to be balanced alongside the understanding of the complexity of people's social backgrounds and the environment into which they will be released.

These doubts have been voiced by Heritage, who comments:

The justification for making this work has often been made in terms of the way in which theatre has a social impact beyond the moment of performance. It is not in the now that this work is tested, but in some indeterminate future: it will reduce risk, increase safety, construct citizenship in some other world that is not the one in which the performance or the dramatic activity has taken place. Performance work is thus established that is in some way not bound by time or space, but becomes boundless. Is this what we want? Is this what we are promising?

(Heritage 2004: 190)

Ultimately, there is little we can promise. Yet although our work may not be 'boundless' and we cannot know the reach of the impact it has, we can witness the changes we feel in the time and place of the project, the small and gigantic changes that seem to happen in the moment.

Much of the work in the arts in prisons appears to be predicated on individual change and agency: an assumption that it is the prisoner who needs to change. Despite wanting to prevent and protect further victims of crime, I believe that is not sufficient; it is also society, with its embedded social inequalities, that needs to change if people who spend time in prison are to become stakeholders in society. We talk about prisoners adopting 'pro-social' roles and that theatre can become a vehicle for exploring and rehearsing these roles, a kind of 'rehearsal for life' (Boal 1979). However, our post-industrialised society with its failing model of monetarist, late capitalist economics offers very little to those on the margins of society. It is hard to substantiate statements about the long-term efficacy of the work given the kind of world that prisoners in the United Kingdom are released into. Prisoners are being released into a world now characterised by austerity and the part-privatisation of services such as the Probation Service. These changes affect the dispossessed most, through cuts to key services which might previously have offered support. The outside world has now become an even more difficult place for ex-prisoners to find a foothold on the ladder to a better life.

References

Baim, C., Brookes S. and Mountford, S. (2002), *The Geese Theatre Handbook*, Winchester: Waterside Press.

Balfour, M. (ed.) (2004), *Theatre in Prison: Theory and Practice*, Bristol: Intellect.

Boal, A. (1979), *Theatre of the Oppressed*, London: Pluto Press.

———— (1995), *The Rainbow of Desire*, London: Routledge.

Crewe, B. (2009), *The Prisoner Society Power, Adaptation and Social Life in an English Prison*, Oxford: Oxford University Press.

Feldhendler, D. (1994), 'Augusto Boal and Jacob L. Moreno Theatre and Therapy' in Schutzman, M. and Cohen-Cruz, J. (eds), *Playing Boal Theatre, Therapy, Activism*, London: Routledge, pp. 87–109.

Fo, D. (1989), *Accidental Death of an Anarchist* (trans. G. Hanna), 6th ed., London: Methuen.

Garrigan, D. (2003), *Refuge*, unpublished.

Glassborow, P. (2011), *Soul Traders*, unpublished.

Heritage, P. (2004), 'Real Social Ties? The ins and outs of making theatre in Brazilian prisons', in M. Balfour (ed.), *Theatre in Prison: Theory and Practice*, Bristol: Intellect, pp. 189–202.

Hollin, C. (ed.) (2001), *Handbook of Offender Assessment and Treatment*, Chichester: John Wiley & Sons Ltd.

Jeffreys, S. (2009), *The Convicts' Opera*, London: Nick Hern Books.

Jones, L. and Manley, S., (2006), *Oh What a Lovely War*, Documentary Film, United Kingdom: LaunchPad Productions.

———— (2011), *Soul Traders*, Documentary Film, United Kingdom: LaunchPad Productions.

———— (2013), *Our Country's Good*, Film of post-show feedback, United Kingdom: LaunchPad Productions.

Kershaw, B. (2004), 'Pathologies of hope in drama and theatre', in M. Balfour (ed.), *Theatre in Prison: Theory and Practice*, Bristol: Intellect, pp. 35–51.

Littlewood, J. Theatre Workshop (2000), *Oh What a Lovely War*, 2nd ed., London: Methuen.

Maruna, S. (2001), *Making Good: How Ex-Convicts Reform and Rebuild Their Lives*, Washington, DC: American Psychological Association.

Matarasso, F. (1997), *Use or Ornament? The Social Impact of Participation in the Arts*, Stroud: Commedia.

McGuire, J. (2013), 'What works' to reduce re-offending 18 years on', in L. Craig, L. Dixon and T. Gannon (eds), *What Works in Offender Rehabilitation: An Evidence-Based Approach to Assessment and Treatment*, Chichester: Wiley-Blackwell, pp. 20–49.

Nicholson, H. (2005), *Applied Drama: The Gift of Theatre*, Basingstoke and New York: Palgrave Macmillan.

Pack, L. (2004), *The Doll's House*, Student Documentary Film, The University of Winchester, United Kingdom.

Palmer, E. (2003), *Offending Behaviour: Moral Reasoning, Criminal Conduct and the Rehabilitation of Offenders*, Exeter: Willan Publishing.

Playing for Time Theatre Company, http://www.playingfortime.org.uk/index.html. Accessed 1 February 2017.

Shailor, J. (ed.) (2011), *Performing New Lives: Prison Theatre*, London: Jennifer Kingsley.

Thompson, J. (1998), 'Theatre and Offender Rehabilitation: observations from the USA' in *Research in Drama Education: The Journal of Applied Theatre and Performance*, 3:2, pp. 197–210

—— (2003), *Applied Theatre: Bewilderment and Beyond*, Bern: Peter Lang.

Wertenbaker, T. (2003), *Our Country's Good*, 4th ed., London: Methuen.

Williams, K., Papadopoulou, V. and Booth, N. (2012), *Prisoners' Childhood and Family Backgrounds: Results from the Surveying Prisoner Crime Reduction (SPCR) Longitudinal Cohort Study of Prisoners*, Ministry of Justice Research Series 4/12, https://www.gov.uk/government/uploads/system/uploads/attachment_data/file/278837/prisoners-childhood-family-backgrounds.pdf. Accessed 23 January 2017.

Woolland, B. (2014), *Stand or Fall*, Oxford: Oxford University Press.

Notes

1 Tribal was the organisation in HMP Winchester that dealt with resettlement issues such as finding housing and possibly training or work upon release into the community.

2 The play *The Accidental Impostor* was adapted from Dario Fo's play *Accidental Death of an Anarchist* by Bethan Clark.

3 The Incentive and Earned Privileges scheme rewards good behaviour. Privileges include the provision of an in-cell television and, at West Hill, being put in a single as opposed to a shared room.

4 Getting a 'tag' is the system whereby a prisoner is released early under the scheme called Home Detention Curfew or Electronic Tagging. Prisoners are released and fitted with an electronic tag around their ankle, which monitors their adherence to a specified curfew.

Chapter 2

Playing for Time Theatre Company: A Model of Practice

Annie McKean

C hapter 1 discussed aspects of the ideology and politics of delivering arts projects in secure institutions. In this chapter I will examine the model of practice that has been developed over the eleven years of delivering theatre projects in West Hill, HMP Winchester. Before staging plays in HMP Winchester I had extensive experience of producing and directing plays in community and education contexts, but no experience of doing this kind of work in a prison. Between 2003 and 2014 the company staged eleven productions with West Hill prisoners. Four of these plays were commissioned for production in the prison; in the case of three of these plays, the playwrights ran workshops in the prison with prisoners in order to develop materials for the writing of the plays. The learning curve for all of us involved in the first production in West Hill was extremely steep; the model of practice that was trialled in that first year has been refined year-on-year. Whilst not advocating what Playing for Time Theatre Company has developed as a model for all work in custodial settings, there may be elements of what we achieved which might usefully inform the practice of others working in this sector.

Framing the work to meet the prison's agenda: Education and transferable skills

A significant number of prisoners have low levels of literacy and learning difficulties. In 2015, the government published data revealing that '46% of people entering the prison system have literacy skills no higher than those broadly expected of an 11-year-old child' (Prisoners' Education Trust 2015). It was possible for Playing for Time to maintain a long-term relationship with HMP Winchester and to stage theatre shows by framing the work within programmes of accreditation. This was a key factor in arguing a case for the work. Prisons in England and Wales have to deliver key performance indicators and meet targets; interventions that address these agendas are more readily supported. There is an emphasis on the delivery of work that increases prisoners' functional skills in literacy and numeracy. Arts projects can be disruptive to prison routines and regimes and therefore have to provide strong justification in terms of what can potentially be delivered. Taking part in a theatre project can offer a gateway into learning, which a prisoner might previously have been unwilling to access, sometimes due to negative experiences of schooling. Playing for Time staff worked closely with the Education Department at HMP Winchester from 2003 when an Open College Network Creative Arts programme was written for the first theatre project. In addition to working creatively with theatre professionals, prisoners would be awarded certification for the work; this could be shown to a prospective employer, demonstrating a constructive use of time whilst in prison.

From the outset, we worked closely with education managers and education staff at the prison in order to deliver work that addresses three key targets: employability and vocational training, literacy, and personal and social development. The work responds to the transferable skills agenda, which is important for prisoners seeking employment upon release. These skills include the following:

Interpersonal skills:
- team building
- communication
- negotiating skills

Thinking skills:
- thinking creatively
- decision-making
- problem-solving
- learning to learn

Personal development:
- confidence building
- enhanced self-esteem
- self-discipline
- sense of achievement

All of these are essential to successful participation in a theatre project in a prison because of the need to build a group of individuals into an ensemble. Prisoner N., who took part in *Our Country's Good* in 2005, appeared to have very little self-belief at the start of the rehearsal period. He struggled to learn his lines and was constantly worried about letting other people down. Afterwards he reflected that:

> Doing something like a play builds your character, it builds your self-esteem, builds your confidence. When you get out for a job interview, you get the confidence to sit in front of somebody.

> (Martinez 2005: 6)

Of course, there isn't an automatic transfer of skills acquired during one intervention in a prison to other contexts. Participants need a variety of opportunities and support to make the transition from inside the institution to the outside world.

From 2006 onwards, a close working relationship was formed with the prison's music tutor and the education manager, also a musician. Their presence contributed to the creation of a more integrative atmosphere; the two acted as a link between prisoners, the external production team and other members of staff in the prison. Their knowledge of the system and ability to support work with prisoners with challenging behaviour was invaluable. A member of the Education Department team was also assigned to work with the creative team, delivering the programmes of accreditation.

Although it is important to see how education and training in prisons can play a key role in improving the employability of prisoners and therefore contribute to reducing recidivism, education has a value in itself in terms of developing the person as a whole. Prisoner R. reflected on how the project made him feel in 2005:

> In the beginning of the project I was going to do backstage work, but then I got involved in the warm-up sessions and games and all of that, and I started to feel more relaxed and next time I was almost acting. I am really glad I have done this work. It is a great way of bringing myself out of the shell. I think it is a great form of release from being in prison. I am really glad I have done that. It is the best thing I have done for a long time.
>
> (Martinez 2005: 3)

Prisoner R. took part in the first production of *Our Country's Good* by Timberlake Wertenbaker in 2005; continuing contact with him for the rest of his time in prison revealed that he was able to hold on to those feelings for longer than the duration of the project. However, it was not possible to assess the long-term impact of the project once he was released from prison. The arts can offer a unique experience that transcends the ticking of boxes and the collection of certificates. Yet, in order to justify the time and expense to the prison for undertaking this kind of work, acknowledgement of the ways in which the work supports prison agendas is important.

A prison officer commented on a marked difference in Prisoner D.'s behaviour when he was taking part in rehearsals for *The Accidental Impostor* in 2011:

> I remember him more than anyone else [...] he was surly, he was arrogant, he was rude, he thought he was everything and to be quite honest with you he was that close probably to being kicked out of West Hill. He then came to the theatre group [...] and then, all of a sudden I don't know what it was, something clicked in his head and he went hell for leather. He was always the first one down at the gate with his paperwork, he was always ready to go, he was there, if for whatever reasons, and it could have been for operational reasons, we had to run late and we couldn't get them out, "come on governor I've got a play to do". His attitude changed drastically [...] he was inspirational towards getting the other prisoners involved, geeing them up and getting them up and that to me was quite an eye opener and that was down to him taking a little bit of pride, a little bit of discipline, putting the two together and finding out, this is what I want to do. And I was impressed by him.
>
> (Allan 2015)

As Prisoner D. said in the documentary that opened the show:

> It gives me something to wake up to every morning. It keeps me motivated. I actually look forward to drama every morning.
>
> (Jones and Manley 2011)

Recruitment: Prisoners and students

Approximately fifteen prisoners were recruited each year to take part in the annual production. This was usually a self-selecting group who responded to a sign-up sheet and attended a recruitment meeting before the rehearsal period commenced. Pre-production workshops with prisoners contributed to the recruitment process. These were delivered three or four months before rehearsals started and some participants subsequently signed up for participation in the theatre project. Release dates had to be checked so as to ensure that prisoners who had signed up would be in the prison for the duration of the project. It was never possible to select prisoners on the basis of the extent to which they would benefit from taking part, although occasionally prison officers encouraged prisoners suffering from depression or those with communication or anger management issues to join us. When the play was cast, all the main roles were given to the prisoners who were interviewed individually by the director, enabling each prisoner to say how large a part they would like and whether there was a particular role or character they would like to perform; they were never formally auditioned and there was always a role for everyone who wanted one.

A similar number of undergraduate students were recruited to take part. Student recruitment for the projects started in the October of each academic year the shows were staged. They had to be cleared to work in the prison through the Enhanced Security Clearance procedure that was managed by the prison, in order to be ready for rehearsals which started in March each year. Students took part as volunteers and were not accredited, except for one or two who took on stage-management roles as part of their Performance Management degree. Students were responsible for sourcing props, costumes, running the box office and writing and designing the programme. Most of the students took part as performers in ensemble scenes and the female students were cast in the women's roles in the play. Taking part in the projects had a profound effect on the students. As with some members of the general public, some students had preconceived ideas and prejudices about crime and punishment in our society. These opinions are often informed by the popular press. Helen summarised a view often expressed by students at the end of a project:

> I think it has changed my perception of what prison is and it has changed me and my ideas of things.
>
> (Jones and Manley 2011)

The experience of working with prisoners gave students the opportunity to hear different people's stories and to understand the socio-economic factors that led some people into patterns of offending behaviour. By the end of a project, many students had experienced a learning journey, which a campus-based experience, working with their peers, could not offer.

The most important contribution that students made to work on these projects was the way in which they supported the prisoners by taking on mentoring roles. This model of practice has a significant impact on the prisoners' sense of self and achievement. As Prisoner M. said in 2011:

> Ella [...] she really encourages me to get into it. She's a brilliant mentor [...] I really enjoy working with her.
>
> (Jones and Manley 2011)

Students were paired with a prisoner and supported that person in all aspects of work on the play. Prisoners have limited opportunities to talk about issues that interest or concern them; therefore, the opportunity to talk to staff and students offered a break from experiences related to prison regimes and the frustrations that characterise everyday life in prison. Further analysis of the student experience is offered in Chapter 7.

Choosing the play

Plays that are developed in collaboration with prisoners can engender a sense of ownership of the work. However, over the last eleven years of delivering these projects, overcrowding and the need to move prisoners on to the next stage of their sentence meant that the population of HMP Winchester was constantly changing. Many prisoners who took part in the autumn workshops were likely to have been moved to Open Conditions or released into the community by the time the rehearsal period commenced in March. Even when rehearsals started in March for performances at the end of April, prisoners could be moved to other prisons or released early. Prisoners were also recruited right up to the moment when rehearsals were due to start and sometimes during the rehearsal period itself. This was one of the reasons why all the plays staged between 2003 and 2014 were scripted, using existing or commissioned plays. The use of a play text created a structure which prisoners recruited late in the day could fit into relatively easily. This also supported the development of prisoners' literacy as plays had to be read, complex vocabulary explained and different language registers explored.

The choice of play for each project was crucial. Plays were chosen for the ways in which themes, issues and content resonated with the prisoners' lives and experiences. Four of the eleven plays were written specifically for the company. In Chapter 5, Woolland discusses how workshops enabled themes the prisoners were interested in to inform the writing of his play *Stand or Fall* (2008). The 2011 production of *Soul Traders*, written by local playwright

Philip Glassborow, was a contemporary version of the Dr. Faustus story. The play provided the participating prisoners with opportunities to examine the potential consequences of making choices and the impact that these consequences can have on others. Workshops were also run with prisoners by the director of *The Fight in the Dog* (2014), with the playwright Rib Davis present, so that the views of prisoners on the stories of the First World War conscientious objectors could be integrated into the play.

Another production that focused on the theme of war was Joan Littlewood's Theatre Workshop play *Oh What a Lovely War*, staged in 2006. Some of the participating prisoners in both these productions had previously served in the armed forces. Research published in 2011 suggested that a high proportion of ex-service personnel suffered from problems related to finance, lack of employment opportunities and high levels of homelessness. There was also an increased risk of alcohol misuse and mental health difficulties, sometimes related to post-traumatic stress. The report suggested that those ex-service personnel who come into contact with the criminal justice system may have been affected by one or more of these factors (Howard League for Penal Reform 2011: 10).

Prisoner T., who took part in the 2006 production of *Oh What a Lovely War*, described how he related to the play:

> I was a soldier for nine years myself so I know what it's like to live in a trench, not like those lads lived then obviously, but I know how cold and wet and miserable it is having spent a week in a trench myself.
>
> (Jones and Manley 2006)

Later, in the same documentary film, Prisoner T. went on to compare the teamwork of putting on a play with the ways in which people in the army have to work together. Several prisoners used their army experiences to contribute to work in rehearsals. For example, the prisoner who played the Drill Sergeant in *Oh What a Lovely War* had been a drill sergeant himself. The lead role in *The Fight in the Dog*, a conscientious objector, was played by an ex-SAS serviceman who led drilling and 'square bashing' sessions for the whole group. As discussed in Chapter 1, the authenticity of the individual experience that is brought to performance work in different contexts often more than makes up for the lack of actor training.

The experiences that the prisoners have of prison, and debates which relate to the purpose and function of the criminal justice system, are rich areas for exploration through theatre work. However, the male prisoners we worked with often stated that they did not want to take part in a play that was set in a contemporary prison; they wanted the experience of taking part to be something that helped them escape from and transcend their current reality. This feeling is powerfully expressed by the character of Tom Jenner in *The Convict's Opera*. In the play, Tom, a convict, is rehearsing for a production of John Gay's play, *The Beggar's Opera*. The play will be staged on the transport ship before it arrives at the penal colony in Australia:

TOM: This is the best of all. This is the best of all that I ever did.
   One or two looks from the COMPANY
   It was hard. 'Cos I can't read. I must have it all read to me. And then I must hold
   it in my head. Sometimes my head wants to burst. But I can do it. By the Lord,
   Harry, I can do it. And when I do it, I am not on the ship. (*Pause*) Obviously I am
   on the ship, But in my head I am somewhere else. So my spirits is not low.
                                          (Jeffreys, Part Two, Scene 10, 2009: 65)

The casting of Prisoner F. as Tom contained multiple resonances in terms of themes within
the play and the character he was playing. He had low levels of literacy and came from an
impoverished background, as had his character. Tom had been sentenced to transportation
for stealing a cabbage; Prisoner F.'s crimes were related to his socio-economic circumstances.
Like his character, who was taking part in the play to get out of the ship's hold, Prisoner F.
said in rehearsals that he was taking part in order to forget about where he was. Neither the
character Tom nor Prisoner F. who played him had ever done anything like this before.
Initially, Prisoner F.'s delivery of the speech above lacked confidence and engagement. When
we discussed the ways in which the speech resonated with his experiences the words gained
a deeper truth and authenticity and his performance of the role was very moving. Although
The Convict's Opera explores aspects of incarceration and punishment, the historical context
of the play distanced it from the prisoners' current reality. A historical lens can be used as a
tool to compare and contrast aspects of the ways in which crime and punishment have both
changed and remain the same, as exemplified by the plays *Refuge*, *Our Country's Good* and
The Convict's Opera.

Humour is often used by prisoners to survive the experience of incarceration; it is a
safety valve and coping mechanism that allows prisoners and staff to relieve the tension and
stresses of life in secure institutions. The plays that have worked best are those that contain
comedy and elements of farce, although they also need to have characters and themes which
are deep enough to be analysed and deconstructed during the rehearsal period.

In 2007, we chose to stage *Ubu the King*, the first in the trilogy of *Ubu* plays by Alfred
Jarry. The play is based on Shakespeare's *Macbeth* and follows the antics of Pa Ubu, who
kills the King of Poland and then goes on to murder all who stand in his way, including
bankers, lawyers and politicians. An early example of absurdist theatre, the thinking behind
choosing *Ubu the King* concerned the creative possibilities and theatrical exploration the
play could afford. The choice of this play gave the cast many opportunities to devise their
own sequences, including songs and choreographic routines. Of all the plays staged with
male prisoners this became the most collaborative endeavour.

The participants created their own aesthetic using the framework of the play and responses
to the design of the piece. For example, the costuming of Pa Ubu's guards in pink PVC
'baloney' sausage outfits and pink umbrellas enabled the actors to parody and subvert the
violence of those characters by playing them within a 'camp' aesthetic that was characterised
by bad taste and irony. Prisoners made up lyrics to existing songs to fit the context of the play

and choreographed those songs in a way that was entirely unselfconscious. Ubu's farcical world, a world without consequences, was sublime and liberating for the participating prisoners who, having overcome their initial puzzlement about the play, threw themselves into rehearsing it with huge amounts of energy and enthusiasm. Masks were worn by most of the prisoners in this show. The grotesque style of the masks used created an aesthetic that was transformative for the performers, because they enabled each actor to fully inhabit their role; they formed a protective barrier between actors and audience, enabling the actors to perform a variety of identities without any inhibitions. The masks gave the actors a licence to behave in a way that would have been considered inappropriate in other circumstances.

We felt that prisoners would relate to a play that explored aspects of greed, the abuse of power and stupidity. However, there were concerns about the amoral nature of the piece, particularly in the context of a prison, where education work is designed to promote pro-social behaviour and a questioning attitude to offending behaviour. We dealt with this issue by creating the character of a 'fool', costumed as a jester. The prisoner playing this role created his own text, written in rhyming couplets, which acted as a commentary on events in the play. The group's discussions about Pa Ubu's actions helped to problematise his behaviour and informed the writing of the jester's script. Questioning and critiquing the consequences of choices made by characters in a play was an integral part of the process underpinning the theatre work delivered by Playing for Time Theatre Company.

We were concerned about the reaction of prison staff to the piece. The play opens with Pa Ubu sitting on a toilet; later he wields a toilet brush as a sceptre and feeds his soldiers faeces from the toilet. The obscene language, mayhem and anarchy that characterises this piece were not what uniformed staff were used to seeing on stage in the prison. However, some of the prison officers who saw the play said that it was their favourite production to date! Their response was very similar to that of the rest of the prisoners who attended the matinee performance for men in the Category C and Category D prisons; both groups enjoyed the scatological humour of the piece and the chaos that ensued when Pa Ubu hurled the puppets made of cake which represented the bankers into the audience. The experience of staging this play demonstrated the closeness of the culture of two groups in the institution: prison officers and prisoners. Prison officers would often comment that they have come from similar backgrounds to the prisoners they were working with but had made different choices. Yet the apparent moral distance between prisoners and prison officers appeared to be momentarily set to one side as both groups demonstrated equal enjoyment of the piece.

Formally quantifying the efficacy and impact of the work is challenging, and often hard to measure in quantifiable 'successes'; however, improved access to education, training and employment is an oft cited yardstick for combating recidivism and improving self-worth, and thus this show yielded one definite success story. The prisoner who played the role of the jester was a very talented dancer. Upon release he felt that he had gained enough confidence to enrol for a higher education course; he was accepted onto the BA in Choreography and Dance at the University of Winchester and graduated in 2011.

Process and product

The first project with women prisoners had a strong element of devising in the workshop process, preceding the writing of the final version of the play. Creative writing was used as a vehicle to develop the script of *Soul Traders* in order for the prisoners to create an authentic voice for their characters. When play texts were used, formal rehearsals using the text were preceded by a period of weeks when themes were workshopped, and then the text was introduced gradually so as not to alienate those prisoners who had low levels of literacy. Our model for workshops and rehearsals was influenced by the theory and practice of Drama in Education methodologies (Bolton 1992; Heathcote and Bolton 1995; O'Neill 1995; Winston 1998) and the work of Augusto Boal (1979, 1992). For example, characters were hot-seated by the rest of the cast and their backstories investigated through improvisation. It was essential that the context of each play was fully explored so that prisoners had a full understanding of the play they were performing. Students were asked to research key elements of the play and given permission to bring research materials and books into the prison so that the prisoners could become engaged with and immersed in the context of the piece. Performative research presentations were rehearsed in small groups so that everyone was given a chance to investigate key areas of context in some depth and present this research to the rest of the cast. Professional theatre directors also incorporated aspects of theatre training into rehearsals; in Chapter 8 Sharp writes about the ensemble training that influenced the rehearsal process involved in staging Timberlake Wertenbaker's play *Our Country's Good* in 2013.

Members of the general public, who had been coming into the prison each year to see the Playing for Time shows, had come to expect productions to have high performance values. It was important that performers were well prepared and confident about performing. Rehearsals had to be structured so that incremental introductions to the play text were made and a schedule developed, which allowed for continuous exploration of the play as well as more conventional rehearsal practices. It was important that each group was able to achieve the highest possible standard that they were capable of. However, it would have been unethical to achieve this by 'drilling' or mindless repetition of lines. It would be wrong to set the prisoners up for failure or condescending comments such as 'didn't they do well for prisoners'. In 2008, one audience member said that he felt he had seen a really good amateur production and had forgotten that he was in prison during the performance. Other audience members have commented on the professionalism of the shows.

Aesthetics

The different aesthetics of our productions have been an important factor in drawing prisoners into the process, as previously discussed in relation to the production of *Ubu the King*. Despite the limitations posed by staging productions in a prison, there has always been a great deal of ambition in terms of creating innovative work. Two large-scale multimedia shows were staged in the last eleven years. This kind of aesthetic and technology allowed the prisoners to play and experiment with film using 'green screen' and live feed techniques. The community documentary film company, LaunchPad Productions, worked with the prisoners and director of the two multimedia shows to create recorded sequences, juxtaposed with live performance. In *Soul Traders* there was interaction between characters on screen and those on the stage. The workshops where the cast made film trailers and news reports helped shape the multimedia aspects of the final piece. There was a sense of liberation about the 'green screen' moments in *The Accidental Impostor* when characters were seen on beaches, outside the Houses of Parliament and in a number of locations quite inaccessible to a prison population. We were amused to find that some audience members thought that we had been given permission to take the prisoners on location filming!

Special permission had to be sought to film the prisoners in front of the green screen and then take the film out of the prison to be edited. Over the eleven years of this work, we were extraordinarily fortunate in being able to take cameras into the prison to make recordings of shows, create pre-recorded sequences to be incorporated into performances and to make four documentaries about the work. The 2011 production of *Soul Traders* opened with the screening of a seventeen-minute documentary tracing the journey of the prisoners during the rehearsal process. This allowed the audience to see how prisoner engagement with the work developed and the ways in which the work impacted on their sense of self and self-esteem. It was clear to the audience that their progress from an almost total lack of experience to capable performers was remarkable.

> I said 'I'm not singing and dancing; I'll just do one song'. Then [Prisoner D.] said, 'Do another' and then 'another'.
>
> (Prisoner J., in Jones and Manley 2011)

From the outset, all shows involved music and singing; rarely did a prisoner refuse to sing but many had been through a similar journey to Prisoner J. When the education manager resigned from the prison service in 2010 he continued to work with us as the musical director composing music for a number of shows. We sometimes added existing songs to shows in 'jukebox musical' style, occasionally tweaking the lyrics to fit the context. The songs in *Ubu the King* were chosen by the prisoners. For other shows, the music had been written in response to the abilities of the cast, including a Sondheim style song, written in 2011 for a prisoner with an exceptional ability to sing challenging music.

Like theatre, singing is a social art form; it is an inclusive activity and can develop an individual's social capital. Singing is life enhancing and there is evidence of the ways in which singing can contribute to physical and mental well-being. Singing can generate happiness and enjoyment, and these positive feelings can counteract feelings of stress or anxiety and help distract people from negative thoughts and feelings. Learning songs can help develop concentration and focus, which in turn can provide a distraction and respite from other concerns (Clift and Morrison 2011). In 2009, a prisoner with serious mental health issues, who self-harmed, was sent along to rehearsals by a prison officer, because the officer said that he thought that 'singing would be good for him'. This man was released before the show was staged, but he came to rehearsals every day, learnt the songs and sang with the cast when these were rehearsed. He stopped self-harming during the four-week period that he was with the group.

Performances

> A couple of months ago there is no way you would have got me standing up in front of people.
>
> (Prisoner D., in Jones and Manley 2011)

Each show was performed five times. There were four performances to the general public and one to the rest of the prisoners in West Hill. Public performances in the prison can not only improve the confidence of the prisoners, as evidenced by Prisoner D.'s comment above, but can also raise awareness amongst the audience about the institution and those who inhabit it. Bringing members of the general public into the prison can raise community awareness about the criminal justice system and challenge preconceptions about prisoners and the prison system. However, bringing an audience in can also be problematic. Thompson warns of the danger of creating a vicarious experience for audience members for whom entry into a prison is a chance to see systems in place, which contributes to a retributive agenda: '[...] a modern day version of the stocks' (Thompson 2004: 57). The performance of power is ever present in the institution; indeed prison staff acknowledge this when considering security measures for the audience coming into and out of the prison. For example, in a steering committee meeting in 2008 the security manager said that the 'sniffer' (drug detection) dogs would be used to check the audience because 'that was what they would expect'. The panoptic nature of prison impacts on the audience as they wait to be searched, hand in their bags and are led through a series of locked gates through fences with barbed wire on the top.

For the audience, the performance begins the moment the gates are opened and they are ushered inside the prison walls. Prisons generally do not offer guided tours to the general public; the opportunity to enter a prison and engage with prisoners offers the general public experience and an opportunity to see inside, first-hand, beyond the political and media discourses surrounding crime and punishment. We hoped that our audiences did not simply engage in the voyeuristic nature of the experience, but were challenged by the reality of seeing people participating in an activity that defies some of the commonly held views about prisoners. Prisoners were able to talk to the audience after each performance and the chance for the audience to mingle and interact with them was important to the process of challenging stereotypes and breaking down barriers. Having the opportunity to discuss with audience members what they had achieved often helped them re-evaluate who they were, or could be, and how they were seen by others. When outsiders are brought into the prison, a transition can be created between the isolation and unreality of being kept away from the general public and a move back into society (Thompson 2003: 102). As many of the prisoners we worked with were close to their release date, the social interactions generated by the work were potentially beneficial.

We would sometimes notice audience members looking at their programmes during a performance. Afterwards, they would say that they had not known whether a performer was a prisoner or a student. There were many occasions when prisoners outshone drama students, in terms of their acting ability, despite never having taken part in a production before. When prison officers were in the audience they were given the opportunity to see the prisoners as more than a name or number; officers were able to recognise that prisoners are people who deserve recognition for what they can achieve. Their talent, skill, creativity and even courage are qualities that may have been previously overlooked in day-to-day encounters. As one prisoner said:

> They look at you with more respect and you feel you are better considered now and some concessions are made as a result of it.
>
> (Prisoner R., post-production feedback, 2010)

From conversations with prison staff it was clear that some of them felt that taking part in the play had made the prisoners easier to work with as improvements in communication skills, confidence and self-esteem had led to more self-control.

Collecting the performers from the wings the day after the first show elicited the same reaction every year. Prisoners talked about feeling 'high' or 'buzzing', a feeling better than drugs or alcohol. During post-production debriefings there was an atmosphere of success and confidence; they were amazed by what they had achieved.

> Unforgettable; it surprised people and even it surprised myself. I shall learn from this and carry it away.
>
> (Prisoner G., in Martinez 2005: 7)

Interviewed for the 2008 documentary about the production of *Stand or Fall*, Prisoner M. said immediately after the final performance:

> Once I was out there, I didn't have no doubt in my mind that we could do it or anything like that. It's just all gone perfect and it's been better every time we've done it. It's just been amazing, yeah, so, it's a big word, amazing but that was. So that's all I can say about it, really, it was just amazing [laughs] it was, yeah.
>
> (Jones and Manley 2008)

The performance of the show to the rest of the West Hill population was always a nerve-wracking event for the prisoners and indeed for the students who took part as performers. However, every year, prisoners in the audience expressed respect and admiration for the achievement of the performers. Many said afterwards that they wished they had had the 'bottle' to take part. On returning to the wings after the evening show, which followed the prisoner matinee, the actors reported that the other guys applauded them and offered positive feedback. Reactions of this sort serve to increase the participants' feelings of self-worth and self-esteem.

One of the most significant aspects of the public performances was that prisoners' friends and family members came to see the shows. For many people, going to visit a family member or friend in prison is often a negative experience. However, the experience of seeing this person achieving a high standard of work in a theatrical production is joyous and allows the performer to be seen in a new light. For prisoners, habituated to receiving negative feedback, the positive responses and applause from the audience are life affirming; the experience of a standing ovation, of being hugged by family members and friends, is often described by prisoners after a performance as the best 'high' of their life. After a performance of *Our Country's Good* in 2005 the mother of the prisoner who played Captain Arthur Philip said in the post-show discussion that she had felt ashamed that her son was in prison. She went on to say that seeing him perform made her feel proud of him for the first time in years.

During the production week there is a strong sense that the institution is momentarily transformed. It changes from being a place where people are dehumanised and disempowered, to one where humanity, empowerment and talent are celebrated. Prisoner D. talked about this after the first performance of *Our Country's Good* in 2013:

> It is important to discover that you are capable of doing things that you did not think you were able to, and that gives you more confidence and security about yourself. You feel good about yourself.
>
> (post-production feedback, 2013)

Thompson notes that taking part in a play can be experienced as the 'sensitising transitory moment between the prison and the rupture to the outside' (2003: 102). For some prisoners, the experience of talking to people from the audience that they do not know can be a moment of transition in which they reconnect with people and 're-present' themselves in ways that might not have been possible before undertaking this work.

Prison staff and the institution

A significant omission in this book is a detailed study of prison staff attitudes to the work, a research project in its own right. Funding cuts, changes in staff, particularly prison governors, and changes in institutional regimes meant that we were constantly dealing with different staff each year. However, there were a small number of individuals, for example the security manager and two heads of Learning and Skills, whose support was unstinting.

It is important that an environment of trust and safety is created in the rehearsal space so that prisoners can become part of the community of artists working together to stage a play. Some prisoners define staff in oppositional terms depending on whether they are seen as having authority over them (prison officers), or facilitating programmes of work (civilians delivering education courses). Therefore, the presence of officers in the rehearsal space can alter the ways in which prisoners work and the dynamics of the group. This is often because prisoners feel that they are under surveillance and being judged.

In 2011, for the first time, uniformed staff were allocated to be present throughout all rehearsals. Overcrowding in the prison had resulted in prisoners from the Category B prison being housed in the Category C prison and therefore some participating prisoners were deemed to be a higher security risk than those who had previously taken part in the theatre projects. Between 2011 and 2013, different officers were detailed to be in the room with the team on a daily basis; many were supportive and helpful. Others, whilst not being overtly obstructive, maintained a stance of polite indifference to what we were doing.

Before 2011, observers sometimes came to visit the rehearsals, including the education manager and the head of Learning and Skills. Contact with the uniformed staff was minimal until the end of the project when some of them came to have a look at the final rehearsals. Prison officers were in charge of security when equipment was brought into the prison and when the audience came into the prison. It is possible that if prison officers had been present on a daily basis from the inception of these projects, a better link between uniformed staff, prisoners and the production team could have been formed. In 2014, the governor arranged for the same member of uniformed staff working at Operational Support Grade (OSG) level to be in the rehearsal room every day. This was very useful for the production team as she was helpful and constantly expressed her support for the work. She was able to act as a trouble-shooter, sorting out things like payments for prisoners, making arrangements for their meals during the production week and generally liaising between the creative team and the prison authorities. However, as an OSG, a lower grade than a prison officer, she did not have the same status and authority and so could be overruled if the prison officers at West Hill did not agree with what she was trying to achieve.

The autonomy of prison officers has been steadily eroded over the last couple of decades as cuts to funding, a target-driven culture and decisions taken at management level have served to decrease the power that prison officers have over key aspects of the running of the establishment (Crewe 2009: 110–12). Power, status and constructs of masculinity contribute to the hierarchical nature of staff relationships. In terms of relationships with prisoners, prison officers are the main conduit and mediators of institutional power and as such can overrule anyone with less status than them (Crewe 2009: 450). Therefore, a female member of uniformed staff with a lower rank than a prison officer was inevitably going to have difficulties asserting the needs of the production team over the perceived priorities of the wing officers.

Conclusion

It is both an advantage and a disadvantage to have worked in the same prison over a number of years. Advantages included the development of trust between the university staff team and staff in the prison, particularly when rules and regulations concerning security were adhered to at all times. However, there are many contradictions that underpin work in such an environment. We were constantly in danger of becoming institutionalised, and institutionalising our practice, by internalising the rules and operating systems of the regime in order to demonstrate our professionalism and trustworthiness. The constant looking over one's shoulder and policing the behaviour of the whole team so as not to commit breaches of security militates against the nature of the creative and collective act of making art and collaborating with all participants. As Heritage points out, we need to be aware that we are 'engaging in a marginal activity in a marginal space' (2004: 194). Looking back over the last few years, it appears that as prison staff got used to the theatre projects being delivered annually, they tended to become more distant from the work. This increased the feeling of marginalisation, the sense of being left to just 'get on with it'. There was less staff involvement; it felt as if the team were part of a greater package of different service providers, without real staff engagement or communication between the different agencies who might interface effectively with the work. It is my opinion that cuts in funding, decreasing staffing levels and constant changes at senior management level were a contributory factor to this sense of disengagement. The failure to create strategies whereby all agencies in the prison communicated with each other and worked together towards the collective aim of the rehabilitation of those involved in the work worsened year on year.

The governor at the time of the first project wrote a letter to the staff team, which acknowledged the ways in which the activity helped to raise the standard and quality of the institution.

> This sort of project is just what we hoped West Hill would be about and your contribution has helped to increase the unit's profile and success.
>
> (Gomersall 2003)

Governor Gomersall also wrote to the participating students and thanked them for their hard work and effort. He retired in 2005 and subsequently, up until 2014, there were six governors in post, several deputy governors acting up in the governing governor role and four heads of Learning and Skills. Whilst all governors were supportive, the nature of the year-on-year cuts made to prison budgets and myriad changes imposed from above, all served to create the sense of a system under continuous pressure. In 2014, there were five or six people working at governor-grade level in HMP Winchester; not one of them came to see the production.

The successful link and work with the Education Department in HMP Winchester also suffered from changes in policy, both locally and nationally. One of the aims of the theatre projects had been to influence the prison system at institutional and social levels by establishing the performing arts as an accepted activity in the prison, embedded in education. The hope was that the arts could be part of a portfolio of activities that had the potential to humanise the institution by reframing its role towards rehabilitation rather than punishment.

For the first three years of Playing for Time's work in the prison there was a part-time drama tutor who followed up the theatre project with smaller related projects. After the second show a disused visitors' room was converted into a drama room. By 2017, this had all gone; the provision of arts activities in both prisons has been pared down to a bare minimum. The drama room in West Hill became an art room, but is no longer used for this purpose as art classes have been discontinued, as have music classes in both prisons. Phase Four of the Offender Learning and Skills Service (OLASS 4) has narrowed the focus of education provision across the prison estate to one of developing skills and routes to employment. The emphasis of work in Education Departments in the prison system has to be on functional skills, specifically literacy and numeracy. Although it is clear that arts provision can contribute to the development of functional skills, unfortunately the pressure is on education managers to deliver programmes that are narrowly focused on these areas. Despite the 2016 Coates review of education provision in prisons and the recognition of the role that the arts can play in the context of rehabilitation in this report, the future of arts work in prisons looks bleak. It remains to be seen whether the government White Paper *Prison Safety and Reform* (Ministry of Justice 2016) will result in any significant changes to regimes that will allow for the development of personal and social education, which includes arts activities.

Playing for Time Theatre Company has now ceased to deliver projects in HMP Winchester. At the end of 2014, the prison management felt that budget cuts and increased pressure to meet government targets made the continuation of the work impossible, and it was with regret that this successful but challenging partnership came to an end.

References

Allan, S. (2015), interview by Annie McKean, Winchester, 2 June.
Balfour, M. (ed.) (2004), *Theatre in Prison: Theory and Practice*, Bristol: Intellect.
Boal, A. (1979), *Theatre of the Oppressed*, London: Pluto Press.
——— (1992), *Games for Actors and Non-Actors*, London: Routledge.
Bolton, G. (1992), *New Perspectives on Classroom Drama*, Cheltenham: Nelson Thornes Ltd.
Clift, S. and Morrison, I. (2011), 'Group singing fosters mental health and wellbeing: Findings from the East Kent "singing for health" network project', *Mental Health and Social Inclusion*, 15:2, pp. 88–97.
Corston J. (2007), *The Corston Report*, http://www.justice.gov.uk/publications/docs/corston-report-march-2007.pdf. Accessed 18 January 2017.
Crewe, B. (2009), *The Prisoner Society: Power, Adaptation, and Social Life in an English Prison*, Oxford: Oxford University Press.

Fo, D. (1987), *Accidental Death of an Anarchist* (trans. Hanna G.), 6th ed., London: Methuen.

Garrigan, D. (2003), *Refuge*, Unpublished.

Glassborow, P. (2011), *Soul Traders*, Unpublished.

Gogol, N. (2005), *The Government Inspector*, (trans. E. Marsh and J. Brooks), 2nd ed., London: Methuen Drama.

Heathcote, D. and Bolton, G. (1995), *Drama for Learning: Dorothy Heathcote's Mantle of the Expert Approach to Education*, Portsmouth: Heinemann.

Heritage, P. (2004), 'Real social ties? The ins and outs of making theatre in Brazilian prisons', in M. Balfour (ed.), *Theatre in Prison: Theory and Practice*, Bristol: Intellect, pp.189–202.

Howard League for Penal Reform (2011), *Report of the Inquiry into Former Armed Services Personnel in Prison*, http://howardleague.org/wp-content/uploads/2016/05/Military-inquiry-final-report.pdf. Accessed 26 January 2017.

Jarry, A. (1997), *Ubu the King* (trans. K. McLeish), London: Nick Hern Books.

Jeffreys, S. (2009), *The Convict's Opera*, London: Nick Hern Books.

Jones, L. and Manley, S., (2006), *Oh What a Lovely War*, Documentary Film, United Kingdom: LaunchPad Productions.

——— (2008), *Stand or Fall: From Page to Stage,* Documentary Film, United Kingdom: LaunchPad Productions.

——— (2011), *Soul Traders*, Documentary Film, United Kingdom: LaunchPad Productions.

——— (2013), *Our Country's Good*, Film of post-show feedback, United Kingdom: LaunchPad Productions.

Littlewood, J. (2000), *Oh What a Lovely War*, 2nd ed., Theatre Workshop, London: Methuen.

Martinez, R. (2005), *Our Country's Good*, Unpublished evaluation.

Ministry of Justice (2016), *Prison Safety and Reform*, https://www.gov.uk/government/uploads/system/uploads/attachment_data/file/565014/cm-9350-prison-safety-and-reform-_web_.pdf. Accessed 26 January 2017.

O'Neill, C. (1995), *Drama Worlds: A Framework for Process Drama*, Portsmouth: Heinemann.

Prisoners' Education Trust (2015), *New Government Data on English and Maths Skills of Prisoners*, http://www.prisonerseducation.org.uk/media-press/new-government-data-on-english-and-maths-skills-of-prisoners. Accessed 26 January 2017.

Thompson, J. (2003), *Applied Theatre: Bewilderment and Beyond*, Bern: Peter Lang.

——— (2004), 'From the stocks to the stage: Prison theatre and the theatre of prison', in M. Balfour (ed.), *Theatre in Prison: Theory and Practice*, Bristol: Intellect, pp. 57–76.

Wertenbaker, T. (2003), *Our Country's Good*, 4th ed., London: Methuen.

Winston, J. (1998), *Drama, Narrative and Moral Education*, London: Falmer Press.

Woolland, B. (2014), *Stand or Fall*, Oxford: Oxford University Press.

Chapter 3

Playing for Time in 'The Dolls' House': Issues of Community and Collaboration in the Devising of Theatre in a Women's Prison

Annie McKean

A version of this chapter was originally published in the Journal *Research in Drama Education*, 11:3, 2006, pp. 313–27.

There's someone here for the Dolls' House
(Overheard as I was waiting at the main prison gate to go into West Hill
for a preliminary visit)

This chapter focuses on aspects of devising and staging a play written for a group of women prisoners. The project raised issues concerning the nature of community theatre in secure institutions. As discussed elsewhere in this book, arts work in a community context is often predicated on notions of intervention and transformation. A central question underpinning this project concerned the nature of transformation through theatre on a personal level, within the institution and through debates with audience members who came to see the piece.

The debate about the suitability of custodial sentences for most women currently in English prisons has intensified recently. Between 1993 and 2003, there was a 19 per cent increase in the female prison population. This increase was because of changes in the administration of community sentences and in sentencing guidelines (HM Inspectorate of Prisons 2005: 3). In 2005, the women's prison population stood at 4,596. By the end of 2016, this number had decreased somewhat to 3,921 (Ministry of Justice 2016a). In 2007, Baroness Corston's comprehensive review of the experience of women in the criminal justice system was published. The Corston Report offered extensive criticism of the ways in which women were incarcerated and treated in prison. The report made many recommendations for improving the ways in which women were treated within the system. A government review entitled 'Women offenders: after the Corston Report 2013–2014' indicated that very little had changed in the criminal justice system. Baroness Corston's suggestion that women who had committed serious offences should be held in more dispersed, smaller custodial units and that there should be alternatives to custody for those women who have committed crimes of a less serious and non-violent nature had not been implemented (House of Commons Justice Committee 2013–2014: 4).

On the last page of a recent government pronouncement on the state of English prisons, almost a postscript, the White Paper 'Prison Safety and Reform', published at the end of 2016, acknowledged that women's needs are different to those of male prisoners. The government's plan was to create five small community prisons, which would focus on resettlement and support for women prisoners. A strategy for setting out the details for improving the safety of women prisoners and reform of the custody system for women was promised for early 2017 (Ministry of Justice 2016b: 61). On 27 June 2018, the Conservative Government announced the scrapping of plans for community prisons for women and instead intends to pilot at least five residential women's centres across England and Wales (Ministry of Justice 2018).

It is against this background that a close reading of the first Playing for Time Theatre Company project in West Hill, HMP Winchester, staged in May 2003, is offered in this chapter.

The context for the project

The worst thing about prison is the loss of freedom…loss of liberty. When you hear the keys and radios, you think, your freedom has gone… you know…the keys that deprive you of your freedom. It's the keys; I just hear the keys all the time…I've become like a dog…that's what I'm like…I react when I hear the keys jingle.

(Garrigan 2003: 3)[1]

Refuge, by Dawn Garrigan, was the first production staged in the prison by Playing for Time Theatre Company in 2003. It was performed by a group of fifteen women prisoners, supported by undergraduate students from the University of Winchester. In 2002–03, West Hill was being reorganised so that it could reopen as a Democratic Therapeutic Community for women prisoners, the first of its kind for women prisoners in Europe. The primary aim of the project was to create a piece of theatre based on women's experiences of the criminal justice system and for this play to be performed by women prisoners to an audience drawn from the local community who would come into the prison. At the time the project was proposed, the Governor of West Hill saw the play as a good way to place women's issues at the centre of the crime and punishment agenda and to use the play as one of the events that would launch the Therapeutic Community.

The funding awarded to the project was linked to the government's social inclusion agenda and was predicated on the links between involvement in the arts and changing people's lives, mainly in terms of raising their levels of educational achievement and enhancing their employability. Project management and administration were funded by the Learning and Skills Council (LSC), using European Social Funding, as were aspects of the delivery of a Theatre Arts programme, which was accredited by the Open College Network (OCN).[2] All women involved achieved accreditation through the project. Final accreditation was therefore important, but the LSC also acknowledged that the nature of the work would enhance the 'soft skills' of the participants, for example communication, self-esteem, goal setting and team building.

Since the show was staged in 2003 there have been a number of research studies designed to demonstrate a clear connection between participation in the arts and changes in behaviour (Arts Alliance 2013; Albertson 2015; Anderson 2015; Hughes 2005). Albertson argues that, in the context of arts projects, subjective changes such as attitude and perceptions of identity should be valued in terms of qualitative research methods applied to arts projects and that the 'quantitative medical model of data collection is inappropriate' (2015: 28). Whilst not disputing the need to provide evidence of the efficacy of arts programmes in secure institutions, the pressure to do so can shift the agenda of projects away from the group and its needs into fulfilling institutional demands, which can sometimes be at odds with the ethos of a project. There were often contradictions between the more utilitarian and pragmatic approaches of funding bodies that required the ticking of boxes, form-filling and report writing in order to fulfil the evidence-based requirements upon which the funding was based and the aims of a project that sought to explore as creatively as possible issues that participants felt were relevant to themselves.

Although the men's prison, HMP Winchester, had a history of inputs from external agencies, including two productions by Pimlico Opera in 2000 and 2001, there had been no similar work undertaken that involved women prisoners in performance projects apart from small-scale in-house work that had been undertaken by myself and University of Winchester students. The prison's drama tutor, who was appointed in September 2002, and the University of Winchester staff who contributed to drama work in the prison, were keen to redress this balance. Women prisoners are marginalised within the prison estate in a number of ways. For example, West Hill was often seen as and described as the 'annexe' to the men's prison by other staff. 'The Dolls' House' was a term that was also informally used by some staff in the main prison to describe West Hill.

In 2003, the sign at the entrance to the prison read 'HMP Winchester, Community Prison'. The descriptor 'community' was subject to much discussion amongst members of organisations who had connections with the prison, particularly those which involved volunteers working alongside prison staff. At the time there was no doubt that the prison was keen to engage in a variety of activities with different organisations. My involvement with both prisons in Winchester had initially been in taking undergraduate students into the two prisons as part of their work on a Community Drama module. I supervised and supported students' work and also ran drama workshops myself as a volunteer with men in the remand prison and with women at West Hill. It very quickly became apparent to me that the experience of women within the criminal justice system was very different to that of men. When I talked to people about the two prisons more often than not they did not know there was a women's prison behind the large Victorian prison that housed the men. I felt it was time to create a piece of theatre that would afford women prisoners the chance to tell their stories to people who knew very little about how prison affects women's lives. A key partner in this work was London-based Clean Break Theatre Company whose experience of working with women offenders and ex-offenders was invaluable. Clean Break was instrumental in bidding for Arts Council funding for the work of the playwright Dawn Garrigan on the project.

The main objective of creating a piece of theatre in order to raise community awareness of the criminal justice system generated concerns. There was continual discussion with the cast members about using their lives in the prison as material for the play. On many occasions life in prison and the problems generated by the impact of incarceration led to cast members being unable to attend rehearsals. The play had been widely advertised and so there was additional pressure on the project team and participants in creating a piece that would achieve a 'good' standard in terms of production values. However, the most important part of the project was the processes that underpinned the work. It would have been problematic to have put pressure on women to rehearse when they felt unable to do so; on the other hand the expectations of other participants and the fulfilment of the project aims had to be met. The tension between process-based work and theatre production is not always easy to reconcile. This is something that Sharp discusses in some detail in Chapter 8. The project also had to be seen as part of a sustainable set of activities and not just a 'one-off.'

Devising and staging the play

> Doing the play and meeting the students has made me feel like a human being again.
> (Prisoner L., in programme: *Refuge*, 2003)

The original intention of the West Hill project was to create a piece of theatre that would allow women prisoners to share their experiences of the criminal justice system with an audience beyond staff and other prisoners. During 2001–02, I conducted a series of semi-structured interviews with individual women prisoners, which recorded a variety of experiences relating to offending behaviour. The interviews offered women the opportunity to reflect upon their time in prison and the impact this had on their family and friends. Extracts from these interviews were later woven into the opening sound montage of the play.

Around this time, a historian had uncovered some names on the parish register of women convicts from London who had served the last six months of their sentence in Battery House,[3] a women's 'refuge' in Winchester, in the 1870s (see Chapter 4). Battery House had a progressive and liberal regime that focused on rehabilitation and reform. A residential school was established in Winchester for the children of the convicts so that when they were released they would not have debts outstanding to people who may have had to be paid to look after their children. We were able to obtain and use primary source material which informed us about the running of Battery House and the attitude of the matron whose ideas on the treatment of women prisoners was more progressive than some of the attitudes held about prisoners in the present day climate. Particularly interesting and moving were the records detailing the women convicts who resided at Battery House, stored in Kew Public Record Office in London. It was through using these records that we were able to draw up profiles of nineteenth-century women convicts whose names might otherwise have disappeared. The material generated through the interviews and the historical materials were explored during a series or workshops attended by the playwright,

Dawn Garrigan, who wrote the play *Refuge*, performed to an audience of over a thousand during the production run in the prison.

Central to the narrative structure of the play was a critique of different prison regimes, past and present. The historical scenes, set in the 1870s, focused on Millbank Prison in London and Battery House in Winchester. These were juxtaposed with scenes in a contemporary women's prison. Key ideas concerning the nature of crime and punishment were debated by the characters of the Matron of Battery House and the prison reformer, Jeremy Bentham. The concept of constant surveillance embodied in Bentham's Panopticon and the efficacy of the 'solitary system' (Foucault 1977: 201), whereby women were forbidden to speak, were juxtaposed with contemporary scenes where women reflected on the disempowering nature of their experiences in prison.

Research into the records of women who spent time at Battery House gave rise to the central nineteenth-century character of Amelia who, at 14 years of age, had killed her child. The fact that she had not been hanged indicated that there had been mitigating circumstances. Through improvisation we speculated about what might have happened to her and parallels were drawn with circumstances that link some contemporary women's crimes with male violence and exploitation. The circumstances of a maidservant and her baby evicted by the employer who raped her and left her to fend for herself were linked to women in custody today who found themselves in prison due to circumstances beyond their control. Scenes in Millbank Prison depicted Amelia deliberately tearing her hands on the ships' ropes from which she was removing the tar. Self-harm is common in women's prisons today and is reflective of the high levels of women in prisons who suffer from mental health problems. At least one of the cast members was a regular self-harmer and, like Amelia, she was also 14 when she had her first child.

A major dilemma faced in the devising and writing of the play was how we could present a piece reflective of women's experiences and also maintain a good working relationship with staff in the prison. It would be difficult to devise a play that offered a detailed and honest critique of women's contemporary experiences of the criminal justice system and perform this in the prison. The first draft of the play would have to be read by the governor and other prison staff, and it was important that the project was not jeopardised through censorship. It was felt that a piece of theatre, in which experiences of the past were juxtaposed with the present, could generate discussion about the future of women within the system. The reaction to the project by many of the staff in the prison raised further questions and issues concerning the nature of community theatre in secure institutions.

Theatre in secure institutions

I have never felt safe in prison. I feel safer on the street because I can run. If I am in danger I can run. In here I feel trapped. I just want to walk in the woods.

(Garrigan 2003: 3)

Trounstine states that what drew her to theatre work with women prisoners was '[…] the power of art in a repressive environment' (2001: 3) and that 'undertaking anything in a prison is like entering a country that doesn't really want visitors' (2001: 45). Thompson similarly acknowledges that theatre that is practised in particular contexts engages with the specifics of their 'discourses and approaches' but recognises that '[w]e are only ever visitors within the disciplines into which we apply our theatre' (2003: 20). Being a visitor as opposed to being a staff member has certain advantages as it enables one to take on the role of the outsider and ask for and sometimes achieve results that would otherwise not be deemed possible. In turn this can and does create suspicion in the minds of those in charge within the institution. This is particularly the case with those in charge of security who fear the disruption that theatre might bring in through the gates of the usually 'closed' institution and that may undermine the system in overt and covert ways. Thompson suggests that work that is most successful is delivered by those situated outside the context; once one becomes part of the system it is all too easy to compromise and bow to the seeming inevitability of what is regarded as possible by permanent staff. A central concern for artists working within secure environments is the nature of collaboration with the authorities in such a setting and whether, in doing so, one colludes with oppression when working within an oppressive environment (Thompson 2003: 29). Although many members of staff in prisons are committed to agendas of reform and rehabilitation, the current system of imprisonment is characterised by agendas of punishment and discipline.

The first theatre project undertaken at West Hill illustrated this disjunction because, despite the support of governors and senior management, many people who ran the prison on a day-to-day basis had a different attitude to working creatively with prisoners. The devising and staging of the play were sometimes seen by staff as disruptive to routines and discipline, and occasionally a threat to security. This became evident in the devising process, where the prisoners wanted to use the play as advocacy and as a vehicle for debating issues related to crime and punishment with an outside audience, however they were concerned about the responses of the staff to the final piece. They felt the play should make statements about their experiences of prison but acknowledged that they had to continue to live in the prison and interact with staff at the end of the project.

One exercise undertaken in a workshop involved symbolically dramatising each activity of a 'normal' day and the interactions between prisoners and officers that these events generated (Boal 1992: 43). After analysing and discussing this work there was a feeling of depression in the room. Finally, one of the prisoners said that the kind of material portrayed in the scenes could not be included in the play: 'we just cannot go there'. Everyone present acknowledged that despite some of the positive aspects of regimes and staff attitudes, the overall experience of prison is often damaging to prisoners, particularly in terms of mental health, and that to dramatise much of this material would end in the project being closed down by prison staff. The ethics of working in this context necessitate a constant questioning about the extent to which people's experiences and views can be fairly represented and the extent to which self-censorship militates against the creation of the 'voice' that this kind of theatre is supposed to 'empower'.

Transformation through participation and personal engagement

> I'm 22. I've been in prison 33 times. Maybe jail is not the thing to stop me. I don't want to go out because it's safe in here. I cannot cope with life on the outside. In prison you are like a sheep who is walking in a group.
>
> (Garrigan 2003: 3)

A psychologist at the prison suggested that for some of the younger women, taking part in the play might have been the first 'normative' activity they had undertaken. Most of these women in their early twenties had dropped out of school and had their first child before they were sixteen. People serving prison sentences struggle to maintain a sense of self and identity whilst dealing with regimes that are often dehumanising and disempowering. Women are perhaps more affected by the loss of personal freedoms and responsibility than many male prisoners (Devlin 1998). At the time the play was staged, over 40 per cent of women either convicted or on remand were primary carers and a significant proportion of this group had their children taken into care; others lost their homes as a result of going into prison (Wilkinson 2004: 161). The prison that we were working in at the start of the project housed prisoners who were, on the whole, in the low-risk category. Many of these women had never been to prison before and were traumatised by the experience. Some of them were serving short sentences, but this had still caused extreme disruption to their lives outside, in terms of what happened to their children whilst they were in prison and where they would live upon release. Working on the project did not solve these problems, but women taking part often made statements about the way involvement in the project served to enhance their sense of self and autonomy. The following quotations are taken from written evaluations of the project by the women as part of the accreditation programme.

> The skills I feel I have developed throughout the process were definitely communication skills, team work and confidence. We built up our self-respect and friendships and also respect for each other. Trust and self-esteem were also built up. It was a good experience and I would love to do it all over again given the choice.
>
> (Prisoner J., evaluation, 2003)

> At the start of rehearsals I was very introverted and found it hard to perform in front of others. My confidence grew as did my self-esteem and that was helped by the team I was working with. Everyone was extremely patient and always pushed me to do my best. I also learnt to be patient and respectful towards others and to listen to others. As time went on I had to trust people, some total strangers, but from being able to trust them I built friendships with them and felt free to talk about my feelings towards being part of such a powerful production.
>
> (Prisoner V., evaluation, 2003)

Most rehabilitative programmes in UK prisons use interventions based on cognitive-behavioural theories and are usually aimed at addressing prisoner behaviour and to some extent making people 'better' prisoners (McGuire 1995: 17); this raises ethical questions about their purpose. Our project did not aim to address the offending behaviour of individuals, or to make prisoners more amenable to the systems in prison. Some prison officers, however, commented that some of the most 'difficult' prisoners became easier for them to work with as their communication skills and confidence improved during the project. These reflections raise further concerns about the extent to which there was collusion with institutional aims of normalisation and what happens to prisoners who do become more compliant. Prisoners who fit into prison systems without challenging in some way the structures that underpin regimes tend to become institutionalised, which makes it harder for them to cope upon release.

During the post-show discussions after the performances some of the prisoners reflected on the impact the project had on their sense of self. One participant stated that she had been considering suicide but that becoming part of the project had enabled her to gain a perspective on how she would cope once released from the system. Another prisoner stopped self-harming during the rehearsal period and said that this was because participating in the play had made her feel 'better about herself'.[4] It has not been possible to evaluate the long-term impact of the project on individual prisoners, so it is difficult to make claims as to the effectiveness of this work on the women's lives upon release. It would be unrealistic to assume that a project such as this would necessarily effect long-term change; however, the benefits that accrued at the time of the project were clearly evident as women reflected in feedback sessions on how they were feeling about the work.

Prison systems infantilise women as evidenced by the language used by staff, e.g. 'girls' rather than 'women' and the phrase 'The Dolls' House' to describe the prison. The prison system is predicated and based on systems and regimes that have been developed for men (Carlen 1983; Stern 1998). For example, the staff at West Hill had abandoned the Home Office accredited anger management course because it had been written for use with men and they discovered it did not work well with the women. Once people arrive in prison virtually all opportunities to make decisions are taken away from them, and this is particularly hard for women who have had complex social responsibilities outside. Once in prison, women have restricted opportunities to deal with the responsibilities they have left behind on the outside. The feelings that result are often '[…] confusion, frustration and disempowerment [which] were for many the worst aspect of coming into prison' (Devlin 1998: 23).

Theatre projects require participants to work closely together and to collaborate in decision-making in ways that are not normally possible in prisons. Applied theatre is often described as giving the participants a 'voice' and 'empowering' them (Thompson 2003: 30–31), but it would be naïve to think that one project alone can radically transform either the individual or the system within which they have to operate. In the end, all that we felt we could do was offer a context in which the issues that came up through the play could be debated, both in the devising process with participants and with the audience after each performance.

Participating in drama involves becoming part of an ensemble, and this can be difficult for people serving time in prisons where the concept of community can be very problematic. One of the challenges of working within the arts in this context is to draw together groups of people from very different backgrounds in order to form a group and a sense of community with a shared focus and aim. It would be erroneous to say that the group functioned completely as a unified group by the end of the project but they did work well as an ensemble on stage. However, the group was always divided by class, race, age and background. The nature of a person's crime can also cause problems within a group. One member of the cast was always on the edge of the group and indeed was attacked by another cast member who was subsequently 'shipped out' of the prison as a result. After this incident, the rest of the cast developed an attitude of tolerance towards the woman concerned, which helped her become integrated into the group. Despite their differences, the factor that united the women was the play. There was an expectation, which was generally shared, that the play we were working on together was important and that bringing an audience into the prison to hear stories about the women and their experiences of prison was a unifying factor within the group.

Another important element in the creation of the community producing the play was the presence at workshops and rehearsals of undergraduate students. Seventeen students took part in the project. Most of them took on technical and understudy roles. It is a common experience for theatre practitioners when staging plays in prisons, for prisoners to be 'shipped out' with little advance notice and consultation. Having understudies meant that the play could still go ahead even if key cast members were lost in the later stages of rehearsals as was the case with one prisoner. In pre- and post-production feedback many women said that the presence of the students brought the outside world into the prison (Elles Productions 2004). Some of the students were close in age to the prisoners, and they were able to share stories and talk about common interests. The production team and all but one student were female. This enabled a particular rapport to develop between the outside group and the prisoners. The project had a great impact on the students in terms of their meeting with and learning about people that they might not otherwise have come into contact with. The project challenged everyone involved in it; for the students, meeting prisoners and hearing their stories was instrumental in challenging the prejudices and stereotyped view they might have held about prisons and prisoners. Their involvement was vital in terms of creating dialogue, friendship and a working relationship built on trust.

Institutional transformation

My problem is that I am institutionalised. I've been in care homes and Young Offenders' Institutions since I was four.

(Garrigan 2003: 3)

The experience of undertaking this project was unlike any other I had worked on before because it was made clear to both the production team and prisoners that any breaches in security or discipline could curtail and even close down the project. This highlights the constant paradox inherent in work within the arts in a system that is about 'containment, observation, punishment, categorisation, restriction [and] separation' (Balfour 2004b: 2–3). Knowing that the project might be terminated made the work extremely stressful, but ultimately more rewarding than other projects delivered in less constrained circumstances. There was a heightened relationship between the production team, students and prisoners that arose from this particular working context. This gave rise to a determination to use the project as a form of resistance to the power structures in the prison as well as attempting to challenge and critique the system using the multiple narratives in the play.

Some staff at officer level stated, at the outset, that the project would fail because it would cause too much disruption, particularly as the change to the Therapeutic Community would result in changes in the population of the prison. The production team experienced difficulties in terms of holding and starting rehearsals on time due to staff shortages, which resulted in prisoners remaining locked on the wings ('lock-downs'). It was almost always left to the team to find a governor in the main prison who could assign a member of staff to fill the gap. Indeed, a third of all rehearsal time was lost due to these 'lock-downs'. It was clear to everyone involved in the project that prison staff morale was very low; staff did not feel that they had been fully consulted about the development of therapeutic work at the prison and training was occurring in a piecemeal way. An additional factor was that many uniformed staff detailed to work in West Hill at that time were approaching retirement. They were placed in West Hill because it was seen as the easier of the two prisons to work in. The attitude of some of these officers was characterised by more traditional views concerning the function and role of a custodial sentence. Many who had been moved across from the Category B male prison had had little or no training to work with women prisoners and did not have the motivation to question regimes based on work with male prisoners in order to meet the needs of the women held in West Hill.

Building work in the space that we were using was very disruptive, and there was no heating during the coldest winter months. Work that operates outside of the frame of daily regime management often serves to highlight inadequacies and shortcomings within the system, and a surprising amount of time was taken up with negotiating different approaches to rules and regimes that went mostly unquestioned. For example, in order to join an education class prisoners had to ask for an application form that was used to apply for another application form that was then used to request admittance to a class. Prisoners called this Kafkaesque system 'an app for an app'. All applications were then discussed in a weekly staff meeting. Because staff in the unit office invariably could not find one or both of these forms it sometimes took four weeks for a prisoner to get enrolled into a class.

Work that is outside the usual routine of life and work in a prison often serves to sharpen the contradictions that lie at the heart of an institution. As a production team we trod a fine line between the notion of 'us' and 'them'. We could not afford to alienate staff at officer level nor could we appear to be on the side of those whom many in the group saw as the oppressors. The processes underpinning the devising of the play allowed for many discussions about prison regimes and staff attitudes to prisoners. The production team tried to maintain a sympathetic though not always neutral stance; given the way in which the production team were sometimes treated by officers, it was hard not to side with the prisoners. For officers who consider their role to be primarily concerned with issues of security, any activities that focus on reform and rehabilitation can become problematic. Some staff believed that access to education is a privilege that has to be earned rather than a right. Work in an area that is obviously skills-based, such as numeracy and literacy, is seen as relatively unproblematic; however, work in the arts creates problems for those people in the system whose attitudes reflect a traditional and conservative view of the purpose of prisons in society. This point was emphasised when a prisoner made a comment during one of the post-performance discussions with the audience. She stated that taking part in the play had 'taken her out of herself'. She went on to say that '[w]hen we are here I'm no longer in prison…you know… in my mind – I'm free'. Immediately, the officer in charge of security for each performance cut the discussion short and ushered the women to the 'back-stage' area from whence they were escorted back to their wings. This occurrence served to highlight the limits of tolerance by prison staff of the work; we felt that this prisoner's comment and the response to it highlighted how elements of the project had moved beyond allowable limits.

Some of the tensions that characterised the early weeks of workshops before we started work on the play were generated by staff anxiety about what the play might say about the running of the prison. After the reading of the first draft of the play in early March 2003, at which a prison officer was present, there was a marked difference in the staff attitude towards the production team. A message had clearly been passed around that the play did not contain the kinds of messages that would reflect wholly negatively on staff or their regimes. For example, the playwright Dawn Garrigan had skilfully created enough contrasts in the two prison officer characters so that they were not stereotyped as wholly negative. A key scene in the play was the strip-search; an officer interviewed for the documentary film acknowledged that this was often a degrading and dehumanising experience for prisoners and was sometimes difficult for staff too. Since staging this show, policy changes for the implementation of strip searches were made in 2007 after the publication of the Corston Report, though this practice continues under certain circumstances. Feedback from prison staff and governors at the end of the project indicated that the project had achieved success, which reflected favourably on the prison. The Number 1 Governor of the prison at that time wrote to the production team:

> The structure and content [of the play] was fabulous. I was so impressed with the seamless way that the perennial issues, liberalism and understanding versus punishment and deterrence, were woven together. As a minor student of social history and prisons, I was captivated by the accuracy of the story lines. The play *Refuge* will provoke thought and discussion for long after it is performed.
>
> (Gomersall 2003)

It was evident that once officers finally saw the play their views shifted, and many of those who had displayed negative attitudes offered compliments when asked what they thought about the piece. One prisoner whose marvellous singing voice was used throughout the piece said that officers commented on her talent. The officer interviewed for the documentary film said that she had stopped seeing the prisoners as 'just a number' and recognised them as individuals with talent and potential (Elles Productions, 2004). A prisoner stated that, having seen a dress rehearsal, the governor took her to one side and said that she could start to have the town visits that had previously been denied her. These are small but significant steps for the participants whose lives whilst in prison were enhanced by taking part in the project.

Transformation and audience

I feel as though I am not able to voice anything. I wasn't even allowed to have an opinion. I have become really introverted since coming into prison. I've really gone into myself.

(Garrigan 2003: 3)

It is surprisingly easy to sell-out a show that is staged in a prison. Some members of the general public have a prurient curiosity about what goes on in prisons. Many are ill-informed, and TV dramas popular at the time, such as the ITV series *Bad Girls*, do not serve to challenge the prejudices and preconceived ideas that people have of life in secure institutions. For some of the members of the audience it was their first time inside a prison. A number of people commented that they were not aware that there was a women's prison in Winchester. There were ethical considerations in terms of wanting the audience to come into the prison and debate issues with the women and see them as people with stories to tell, and a concern about the inevitable voyeurism that would bring some people into the prison to see the show. The women involved were very clear about what they wanted the audience to understand.

I wanted to show the general public that just because I was in prison I wasn't a bad person. There's a lot of biased people on the other side of the gate; I used to be one of them. I wanted people to be able to ask questions and me to be able to tell them the truth about prison life. I wanted them to know how it really is for us in prison. Just for once I wanted to put my views across, not the Governor's views, or the officers' views, but mine. After a year inside I wanted to be listened to.

(Prisoner L., evaluation, 2003)

There were restrictions due to security which made entry into the prison complicated for the audience, such as the request not to bring in bags and mobile phones. Many people said that the theatre started as they were let into the gatehouse in groups. Each audience member was subjected to scrutiny by 'sniffer' (drug detection) dogs. Even if you have nothing to hide, this can be an intimidating experience and acted as a prelude to what was to come in terms of the nature and content of the play. Responses to the play came through the post-performance discussions and questionnaires. Some people wrote letters and sent cards after the event. Many people commented on the power of the context of the performance. To see a play about the criminal justice system set and performed in a prison by prisoners offered an additional dimension to the experience, which would not have been the same in an outside venue. The contemporary sections of the play, where characters talked of their hopes and dreams and the ways in which these had been destroyed by the experience of prison, were given additional weight and poignancy because these speeches were delivered by prisoners.

Several people commented on the negative representation of key male characters and this was discussed by the women, the playwright and the audience on the last night of the show. As has already been stated, historical and contemporary scenes had been shaped in workshops and improvisations often based directly on the participants' experiences or on those of women that they had become close to in prison. The play reflected these stories and did not attempt to offer perspectives that might have provided a more balanced view. Some audience members confessed that the play had made them rethink the usefulness of prison sentences for many of the women who end up in prison.

The transformative power of theatre in secure institutions

Doing this play has made me realise that there is more to life than prison and drugs. Life is good and I am looking forward to living mine.

(Prisoner V., in programme: *Refuge*, 2003)

The contradictions that have to be dealt with in terms of setting up what might be considered radical theatre practice, whilst at the same time trying to accommodate some of the agendas of the institution, have already been mentioned. Thompson considers the role of theatre in terms of whether its effect is that of humanising the system of imprisonment or whether it can also transform the system it is working within (1998: 10). It is my view that such projects can effect changes within secure institutions and that these can occur at many levels, including changes in attitudes to creative work and sometimes changes in regimes. However, transformation also requires changes in policy and ideology, not to mention funding. These are difficult areas for arts practitioners to engage with. Education priorities in the prison service have been focused, in recent years, on meeting key and basic skills targets with a focus on functional skills, literacy and numeracy. The arts have suffered as a result and so the initiation of creative projects requires an understanding of a variety of prejudices and preconceptions with which this work will be regarded.

The play *Refuge* was an attempt to engage with a number of narratives; however, the primary focus was that of telling stories about women's experiences of crime and punishment without necessarily offering a critique of the whole system. The materials for the play were derived from stories told in workshops and creative responses to materials taken from historical and contemporary accounts of women's experiences of the criminal justice system. For most of these women, their offences were committed as a result of social circumstances, some of which included involvement in offending behaviour as a result of relationships with men engaged in criminal activities. However, these stories were of the moment, and necessarily only gave a partial picture of what the experience of offending behaviour meant for these women. The play was written in a dialogical style with no attempt to provide answers or solutions, but rather to raise a debate that would be different with each audience. It was the hope of the team that having gained the respect of some of the more sceptical members of the prison staff, future projects could begin to address some of the issues that the play had raised and that greater staff involvement could be engendered.

Refuge was taken on a tour of schools and colleges and performed by the student cast in September 2003. The tour was funded by the Hampshire Crime Prevention Panel who came to see the play in the prison and immediately offered funding for the development of the project into schools. A new cast member for the tour was a male prisoner who was on release on temporary license and studying drama at the University of Winchester.

Postscript

It's a sentence for life. To lock someone up is not a solution. Definitely not. There must be a better way than this.

(Garrigan 2003: 3)

The process did not stop at the end of the project. The next West Hill project was to be a participatory theatre piece with women performing and running workshops with young female offenders. The Wessex Youth Offending Team were partners in this project and funding was to come from the Higher Education Innovation Fund. However, on 8 March 2004, the staff team who worked in the Therapeutic Community (TC) were told it was closing down and they and the TC women would be moving to HMP Send in Surrey. Three days later the staff who were still on duty at 5.30 p.m. were told that West Hill was closing as a women's prison and would be turned into a Category C male training prison. The rest of the staff found out informally the next day. They were told the women would be 'shipped out' within six weeks. Two weeks later they had all gone. A week later the men were moved in. At that time in the South and South East of England, the male prison estate was overcrowded by 17 per cent. This decision was made by area managers in consultation with the Ministry of Justice. There was no consultation with HMP Winchester governors and staff about this decision. The redesignation of West Hill from a female to a male prison raises a number of questions concerning empowerment and ownership not just in terms of the prisoners but also in terms of the work of managers, officers and other staff in the then women's prison. This is supported by the external evaluator of the project who commented that '[n]o matter how positive the project, if it is isolated within a negative or unchanging environment, the effectiveness of the project is severely limited' (Balfour 2004a: 15).

The dialogue that arts activities facilitates can begin to make inroads into a system that is essentially monological, but it would be naïve to assume that change is possible beyond the immediate circumstances of the project and the context in which it is located.

The success of this first project laid the foundations for future work. Although the women were moved to other prisons, the new governor and the head of Learning and Skills were keen to support the continuation of theatre projects at West Hill with male prisoners. However, this first play remains for me the most successful in terms of the nature of the collaboration between the women and the creative team and the ways in which the women had ownership of the work. I have never forgotten the first interview I did with a woman prisoner. I asked her to imagine a photograph that would be emblematic of her time in prison. Her response was the trigger for my decision and determination to create a piece of theatre that would act as a platform for women's voices.

> What would be my lasting image of prison? The scussy toilets at Holloway. Stainless steel with lime scale and stains. It's like going down the drain. All those lives, those wasted lives.
>
> (Garrigan 2003: 3)

References

Albertson, K. (2015), 'Creativity, self-exploration and change: Creative arts-based activities' contribution to desistance narratives', *The Howard Journal of Criminal Justice*, 54:3, pp. 277–91.

Anderson, K. (2015), 'Documenting arts practitioners' practice in prisons: "What do you do in there?"', *The Howard Journal of Criminal Justice*, 54:4, pp. 371–83.

Arts Alliance Report (2013), *Re-imagining Futures: Exploring Arts Interventions and the Process of Desistance*, London, http://artsevidence.org.uk/media/uploads/re-imagining-futures-research-report-final.pdf. Accessed 19 January 2017.

Balfour, M. (2004a), *Report on 'Playing For Time Theatre Company': Prison Theatre as Education and Empowerment*, unpublished.

——— (2004b), *Theatre in Prison: Theory and Practice*, Bristol: Intellect.

Boal, A. (1992), *Games for Actors and Non-Actors*, London: Routledge.

Carlen, P. (1983), *Women's Imprisonment: A Study in Social Control*, London: Routledge and Keegan Paul.

Corston, J. (2007), *The Corston Report*, http://www.justice.gov.uk/publications/docs/corston-report-march-2007.pdf. Accessed 18 January 2017.

Devlin, A. (1998), *Invisible Women: What's Wrong with Women's Prisons?*, Winchester: Waterside Press.

Elles Productions (2004), *The Dolls' House*, Documentary Film, Winchester.

Foucault, M. (1977), *Discipline and Punish: The Birth of Prison*, London: Penguin Books.

Garrigan, D. (2003), *Refuge*, unpublished.

Gommersall, J. (2003), *Unpublished Letter*, Winchester.

HM Inspectorate of Prisons (2005), *Women in Prison: A Literature Review*, London, https://www.justiceinspectorates.gov.uk/hmiprisons/wp-content/uploads/sites/4/2014/07/Women-in-prison-20061.pdf. Accessed 18 January 2017.

Home Office (2003), *Prison Statistics, England and Wales 2002*, London: The Stationery Office, https://www.google.co.uk/?gws_rd=ssl#q=Home+Office%2C+(2003)+Prison+statistics%2C+England+and+Wales+2002%2C+London%2C+The+Stationery+Office. Accessed 18 January 2017.

House of Commons Justice Committee (2013–2014), *Women Offenders after the Corston Report: Second Report of Session 2013–2014*, Summary, p. 4, London, https://www.parliament.uk/documents/commons-committees/Justice/Women-offenders.pdf. Accessed 18 January 2017.

Hughes, J. (2005), *Doing the Arts Justice: A Review of Research Literature, Practice and Theory*, London: The Unit for the Arts and Offenders.

McGuire, J. (ed.), (1995), *What Works: Reducing Re-offending*, London: Wiley & Sons.

McIvor, G. (ed.) (2004), *Women Who Offend*, London: Jessica Kingsley.

McKean, A. (2006) 'Playing for Time in the Dolls' House', *Research in Drama Education,* 11:3, pp. 313–17.

Ministry of Justice (2016a), *HM Prison Population Bulletin*, Prison Population Figures, London, www.gov.uk/government/statistics/prison-population-figues-2016. Accessed 18 January 2017.

—— (2016b), *Prison Safety and Reform*, London, https://www.gov.uk/government/uploads/system/uploads/attachment_data/file/565014/cm-9350-prison-safety-and-reform-_web_.pdf. Accessed 18 January 2017.

—— (2018) *Female Offender Strategy*, London, https://www.gov.uk/government/news/secretary-of-state-launches-dedicated-strategy-to-break-the-cycle-of-female-offending. Accessed 3 July 2018.

Stern, V. (1998), *A Sin Against the Future: Imprisonment in the World*, London: Penguin Books.

Thompson, J. (ed.) (1998), *Prison Theatre: Perspectives and Practice*, London: Jennifer Kingsley.

—— (2003), *Applied Theatre: Bewilderment and Beyond*, Bern: Peter Lang.

Trounstine, J. (2001), *Shakespeare Behind Bars: The Power of Drama in a Women's Prison*, New York: St. Martin's Press.

Wilkinson, C. (2004), 'Women's release from prison: The case for change', in G. McIvor (ed.), *Women Who Offend*, London: Jessica Kingsley.

Notes

1   The quotes from Dawn Garrigan's play *Refuge* (2003), used throughout this chapter, came from interviews conducted with women prisoners in 2001–02. They were part of an opening

sound montage at the beginning of the play that the audience listened to, seated in darkness, before the theatre lights were brought up for the first scene.

2   The Learning and Skills Council was funded by the UK Government and the European Social Fund. Its work was focused on increasing the skills of people in the United Kingdom with a view to making them more employable. The Open College Network offers nationally accredited courses of a vocational and non-vocational nature. It is one of the accrediting bodies for work in further education.

3   The descriptor 'Battery House' was used throughout the play *Refuge*. The author of Chapter 4 uses the descriptor 'The Carlisle Memorial Refuge' which was also known as the Carlisle Home, the Carlisle Refuge, the Winchester Home and Battery House.

4.   4 April 2003 interview with the prisoner reported to the drama team by her personal officer.

Chapter 4

The Carlisle Memorial Refuge, Winchester 1868-81: 'That Most Difficult of All Social Questions' - A Nineteenth-Century Approach to the Rehabilitation of Women Prisoners

Pat Thompson

This chapter presents the research that was used for the historical sections of the play *Refuge*, by Dawn Garrigan. It outlines the result of investigation into the lives of nineteenth-century convict women who underwent an experimental regime in a provincial penal establishment and how this research was used within Playing for Time's first project in 2003. It analyses how the women prisoners at West Hill, HMP Winchester, used and reacted to historical sources that offered parallels with their own situation. The chapter also offers comparisons and contrasts between the treatment of women prisoners in the nineteenth century and the treatment of women in the criminal justice system today.

Just as they are today, the issues that beset the treatment of women prisoners were problematic to the Victorians; the debates over the nature and purpose of imprisonment and whether the penal regime was appropriate for women were prolonged and controversial. Common to all arguments, however, was the ideal that the offender should be fit for honest employment upon release, whether this was to be achieved by enforced reflection upon the wickedness of a criminal life, by the imposed inculcation of habits of work or by overall reformation. Contemporary debates include these and other concerns, to be discussed throughout the chapter, and it is the commonalities between these debates, and indeed the different experiences of nineteenth-century female convicts and contemporary female prisoners, which made this a rich backdrop for the theatre project undertaken with women prisoners in 2003.

Initially, this had not been the intended purpose of the research undertaken. By chance, a few years before, I noticed that the 1871 Census for Winchester included the names of women identified as 'convicts' living at an address opposite the County Gaol (Census for Battery House 1871). 'Convict' was a term applied to those men and women whose gravity of crime or continual petty offences would have earned them a sentence of transportation. When transportation ceased, a sentence of penal servitude would be spent at convict prisons such as at Portland or Woking Female Prison. County gaols, such as that at Romsey Road in Winchester, were used mainly for those awaiting trial, while borough gaols were used mainly for the incarceration of less serious offenders. This inclusion in the census was therefore puzzling because this gaol was not designed to hold convicts, male or female, and there was no obvious reason why women of this category should be living in Winchester.

Like most historical investigation, searching for an answer was similar to following a trail of clues, with numerous dead-ends. The different names by which the address was known meant that an initial visit to the Hampshire Record Office was less than illuminating and there the matter rested. However, on a later visit to the National Archives at Kew, I browsed voluminous collections of material in the catalogues of the Home Office Guides, which included a reference to female convict prisons. This jogged the recollection that the puzzle of women convicts in Winchester remained to be solved. By this time, a monograph on Victorian women prisoners, a work on an aspect of criminal life then largely unexplored, had been published (Zedner 1991). This mentioned 'refuges' for some convict women who were nearing the end of their sentences and a reference to annual reports of the Directors of Convict Prisons; these, like most official reports, were published subsequently as Parliamentary Papers. Could this have been the case in Winchester?

Historical research is not a matter of discovery through a straightforward sequence but dependent on sources that have survived. The problem is compounded when tackling a topic representative of 'history from below', that is, the lives of ordinary working class people who were neither rich, nor famous, nor members of the Establishment, those who had been the traditional subjects for historical research. It was only from the mid-1960s that the lives of the less eminent became recognised as a legitimate field for historical enquiry, and thus an investigation into the lives of men both poor and criminal resembles a jigsaw with many pieces missing. It is even more recently that investigation into the experiences of women in the past was recognised as historically respectable; consequently, the lives of those who were criminal and poor *and* female are even more difficult to access.

One of the perennial problems for those studying 'history from below' is the scarcity of sources produced by the marginalised themselves. Apart from the greater incidence of illiteracy and lack of opportunity, any writings produced by the 'unremarkable' were regarded by traditional historians as possessing little importance or interest. These attitudes, and the limitations of their lives, are even more pronounced if the writer was a woman. In the past, the poor – male or female – were noted by their social superiors, but usually only if their behaviour impinged unfavourably by being undesirable or problematic. Hence the lives of the poor, criminals and women, are refracted through the eyes of the upper and middle classes. However, when investigating the past, information is found in a variety of sources. Gradually, little pieces of initially random facts begin to cohere and a larger picture begins to emerge, even though some queries may never be answered satisfactorily, because the information may have been lost, misfiled or never thought worth recording. Searches at the British Library and in the *Dictionary of National Biography*, local newspapers and monographs, such as *Mary Carpenter's Reformatory Schools for the Children of the Perishing and Dangerous Classes* published in 1872, yielded information that could be pieced together. Return visits to the National Archives unearthed details of women convicts held at Woking Female Prison who had been sent to refuges, including that at Winchester. At last, a coherent, albeit incomplete, picture began to emerge.

The Carlisle Memorial Refuge,[1] sited opposite the County Prison in Winchester, was a locus for the rehabilitation of female convicts during the years 1868–86. It had been recognised that, because of the very restricted range of employment open to women in the nineteenth century, the chances of a female released from prison finding work were much lower than for a man and explained the much higher rate of recidivism among the former. The Refuge represented the idea for a fruitful transition between imprisonment and liberty. This design had several roots, including the temporary shelters set up for newly discharged women prisoners by the British Ladies' Society for the Reformation of Female Prisoners. Inspired by the well-known labours of Elizabeth Fry among women prisoners at Newgate, it was part of the great Victorian impetus, not universally accepted but remarkably effective, to rescue and protect the more vulnerable members of society. In the 1850s, with the end of transportation to Australia, there came a crisis in English prison administration that led to the government's involvement with the rehabilitation of female convicts. This necessitated the building of convict prisons for those men and women who, with their criminal past and possible criminal future, would formerly have been shipped safely out of sight. There was a general perception among the public that convicts were released prematurely within Britain, without evidence of reformation or adequate supervision upon release. It was this unease that led to an examination of the ideals of Sir Walter Crofton (1815–97), one-time resident of Winchester. The system of prison discipline that was developed in Ireland in the years between 1854 and 1862 by Crofton, following his appointment as Chairman of the Irish Board of Directors of Convict Prisons, was very highly regarded by many late Victorian penal reformers.

Influenced by the positive regime of Alexander Maconochie, who had been in charge of an Australian punishment establishment that had been earlier a byword for brutality and despair, Crofton devised a system that was both punitive and reformative. As in England, convicts were required to pass through three stages: the deterrent first stage, where female convicts spent four months in isolation, passing the time in contemplation of their sins and the tedious and unpleasant task of picking oakum. This was a task often assigned in prisons and workhouses; it entailed the disentangling of the tarry ropes used in sailing ships and caused the splitting of the skin on fingertips, a condition that did not excuse further picking. In the later stages of the sentence the women could become more in control of their own lives, firstly by working communally in a sewing room and being visited by philanthropic 'ladies', earning gratuities and privileges by demonstrating industry and self-discipline. It was Crofton's third stage that was the most radical. Here, convicts transferred to 'intermediate prisons' where small groups of convict women lived in 'houses of refuge' that tested their self-control, integrated them more closely into the wider community and increased their chances of employment upon release. It is argued today by some criminologists that finding employment in itself is not a solution for recidivism. Rather, becoming self-supporting through honest means, and thus rejecting criminality, is more an outward demonstration of the ex-offenders having adopted a new self-identity (Maruna 1999: 10). However, gaining employment was a Victorian yardstick for measuring reform, and the housework domain offered a constant demand for domestic servants, particularly if they were already trained.

Against the background of increasing vocal public concern about the entire system of penal servitude, the baton of change was picked up by the prestigious National Association for the Promotion of Social Science (NAPSS) at whose conferences Crofton was a frequent contributor. At the congress in 1863, and under the aegis of the Reformatory and Refuge Union (RRU), a committee was formed to exert pressure on the Home Secretary. It urged the adoption of Crofton's principles as being the best way of effectively dealing with 'that most difficult of all social questions, the reformation of our female convicts' ('Memorial of Reformatory and Refuge Union' 1864). The committee volunteered to establish pre-discharge refuges in England, under the supervision of 'competent ladies', if the government would authorise the sending of convict women to undergo the same regime as in Ireland and make the payment of seven shillings (35p) per head, per week ('Letter from Directors of Convict Prisons [DCP] in England to Home Office', 3rd August 1865). The DCP consoled themselves that, if reconvictions were reduced as a result of the experiment, the expense would be recouped. They were therefore inclined to view the RRU's suggestion favourably ('Letter from Home Office to Directors of Convict Prisons', 4th January 1865). Thus, the RRU were prepared, in January 1865, to guarantee suitable refuges capable of accommodating 100 female convicts altogether, and agreed that these refuges should be under government inspection and certification. On 24 August, premises in Queen's Square, Bloomsbury, in the British Museum area of London, were ready for occupation by female convicts for a short period at the end of their sentences ('Letter from secretary RRU' 30th January 1865).

The Carlisle Memorial Refuge was staffed by a lady superintendent and three matrons: one for the supervision of laundry, another to oversee needlework and third for stores and general work ('Letter from DCP to Home Office', 3rd August 1865). It could accommodate 50 Protestant women convicts drawn from the London prisons at Millbank, Brixton and Fulham. Three years later it was decided to move the location to Winchester, Hampshire, where it was known variously as Battery House, the Carlisle Home, the Carlisle Refuge, the Winchester Home and the Winchester Refuge, being and remaining the only refuge outside London. This decision was based on the fact that, although it had originally been thought that an experimental venture was better located in London, Walter Crofton's purchase of premises in Winchester presented several advantages. It removed the threat of removal by landlord (landlords were reluctant to let out their properties for purposes seen as unsavoury), and the nearby railway station afforded ease of communication. Moreover, its proximity to the home of Walter Crofton gave an assurance of his 'personal attention' ('Letter from Walter Crofton' 17th April 1868).

The staff at the Refuge

A 31-year-old single woman, Eliza Pumphrey, was appointed as lady supervisor at the Winchester Refuge's inception in 1868 and probably was always aided by three 'matrons', their names in 1871 being Isabella Harding, a spinster of 25, L. Walter, also a spinster, aged

28 and E. Brook, a widow of 30 (Census for Battery House 1871). By 1881, Miss Pumphrey's three staff had changed, but she had also gained the services of her niece Caroline Pumphrey, noted in the census as a 'teacher matron' (Census for Battery House 1871). The cooking was always done by one of the convict women. Although young, and probably recommended by word of mouth, Miss Pumphrey must have been a woman used to command and to be obeyed, as one would expect of a 'lady', for the majority of the 45 convict women were older than she. The youngest inmate was 22, the oldest 56. That she was regarded as possessing both sufficient status and experience is indicated by her appearance as a witness before the Royal Commission of Enquiry into the Working of the Penal Servitude Act in July 1878. The Refuge was in close proximity to Walter Crofton's home (he was actually sleeping there on the night of the 1881 Census), while his wife personally had overall supervision of the establishment. The doctor and the chaplain, who initially had given their services free ('Memo from Walter Crofton' 10th February 1869) were, by 1878, receiving a salary of £30 per annum and £50 per annum, respectively. For this, the chaplain performed a daily service in the room set aside as a chapel; the doctor saw the prisoners once a week and visited any who were sick two or three times a day, providing much medicine from his salary ('Report of Commissioners on the Workings of the Penal Servitude Acts' 1878/9: 604).

The prisoners

Now, in 2018, there are currently twelve prisons for women in England, one in Scotland and no prison for women in Wales. Women in Northern Ireland are held within a male young offenders' institution (Women in Prison 2018). Women are held an average of 60 miles away from their home or court address, although it is often significantly more, meaning most women are detained a good journey away from their families and local communities (Gulberg 2013). Similarly, the women convicts who passed through Eliza Pumphrey's hands were not born locally. Of the 45 women living in Carlisle Refuge on the census night of 1871, half were born in London, the other half mostly from the northern counties. Ten years later, only five of the 9 women were from London, the birthplaces of the remainder being more geographically spread, including one entry of a woman from 'Quebeck, America' (sic).

The employment of the women when at liberty was typical of those of Victorian working class women. Of the 23 sent there in 1878, six were noted as being married; to the middle-class Victorian mind being married was employment in itself and rarely in official documents were married women, as opposed to spinsters or widows, recorded as having an occupation. Of the remaining seventeen, only eleven had an occupation recorded, employment such as domestic service and the making of clothes being well represented ('Reports of Directors of Convict Prisons' 1878: 540–41). A similar pattern prevailed in those nineteen women sent two years later, with some detail such as 'lace dresser' and 'shoe binder' ('Reports of Directors

Playing for Time Theatre Company

of Convict Prisons' 1881: 536–37). In both 1871 and 1881, the combined number of spinsters and widows equalled the number of those claiming to be married.

Comparing the reasons for imprisonment of the women then with the present day, theft features highly in both eras. In 2014, 'more women were sent to prison to serve a sentence for theft and handling than for violence against the person, robbery, sexual offences, burglary, fraud and forgery, drugs, and motoring offences combined' (Bromley Briefings 2015). At Battery House, the crimes for which the women had originally been sentenced were typical of those of Victorian female criminals, with theft in various forms predominant, and currency offences also recorded. Four of the 23 women in 1878 had not been sentenced before, including a 'jealous' woman who had received a sentence of fourteen years for threatening to poison her 'immoral' husband ('Reports of Directors of Convict Prisons' 1878: 541). Only a single case with no previous convictions was sent from Woking Prison in 1880, that of a 50-year-old woman who claimed that her son had been made drunk before committing arson and that she declared the offence to be hers in order to save him ('Reports of Directors of Convict Prisons' 1881: 536). Her case, with others, was included in returns compiled by the Woking Prison chaplain, which itemise a number of facts about each woman and her character. Thus, we have such snapshots as:

33 year old charwoman, 10 previous convictions and 3 sentences of penal servitude, in prison at 12, imprisoned for stealing, convicted at 15, lost parents at 7 years of age; prostitution and drunk; hardened.

24 year old dressmaker, theft of 2/6 [25p] and cotton dress from a child, no previous convictions; cruel husband, her prosecutrix, [i.e. the woman who brought the case against her], the woman with whom he lived and had a child; asserts innocence; a very sad case; hopeful.

25 year old with 2 previous convictions, charwoman, drunk, doubtful.

A 22 year old needlewoman, guilty of forgery with a previous conviction of a similar offence, attributed to her 'love of dress and gaiety'.

('Reports of Directors of Convict Prisons' 1881: 536)

According to the lady superintendent, in 1878, many were factory hands, together with Welsh women from the mines, as well as a great many hawkers and London thieves and pickpockets. One of these last always 'puts up to be a lady; she is very grand' ('Reports of Directors of Convict Prisons' 1878: 540–41); some dressed smartly and generally wanted to appear better than they were. However, she went on to say, while most of the women were not married, they were faithful to the men whom they called their husbands and very few were prostitutes. Many had been led into crimes by their men, particularly in cases of robbery with violence, and it was not uncommon for their men, once themselves released from

84

prison, to seek out their women who had entered service and reintroduce them to a life of crime ('Report of Commissioners on the Workings of the Penal Servitude Acts' 1878/9: 601).

If we compare the demographic of modern day female prisoners, the role of relationships in their lives can also be seen to play a part in their offending behaviour; a survey of prisoners found that nearly half of all women (48 per cent), compared to just over one-fifth of men (22 per cent), reported having committed offences to support someone else's drug use (Light, Grant and Hopkins 2013). It is also important to note that 46 per cent of women in prison report having suffered a history of domestic abuse (Corston 2007) and 53 per cent of women in prison reported having experienced emotional, physical or sexual abuse as a child, compared to 27 per cent of men (Williams et al. 2012).

The chaplain at Woking Prison recorded his opinion on the outlook for the 23 women who were sent to the Refuge in 1880. For two it was 'very hopeful', for five 'hopeful', for four it was 'doubtful' and he was 'unimpressed' by six of the women; the remaining were categorised as 'hardened' or even 'hardened and bad' ('Reports of Directors of Convict Prisons' 1881: 536–37). The original idea had been that the most responsive women should be sent to refuges. These included those who had never been to a refuge before and who had obtained the requisite number of marks for good conduct and who had no reports for the previous three or four months. The chaplain's comments indicate that most women did not meet the criteria for entry into a refuge and that the high standard for selection had to be modified. Indeed, records appear to imply that medical grounds became the only grounds for ineligibility.

Regime

Then, as now, prison reformers urged the greater effectiveness of small units. There was space at Carlisle Refuge for 55, but numbers held were erratic. In 1868, numbers had varied between nineteen and forty and in 1878 it was reported that as many as 65 women had been held, but currently there were 34. It appears that the smaller numbers sheltered enabled the regime to be benign and congenial, as can be seen by the fact that some stayed beyond the statutory nine months because it was, in the words of Eliza Pumphrey, 'more a home than a refuge' ('Report of Commissioners on the Workings of the Penal Servitude Acts' 1878/9: 601). When asked by a member of a Royal Commission whether she looked upon herself as a 'friend as well as the manager', she replied:

> Yes, that is what they want; they want someone to look after them, they are like a lot of little children, some of them have no friend.
>
> ('Report of Commissioners on the Workings of the
> Penal Servitude Acts' 1878/9: 601)

Some women opted to stay for as long as two years, the food and treatment being identical to those of their detained sisters. Two women had, in fact, stayed in the refuge as they had no home to which to return, and had died there. Others returned because they were ill or in need of a holiday. What was known as 'liberty clothing' (a tight sleeveless vest, which buttoned up the front and also had rows of buttons along the bottom which could be attached to petticoats and a skirt) and not prison uniform was worn by the residents ('Letter from Directors of Convict Prisons to Home Office', 3rd March 1865). It is probable that Carlisle House continued the working pattern prescribed at the original London site where the women observed a rota whereby they worked for a fortnight each on laundry, needlework and housework, thus giving all women a fair chance of acquiring skills ('Carlisle Memorial Refuge, Reformatory and Refuge Journal' 1865/6). There was a grand piano in the living room used by some of the lady visitors to 'amuse and humanise' with singing and music for an hour an evening and whose attendance was said to be more systematic than that of their counterparts in London ('Carlisle Memorial Refuge, Reformatory and Refuge Journal' 1865/6). Less amusing, perhaps, were periodic lectures by a Rev. Collier on 'interesting and instructive subjects', and the occasional speakers sent by the Temperance Association (Carpenter 1872:143). It is interesting to note here that Jack Straw, in his role as Justice Secretary under the last Labour Government, issued a Prison Service Instruction in 2008, in response to tabloid indignation about too much 'amusement' for prisoners at Whitemoor prison attending Comedy School workshops, triggering a push not simply towards the instructive, but the forbidding of any 'recreational, social, or educational activity' unless it meets 'the public acceptability test'. The Victorian public, in the form of the lady visitors, perhaps understood the rehabilitative potential of the arts more keenly.

The regime was designed to have a humanising effect. Should any punishment be required, usually for continual quarrelling as there was no petty thieving from each other, the perpetrators were locked in their bedroom, for at the most three days, on a gruel and bread diet. This seems to have been a relatively rare occurrence, perhaps three times a year. But generally, Pumphrey said, she stayed with the offenders in their bedroom to talk to them for a little while, sometimes making the threat of deducting some of the money that they received for their work. It was her policy, should one of the women prove to be a bad character, to move three 'good women' whom she could really trust, into the same bedroom, and 'then we get rid of her bad conduct; she will then get too much ashamed to go on with it' ('Report of Commissioners on the Workings of the Penal Servitude Acts' 1878/9: 598–607). Agreeing with the suggestion of a member of the Royal Commission that the greatest means of punishment was the threat of being sent back to prison, she supplied the information that of the 1,016 women who had passed through Carlisle Refuge since 1868, sixteen had been returned. There were no locks on the doors of rooms in which work was carried out, and the front and back doors were always open during the day. Despite this, only two women in thirteen years had absconded, it being said that they were mentally unstable ('Report of Commissioners on the Workings of the Penal Servitude Acts' 1878/9: 598–607). The low proportion of women who did not have to be returned to a conventional prison, or who failed to take advantage of the physical freedom, argues strongly that they were highly responsive to the treatment that they received at the Carlisle Refuge.

A group of women, mixed in terms of age, offence and character, but from a background of socio-economic and emotional deprivation, many for whom the possibility of reform seemed doubtful, found themselves in a regime of care that perhaps they had never experienced before. These included an uncrowded house, healthy food, a regime that demonstrated trust and respect and, above all, contact with adults who took a warm parental interest in their welfare and who believed in their potential. When asked about the 'incorrigible' to whom she could hope to do very little good, Pumphrey replied 'I think there is good in all of them if you can only find it out' ('Report of Commissioners on the Workings of the Penal Servitude Acts' 1878/9: 606). All this provided an environment in which the women could perceive the possibility of change in themselves and in their future. In the light of new experiences, the convict women were enabled to reconstruct their identity. According to Shad Maruna, today's ex-offenders overwhelmingly attributed their change to outside forces, usually the 'generosity of some forgiving person or person who can see past the ex-offender's mistakes' (1999: 10). At the Carlisle Refuge, this generosity of spirit was evinced by Eliza Pumphrey, the 'lady visitors' and, later, the employers whose support allowed the woman to finally become, again in Maruna's words: 'her "true self" (a good or, non-criminal person)' (1999: 10).

Financial incentives

The government provided financial incentives for the women dependent on their behaviour, labour and good conduct after release from the Refuge. This conduct had to be certified by a superintendent of police or by a clergyman, the latter disposing of it for the woman's benefit, for example in the purchase of a mangle. The money was thus used as an incentive to try and ensure the woman kept to an honest path when at liberty. If any woman chose to stay at the Refuge beyond her release, she paid for her upkeep with any profit obtained through her labour. Through their work, in the laundry or in needlework, women were not only given some financial safety net upon release, but there was some attempt to encourage them to use the money to support themselves. More important, one would imagine, was the training, which must have been sufficiently thorough to allow the women to compete successfully with free labour. Envisaged as a utilitarian activity, it also gave the women self-respect and hope for the future.

Reform

The Carlisle Refuge seems to have succeeded in its ultimate purpose. The criminal records of the women showed many had led a life of crime since the age of ten or twelve, had spent innumerable periods in local gaols and up to three periods in convict prisons where initially they had been 'very outrageous and refractory'; since release, however, they had lived for many years in domestic service, under the constant observation of the authorities of the refuge (Carpenter 1872: 142). In 1868, of the 53 women discharged, 36 had found employment, four had returned to their old ways, five were untraceable and the remaining eight were 'doing well' ('Carlisle Memorial Refuge, Reformatory and Refuge Journal' 1865/6). To monitor their progress, letters from both the employers and former convict women were required, and visits were made by Miss Pumphrey and others involved with the Refuge, such as the Rev. Ashton Wallis. These visits were described as requiring much time and self-sacrifice, as well as thoroughness and discretion in distinguishing between those who were not merely reconvicted and those who were doing well (Carpenter 1872: 141). It must be borne in mind that the supporters of refuges would naturally perceive results in the most positive light; nevertheless, it can be claimed that the Carlisle Memorial Refuge succeeded in its ultimate purpose.

The children of convict women

It had been argued that the child of a female convict left destitute by the mother's imprisonment was a 'peculiarly fit' subject for the protection and training provided by industrial schools ('Letter from Rev'd Sydney Turner to Home Office', 11th June 1870). These were residential institutions set up from 1857 where destitute, homeless, neglected or disorderly children were taught basic literacy skills and trained to equip them for work appropriate to their station in life. Such a child was 'almost certain to have been brought up in the habits and amid the associations of vice and crime' ('Letter from Rev'd Sydney Turner to Home Office', 11th June 1870). While a convict mother was incarcerated, the child would be taken care of by some relative or companion of the mother, or was sent to the workhouse, and in either case was reclaimed by the mother and brought again under her influence. In the opinion of an Inspector of Industrial and Reformatory Schools:

> This process if more than once repeated till the Child qualifies itself by begging or stealing for penal or reformatory treatment – or if a Girl – takes to the streets. To interfere at an earlier age for the rescue of such children seems to me an act of policy as regards Society quite as much as of mercy towards the children themselves.
>
> ('Letter from Rev'd Sydney Turner to Home Office', 11th June1870)

Moreover, Eliza Pumphrey believed that leaving convicts' children to informal care led to the mothers' reoffending, stating that when the children were left with friends for the seven, ten or more years of their sentence, the friends had a hold over the mothers; when liberated the mother then returned to thieving in order to repay these friends the cost of caring for their child. According to a report by the Prison Reform Trust in 2015, currently: 'two-thirds of imprisoned women are mothers of children under the age of 18. A third of these women have children under the age of five, and a further 40% have children aged between five and ten' (Minson, Nadin and Earle 2015: 2). 'In a survey of 1,400 women serving a first sentence in Holloway prison, 42 did not know who was looking after their children' (Minson et al. 2015: 7). The impact of prison on mothers and their children is both an historic and current problem.

Walter Crofton was instrumental in the provision of care for the children of the women living in the Carlisle Refuge. In 1875, or earlier, the St Andrew's Industrial School, primarily for the children of female convicts, was established at Westgate House, 8 Upper High Street, Winchester. The annual reports of the inspector, usually the Reverend Sydney Turner, of St Andrew's Industrial School opined that the children were happy, healthy, thriving, well-behaved and making satisfactory progress at a nearby elementary school. The 'training' received for girls comprised of learning to knit and sew, and helping in the kitchen, laundry and with housework; for boys, it entailed working in the garden and keeping the premises clean ('Report of Commissioners on the Workings of the Penal Servitude Acts' 1882: 146). To the argument that the woman would be left unrestrained to pursue her criminal course should the children not be reclaimed, Turner had countered that 'women of this class act more by impulse than by calculation. They care very little about the future of their children but feel very strongly any present separation from them'. He stated that the chief difficulty of the managers of two existing refuges for the children of convicts, one in London and the other in Liverpool, had been the 'eagerness of the mothers to remove their children from such institutions' ('Letter from Rev'd Sydney Turner to Home Office', 11th June 1870). Given that many of the women discharged from the Carlisle Refuge entered into service, where they would be unable to have their children live with them, it is uncertain whether this was a problem for Miss Pumphrey. She told the Royal Commission in 1878 that, when the children of St Andrew's were taken for a walk, their mothers were able to watch them from the Refuge windows. It is interesting to reflect here on the situation of some of today's women prisoners who prefer not to have their children visit them but who would nevertheless be able to identify with the emotional deprivation experienced by their Victorian counterparts. Eliza Pumphrey provided further evidence of her charges' maternal feelings by relating that, when permitted, the women worked very hard at needlework to earn up to fourteen shillings (70p) a week for the benefit of their children. This was further evidence of an enlightened regime that acknowledged the women to be individuals with the same 'normal' feelings as their respectable sisters.

The closing of the Carlisle Memorial Refuge

By 1886, the Carlisle Memorial Refuge and St Andrew's had closed, ending eighteen years of Winchester's involvement with an enlightened regime for the care and reformation of adults and children of the 'perishing and dangerous classes'. The number of women committed to penal servitude declined steadily during the latter half of the nineteenth century. This is perhaps less due to the fact that the du Cane regime of deterrence in convict prisons was cutting crime rates, than that there was a growing recognition that long sentences were inappropriate for many of the continual recidivist women who tended to be mentally ill, socially inadequate or 'hopeless drunkards'. After nearly 150 years, today's society has made very few innovations to address this problem.

West Hill, HMP Winchester: Twenty-first-century women prisoners and history

History is a subject that deals with human behaviour and experience in the past, demanding both an analytical methodology and an imaginative, empathetic approach to the people whose lives are being scrutinised. I anticipated that using these primary sources with the women, handwritten and often expressed in archaic language, could be a challenge, particularly in the short time frame and for those with low levels of literacy. However, it proved not only possible during the workshop period, in November 2002, when I went into West Hill, HMP Winchester for two afternoons, but provided stimuli that the participants met with excitement and interest.

The very first activity upon meeting the women was to ask how, in a hundred years' time, it would be possible to find out about them. The answers came readily and included certificates of birth, marriage and death, appearances in newspapers, their own criminal record. That was fine – but how would we know about them as people: their hopes, ambitions, emotions? Well, diaries perhaps, or audio-visual media – but were there any drawbacks in the use of these for accurate information? And what about their everyday lives – who would keep their shopping lists for posterity or follow them round for a week to record their activities? Gradually, we drew up a picture of the ephemerality of informal evidence and the difficulties of obtaining an accurate portrait from what did survive. Time spent at the National Archives had uncovered official forms revealing some details of women who were discharged from convict prisons into refuges for the remainder of their custodial sentence. They gave information on the woman's appearance, age, initial offence and her conduct during her incarceration. Photocopies of some of these nineteenth-century prison records were distributed to the prisoners, working in pairs, to encourage confidence and participation.

First we investigated what we could tell from these official records, where the emphasis is, of course, on the offences rather than the prisoner as a person. This focus was, and remains, common; to overcome it, the West Hill prisoners were asked for questions they would like to ask the woman whose record they held. Answers were suggested and, although this task was treated with a note of levity, it was emphasised that these answers could only be surmised due to a lack of evidence. When asked what evidence for their answers might be, the women were able to draw on what we had discussed earlier and showed some ingenuity. For example, when one of the West Hill women said that she would like to know how the nineteenth-century woman got on with her husband, another suggested that hospital records should be consulted to see how often she had been beaten up. They were able to pass comments on each other's suggestions, pointing out any drawbacks or what other source might be required. The session passed quickly, with the women becoming increasingly empathetic to their historical counterparts and showing an awareness I had not expected of the limitation of the evidence they were handling. As one declared: 'I wouldn't like to think the only thing that survived about me is what some prison bastard said'.

In the second session, some of these facts were picked up again, with some of the 'case studies' causing further reflection from the group. There was curiosity as to the type of crime committed by the female convicts and a noticeable reaction to the role of men in initiating or provoking crime. When it came to the regime and staff of the Carlisle Refuge, the problem arose of the accessibility of the information. In Victorian official sources, the language tends towards the unfamiliar and the verbose. To surmount this difficulty, I took on the role of Miss Pumphrey who answered the questions devised by groups of three or four. Some of the questions tended to be framed assertively, for example, 'who asked for these "lady visitors" to come in?' and 'why didn't she teach them to be other things but servants?' These questions evinced a form of class-consciousness that was in danger of being anachronistic and that may have been directed to me as much as to 'Miss Pumphrey'. However, the hot-seating did enable misconceptions of the past to be modified and enabled the caring as well as the controlling aspect of the refuge to become overt. Interestingly, by the end, I felt a distinct identification with Eliza, and that the women did too was indicated by a replacement of the word 'she' with 'you'. With this session drawing to a close, I asked the group how they would measure the success of any penal experiment, past or present. While remaining dubious about the benefits of being a domestic servant, the group actually seemed pleased that Walter Crofton had been vindicated and that a regime based on an understanding of the women and their circumstances had fulfilled the hopes of its founders.

The social conditions of the convict women may have been different in some external features, but their personal reactions and the way they adapted to their circumstances were perhaps recognisable to women in the twenty-first century. The domestic training that led to employability and hence to integration into wider society also led to independence and perhaps a sense of increased worth. The lives of the women in the Carlisle Refuge illustrated that, while it is difficult to escape the label of criminal, with support people can overcome disadvantage and put their criminal past behind them.

The limitations of time prevented the exploration of two issues that were potentially very sensitive. One of these was of the awareness raised in the last quarter of the century of the causes of continual recidivism and the inadequacy of conventional sentences for women whose personal or medical problems were the basis of their criminal activity. The workshop sessions took place before the Corston Report was commissioned, following a national spate of suicides among women prisoners, and it would have been interesting to know what suggestions the West Hill women would have made. The second issue, which had even more potential to be distressing to at least some in the group, was that of the fate of children of the convict women. When considering the impact of the two comparatively short sessions on the women in the group, I hoped that the examination of the lives of their nineteenth-century counterparts gave an opportunity, albeit superficial, for an evaluation of their own situation. Additionally, these workshops informed the processes that underpinned the writing of the play that was staged in April 2003.

It is easier to assess the impact of the activities on myself. Used as I was to visiting a variety of prisons and conversing with prisoners, it was a new experience to undertake this type of work in such an environment. It proved to be a true learning experience. The shared discoveries of the lives of real people in the past provided a real excitement for both me and for the women who were unexpectedly curious and willing to undertake an academic exercise. My underestimation of the capabilities and insights of the West Hill women received a salutary and chastening correction. Equally unexpected was the swiftness with which a rapport with the group was established and their eagerness to engage with materials that demonstrated in part a more enlightened approach to working with women offenders today. The wryly perceptive comments made by some women were also unanticipated; most unexpected of all was the frequency of our laughter. It would be pleasant to think that such a relaxed atmosphere prevailed at the Carlisle Refuge.

The Wedderburn Report by the Prison Reform Trust's Committee on Women's Imprisonment in 2000, the Corston Report in 2007 (a 'Review of Women with Particular Vulnerabilities in the Criminal Justice System'), the 2011 report of the Women's Justice Taskforce (Reforming Women's Justice), and the Scottish Government's Commission on Women's Offenders in 2012, all conclude that prison is rarely an appropriate, necessary or proportionate response to women who get caught up in the criminal justice system, and that considered reform is needed to reduce women's imprisonment. The Corston Report addressed the problem of appropriate treatment of women prisoners rendered particularly vulnerable by domestic and personal circumstances and socio-economic factors (Corston 2007: 2). Juliet Lyon, Director of the Prison Reform Trust, welcomed the Report's recommendation that large prisons that operated as 'social dustbins' be done away with. Instead, the report argues that what is required are small units coupled with proper supervision and support. This sounds very much like the Carlisle Memorial Refuge. The similarity does not end there. The possibility that women prisoners can desist from crime if they are offered the opportunity for changing their self-identity also offers a continuum between past and present. For, Lyon claims, under the Corston proposals: 'many women who offend, will have their first real opportunity to take responsibility for their lives, and those of their children and most will take it', arguing that: 'Women have been marginalised within a system largely designed by men for men for far too long' (2007: 2). If, for some, the only record we have of them 'is what some prison bastard said', the least we can do is explore the possibilities of their stories in the present.

References

'Bromley Briefings Prison Factfile' (2015), http://www.thebromleytrust.org.uk/files/bromleybrie fingsautumn2015.pdf. Accessed 31 January 2017.
'Carlisle Memorial Refuge, Reformatory and Refuge Journal' (1865/6), Hampshire Record Office, TOP/343/3/833/3.

Carpenter, M. (1872), *Reformatory Prison Discipline*, London: Longman Green.

Census for Battery House (1871), Hampshire Record Office, M 327, RG10/1209/f 32 & 32.

Corston, J. (2007), *A Review of Women with Particular Vulnerabilities in the Criminal Justice System*, London: Home Office.

Ford C. (1868), 'Efforts on behalf of criminal women', *Reformatory and Refuge Journal, 1867/9 Report of the Carlisle Memorial Refuge*.

Gullberg, S. (2013), *State of the Estate: Women in Prison's Report on the Women's Custodial Estate 2011–12*, http://www.womeninprison.org.uk/perch/resources/stateoftheestatereport.pdf. Accessed 31 January 2017.

'Letter from DCP to Home Office', 3rd March (1865), The National Archives, Home Office 45/9318/16208/4.

'Letter from DCP to Home Office', 3rd August (1865), The National Archives, Home Office 45/9318/16208/10.

'Letter from Home Office to Directors of Convict Prisons', 4th January (1865), The National Archives, Home Office 45/9318/16208/2.

'Letter from Rev'd Sydney Turner to Home Office', 11th June (1870), The National Archives, Home Office 45/9320/16629b.

'Letter from secretary RRU' 30th January (1865), The National Archives, Home Office 45/9318/16208/3.

'Letter from Walter Crofton' 17th April (1868), The National Archives, Home Office 45/9318/16208/20.

Light, M., Grant, E. and Hopkins, K. (2013), 'Gender differences in substance misuse and mental health amongst prisoners', *Results from the Surveying Prisoner Crime Reduction (SPCR) Longitudinal Cohort Study of Prisoners*, London: Ministry of Justice.

Maruna, S. (1999), 'Desistance and development: The psychosocial process of going straight', *British Criminology Conferences: Selected Proceedings*, 2, pp. 1–25.

'Memo from Walter Crofton 10th February' (1869), The National Archives, Home Office 45/9318/16208/22.

'Memorial of Reformatory and Refuge Union' (1864, undated but approximate), The National Archives, Home Office 45/9318/16208/1.

Minson, S., Nadin, R. and Earle, J. (2015), 'Sentencing of mothers: Improving the sentencing process and outcomes for women with dependent children', Prison Reform Trust, http://www.prisonreformtrust.org.uk/Portals/0/Documents/sentencing_mothers.pdf. Accessed 1 June 2016.

'Report of Commissioners on the Workings of the Penal Servitude Acts' (1878/9), Parliamentary Papers, vol. xxxvii.

'Report of Commissioners on the Workings of the Penal Servitude Acts' (1882), Parliamentary Papers, Twenty-fifth Report, vol. xxxv.

'Reports of Directors of Convict Prisons' (1878), Parliamentary Papers, vol. xliii.

'Reports of Directors of Convict Prisons' (1881), Parliamentary Papers, vol. lii.

Williams, K., Papadopoulou, V. and Booth, N. (2012), 'Prisoners' childhood and family backgrounds: Results from the Surveying Prisoner Crime Reduction (SPCR) longitudinal cohort study of prisoners', *Ministry of Justice Research Series 4/12*, https://www.gov.uk/

government/uploads/system/uploads/attachment_data/file/278837/prisoners-childhood-family-backgrounds.pdf. Accessed 31 January 2017.

Women in Prison, (2018), Key Facts, http://www.womeninprison.org.uk/research/key-facts.php. Accessed 25 May 2018.

Zedner L. (1991), *Women, Crime and Custody in Victorian England*, Oxford: Clarendon Press.

Note

1 It was named after the Earl of Carlisle who, as Lord Lieutenant of Ireland, had been instrumental in implementing Crofton's reforms in that country. Roman Catholic female convicts were sent to Eagle House Refuge in Hammersmith, London. By 1875, there were two more refuges in London, Elizabeth Fry House in Hackney and Russell House in Streatham.

Chapter 5

Stage Fright: What's so Scary about Dressing Up?

Brian Woolland

A version of this chapter was first published in *The Journal for Drama in Education*, 25:2, Summer 2009.

Introduction

In the autumn of 2007 I led a series of theatre workshops in West Hill, HMP Winchester in preparation for a commission by Playing for Time Theatre Company to write and direct a play – to be performed by twelve prisoners and ten students from the University of Winchester. The resulting play, *Stand or Fall*, was rehearsed in the Spring of 2008 and given five performances in West Hill, HMP Winchester to invited audiences in April 2008.

This chapter is firstly a brief account of that process; and secondly a reflection on the extraordinary way in which creating drama and theatre in this very particular and peculiar social context reanimates debates and triggers anxieties about the power and evils of theatre that had been prevalent in early seventeenth-century England – when Shakespeare, Jonson, Middleton, Marlowe and Webster were writing their great plays. It then goes on to explore how these anxieties and debates provoke insights about theatre in our own society in the early twenty-first century, with its contradictory attitudes to education, punishment and pleasure.

The context and the project

In 2006, I had seen the Playing for Time production of *Oh What a Lovely War* and I still think of it as one of the most moving and profoundly affecting theatrical and cultural events I have experienced. I had previously seen three professional productions of the play, including the National Theatre's touring production; all lively, provocative productions, but none of them came close to the experience of seeing prisoners playing squaddies and officers in a prison gym. Whenever we see a play, the theatre space in itself is significant, even if it is usually filtered out of our reading. With this production of *Oh What a Lovely War* the audience could not help but read the culturally specific context of the production at the same time as reading the performances. And it was this that made the theatre event so profoundly affecting – that these men were themselves cannon fodder (indeed, several had served in the army), imprisoned not only for specific crimes, but also by social and political circumstances. When I received the commission to write and direct a play for Playing for Time, I resolved to try to write a play that would have similar resonances for the performers and the audiences.

Preparations and workshops

I felt from the outset that if I was to write a play for prisoners to perform it was essential to understand as much as possible of the prisoners' situations and about institutional life in a modern prison. With the help of Annie McKean, Artistic Director of Playing for Time, and Richard Daniels, Education Manager at HMP Winchester, I set up a series of drama workshops in autumn 2007, many of which drew heavily on the techniques and methodology of drama in education, aiming to empower the participants and allow their voices to be heard and to affect the work.

Some of the workshops were light-hearted, some were serious. Amongst other things we explored possible relationships between family histories and personal identity and some of the ways in which peer pressure can affect decision-making. The discussions we had during those workshops, the improvisations, the theatre games and the pantomime we put on in December – nominally *Jack and the Beanstalk*, but in practice a strange mad hybrid of panto, *Monty Python*, *Punch and Judy* and *Pulp Fiction* – all informed the writing of *Stand or Fall*. The other work, the more 'serious' theatre workshops, was more difficult – in as much that we kept on 'bumping into' the past experiences of some of the men, which they found very uncomfortable: childhood, relations with parents, perceived abandonment by wives and girlfriends. One of the things that became apparent early on in these workshops was that all those taking part were as terrified of change as they were desperate for it. At each of the sessions we talked about the play that had yet to be written. During one of these discussions, Vinnie said he wanted to take part 'in something uplifting […]. It may sound stupid', he said, 'but I'd like it to be a thing of beauty'.

Stand or Fall

Drawing on the experience of *Oh What a Lovely War* and the preparatory theatre workshops, I sought (in writing *Stand or Fall*) to create a piece of theatre with powerful resonances between the situations that the prisoners and the students were in and the social circumstances of the characters they would play. Balancing this, I recognised that it was important to create sufficient distance between prisoners and their character(s) to allow them to reflect critically on the decisions made by those characters – thus the methodology, although directed towards performance, was close to and drew heavily on my experience of educational drama. It was important to create a fictional world with which all participants could identify, a world which would have metaphorical resonance for them, whilst avoiding direct allegory.

And, perhaps most importantly, recognising Vinnie's desire to be a part of something 'uplifting', to write a play in which at least some of the characters made difficult decisions that resulted in positive change.

For many years, I had been fascinated by an incident recounted by Terry Coleman in his book, *The Railway Navvies*:

> The navvies were careless, and lived up to their reckless reputation with bravado. In the Kilsby Tunnel on the London and Birmingham Railway, three men were killed as they tried to jump, one after the other, over the mouth of a tunnel airshaft in a game of follow my leader.
>
> (Coleman 1965: 27)

It is relatively easy to see how one man might jump to his death as an act of daring, but for a second and then a third to follow begs extraordinary questions about peer group pressure, about the brutality of a culture that could condone if not encourage such actions; and about the ways that meanings of a concept such as courage are at least partly contingent upon cultural and social contexts.

The following is a very brief synopsis of *Stand or Fall*:

Two men, three generations apart, struggle to escape the labels that have been pinned to them.

1878. Slen McGuire has tramped all over England, taking any work he can get. He's worked on farms, now he's a navvy on the *Deadwood Tunnel*. Regarded by 'civilised society' as 'an ungodly, reckless pack of rascals' (Woolland 2014: 5), the navvies may be as hard and dangerous as their work, but many of them are also warm-hearted, witty and honourable. When people lose count of the number of men killed or injured on the works, what else is there for a man to do with his wages than gamble and drink? Three of the men, including Slen, agree to a wager that each can jump across the mouth of the tunnel airshaft. A date is set. 'And we'll have such a randy[1] they'll never forget it…. Never. Go down in books it will' (Woolland 2014: 29). Then the eight year old son of Bonny, the woman Slen lodges with, is killed in yet another tunnel accident. And Slen makes a decision that will change his life. After a spell of imprisonment for poaching, trying to get food for Bonny 'and her little brood of nippers' (Woolland 2014: 31), he is walking back to the navvy camp when he comes across the great randy gathered around the tunnel airshaft. A group of missionary women have tried to dissuade them from jumping; but two of the men have already failed to get across. As a cheer greets Slen's arrival, the women leave in horror at the prospect of yet another senseless death.

2008. Kevin McGuire has plenty of problems of his own. The pressures are bearing down on him from every direction. Steve, his closest friend, is killed in a dreadful accident;

Kevin is in prison for a drugs offence; his Mum thinks he's a waster and his cell mate is threatening him. While researching his own family tree, as part of an education project, Kevin discovers that his great grandfather was Slen McGuire, and he unearths a family history that is initially as shocking as it is ultimately inspirational: he discovers that although the history books all tell of Slen McGuire as one of three men who fell in the airshaft jump, the history (which originated in stories told by the missionary women) is wrong. Slen refused to jump, walked away from the randy and went back on the tramp.

Courage and pleasure

The play interweaves these two stories, moving between Kevin's growing determination to pursue the truth about his own family history and events leading up to the airshaft jump. The first of the men to jump the airshaft has to battle inner demons; and his jump, although foolish to many people in a modern audience, is an act of courage. He struggles with himself to do what he thinks is right. The play neither condones nor judges his action. Slen refuses to jump, although he has agreed to. When we first started working on the play, many of the prisoners branded Slen's actions in walking away from the jump as 'chicken'. The framing device of the play, however, and the distance between navvy life and their own, allowed us to explore and interrogate the concept of courage in increasingly challenging depth. For many of the prisoners, taking part in the project itself was an act of courage. Of the five performances, one of the matinees was to an audience of fellow prisoners. This was the performance that all of them were most nervous about. As Prisoner D. said, when asked to comment on how he was feeling just before this performance, 'Everything's just a blur. I'm just terrified. I'd rather be up there fighting fifty blokes than doing this at the moment – to be honest with you' (Prisoner D., Jones and Manley 2008).[2] In the event, the prisoners watching the matinee performance were totally attentive. A senior officer watching the performance said he had never seen prisoners concentrate so hard for so long. That was immensely gratifying for all of us, but it did not take away from the mockery and hostility they had to deal with during the rehearsal process: ridicule from fellow inmates for being involved in drama and hostility towards the project itself from some (though by no means all) prison officers; mockery and hostility which took many forms, much of it rooted in resentment that the men were enjoying themselves.

The rehearsal process was tough, demanding and rigorous. When officers and fellow prisoners passed by the prison gym or chapel (where rehearsals took place), however, they often heard laughter and singing. During the final week of the production, BBC *South Today* and ITV's *Meridian* featured extracts from a performance in their local news bulletins; and local newspapers ran short articles about the production. One of these local papers published several letters claiming that the theatre production was evidence that life in prison was getting cushier, in essence arguing that although a prison sentence was supposed to be a punishment, these prisoners were clearly getting fulfilment and pleasure. Most people have no direct experience of prisons, so the reaction is to an extent understandable, but I think it also reveals a more general fear of pleasure. During the time that has passed since the final performance of *Stand or Fall* I have often reflected on the project and reactions to it. Thinking about this resentment of pleasure triggered thoughts about the way that theatre has, historically, often provoked hostility and mistrust.

Anti-theatricality in early seventeenth-century England

It is perhaps surprising to us now, who think of early seventeenth-century London as being home to a theatrical golden age, that theatre at this time, and in this place, was highly contentious. Driven by the growing power of Puritans, attacks against theatre, which ultimately resulted in the enforced closure of all theatres in 1642,[3] were founded on the argument that it was dangerous and corrupting. There were four main strands to this argument:

1. Actors are 'rogues' and 'villains'. Presenting them on a public stage is not only corrupting, but a form of adulation of criminality. 'Who can better play the ruffian than a very ruffian?' (Munday in Pollard 2003: 80).[4]
2. Actors often play above and below their social class. Furthermore, they play across gender. This encourages actors and audience members in the belief that social class, gender and sexuality can be construed as being transitory, not fixed – which has the potential to subvert the established social order.
3. Because actors pretend to be other than what they are, theatre actively encourages hypocrisy, deceit and dissimulation. This line of argument appears to contradict the first, but it did not prevent both lines of argument being used in the same pamphlet or speech.
4. In the public playhouses, men and women could mix together freely outside of normal social constraints, which was potentially corrupting in itself.

The Puritans' arguments were rooted in deep anxieties about sexuality, gender and social identity; manifestations not only of the alarm that putting on costumes, face-painting and, indeed, role playing of any kind adulterates the essences that God gave us, but a dread of pleasure itself and of change of any kind. They believed that theatre posed a genuine threat to the stability of the social environment, not least because theatre is essentially designed to create arousal. But the arguments also reveal that they were terrified of metaphor, of the possibility that meaning is unstable – whether reading the text of a play or the 'character' of an actor. Fundamentalists of all religious persuasions (then and now) seek to tie meaning down to single highly controlled interpretations. Meaning beyond the literal is profoundly threatening because it gives power to the reader, because it evades control. The easy way to deal with the unpredictability of human beings is to categorise them; and, better still, to ensure that they remain within the bounds of that categorisation: lord, lady, ruffian, rogue; student, prisoner, amateur, professional.

Anti-theatricality in early twenty-first-century England

It's easy to see prisons as institutions entirely separate from the societies that establish and maintain them. As in schools and colleges, and probably in most institutions, officers, inmates, education staff and even volunteers and occasional visitors all refer to that place beyond the prison walls and gates as the 'real world', implying that 'inside' is somehow fictional. There are, of course, numerous ways in which prison conditions insulate and isolate those within (both staff and prisoners), but if The Out is 'reality' and Inside is in some ways a fiction, it is a disturbingly and paradoxically 'truthful' reflection of The Out. So the attitudes that developed towards the rehearsal process and the production of *Stand or Fall* were extraordinarily revealing – not only of the micro habitat inside the prison, but of much broader attitudes in the outside world. It was in every sense a microcosm; and the ways in which those seventeenth-century attitudes to theatre reappeared are fascinating for what they tell us about the power of theatre, and the anxieties it arouses.

The clearest re-emergence of the seventeenth-century arguments came in the reassertion that presenting 'rogues' and 'villains' on a public stage is corrupting and a form of adulation of criminality. This strand of the argument surfaced almost without modification. As I have already indicated, many, both inside and out, perceived allowing prisoners to take part in a theatrical performance as a reward for their criminality.

When Puritans argued that theatre subverts the established social order and actively encourages dissimulation, they did so in a spirit of anxious condemnation. But if, instead of fearing change, we embrace it as essential to our humanity, this same argument becomes an endorsement of the power and the importance of theatre. The production gave both prisoners and students the opportunity to take on unfamiliar roles at two levels. Having signed up for the project, the prisoners were required to attend rehearsals as rigorously as professional actors. The play had been written specifically for them, but although they could relate to the brutality of the navvy world, none of the characters they played were a version of themselves. For the students, too, the demands were great: they had to be present at rehearsals during term time whenever they did not have lectures and from early every weekday morning throughout the Easter vacation, they acted as mentors for the prisoners, helping them not only with line learning, but also with literacy and with many of the practical tasks that mounting a major production involves. They too were required to behave as professionals – and yet, in 'reality' most of them were students on the first year of a degree, barely seven months out of school at the start of rehearsals. The theatre project did indeed actively encourage dissimulation. But, whatever the Puritans might have argued, dissimulation is not synonymous with hypocrisy and deceit. Indeed, by taking on highly responsible roles, both prisoners and students were liberated from the confines of rigid social roles and expectations, although several initially found this profoundly unsettling and challenging. Many in both groups had had little if any previous contact with the social groupings from which the others came. They learnt to co-operate, to collaborate, to solve problems through collective action – all in the company of people with whom they would never normally mix.

We were also made very aware of the fourth argument: that men and women mixing together is potentially corrupting. Students were regularly reminded about the need to dress appropriately and to keep a professional distance between themselves and the men. But this collaboration between prisoners and students also had immense potential as a learning experience for all concerned – not least because those very social barriers that the seventeenth-century Puritans saw as so essential for the maintenance of a stable society were undermined by the need for cooperation. As one of the students said in a feedback session, '[i]t got everyone working at the same level. And to work as a group everyone's got to feel at the same level'.

Skills and insights

Few would dispute that the criminal justice system is self-perpetuating. Figures released by the Home Office soon after the production of *Stand or Fall* indicated that more than half of the prison population were serial reoffenders.[5] I lost count of the number of times I heard officers (and even the most positive teachers on the education staff) musing about prisoners who had just been released, wondering when they would be back inside. Eleven of the twelve prisoners on the project, however, passionately expressed their sense that they had changed as a result of their participation; that it had vastly increased their confidence and sense of self-worth. There was a concerted attempt by prison education staff to codify the key skills that the participants were gaining (literacy, time management, personal organisation, communication, team work amongst others) so that their participation in the project could be seen to have tangible benefits. But the sense I got from my own informal conversations with the men was that it was the insights that the project gave them that were at least as affecting as the acquisition of skills: understanding behaviour (their own and others'), glimpsing their own potential for growth and change, seeing humanity in themselves.

It is a truism of therapy that people can only change when they want to change themselves. Participation in the project was immensely hard work for all concerned – there was nothing cushy about it at any level; the play itself is a challenging piece, the rehearsals were very demanding – but it was also richly enjoyable. And it was the very pleasure that they took from it, which triggered the desire to change.

As Prisoner S. said in an interview for the documentary *Stand or Fall: From Page to Stage*:

It's not about being the best actor or anything like that. It's a confidence builder. I talk about it all the time on the wing. It's good. Everyone's coming together. That's really good.

When we go back to the wing [at the end of a day's rehearsal] I'm buzzing, I'm absolutely buzzing, I really am buzzing. There's no feeling like it.

(Jones and Manley 2008)

I am in no position to judge whether the play, *Stand or Fall*, itself had a positive effect on those who took part in it, but I have no doubt that the experience of participation and of long-term collaboration gave all involved hitherto unseen glimpses of their own human potential. Theatre may not of itself change people, but it can give us a glimpse of other ways to live our lives; of new possibilities.

Metaphor, pleasure and change

I was wryly amused by the response to the play of an officer (who knew that I was the director but not that I had written it). He thought the men and students had 'all done very well' but that he 'hated the play' and found it deeply offensive. I was curious as to why he felt so strongly. In response to my probing (I still didn't let on that I was the writer), he insisted that the play was blasphemous and anti-religious. One of the characters in the play is indeed very scathing about the attempts by the missionaries to convert some of the navvies to Christianity, but that's not what so upset the officer. What he really found so disturbing was that three of the characters (Slen, the navvy; Kevin, the prisoner; Arabella, daughter of a wealthy landowner) each sought and found a kind of redemption without recourse to religion; each took hold of their own life, fighting prejudice, brutality and immense social pressure in order to change themselves. I later discovered that the officer was himself a born again Christian, a latter day Puritan. Maybe it was his response that set me thinking again about anti-theatricality. And maybe his predecessors, the seventeenth-century Puritans, were right to be so alarmed, for what this project taught me in the most moving and tangible of ways, was that theatre is every bit as powerful an agent for change as they feared. I would, however, reframe this, and suggest that those qualities which the Puritans most feared about theatre are the very things we should value most highly in it.

In the week following the production, during a session of evaluative appraisal of the production and the process of workshops, rehearsals and performance, Prisoner D. reflected, 'I'm normally in the audience taking the piss – you know what I mean. But I thought I'd give it a try this time. And I'm glad I did. Best thing I've ever done' (Prisoner D., Jones and Manley 2008).

References

Coleman, T. (1965), *The Railway Navvies*, London: Hutchinson.
Jones, L. and Manley, S., (2008), *Stand or Fall: From Page to Stage,* Documentary Film, United Kingdom: LaunchPad Productions.

Levine, L. (1994), *Men in Women's Clothing: Anti-theatricality and Effeminization, 1579–1642*, 1st ed., Cambridge: Cambridge University Press.

MacGill, P. (1912), *Songs of a Navvy*, Windsor: Patrick MacGill, University of California Libraries, https://archive.org/details/songsofnavvy00macgiala. Accessed 15 February 2018.

—— (1916), *Children of the Dead End*, London: Herbert Jenkins, University of California Libraries, https://archive.org/details/childrenofdeaden00macgrich. Accessed 15 February 2018.

Pollard, T. (ed.) (2003), *Shakespeare's Theater: A Sourcebook*, Oxford: Wiley-Blackwell.

Sullivan, D. (1983), *Navvyman*, 1st ed., London: Coracle Books.

Thompson, E. P. (2013), *The Making of the English Working Class*, London: Penguin Modern Classics.

Woolland, B. (2014), *Stand or Fall*, Oxford: Oxford University Press.

Notes

1 In this context, the word 'randy' meant a loud, disorderly, drunken gathering.

2 A documentary film about the development of the production from early workshops, through rehearsals to the final performance, was made by LaunchPad Productions: *Stand or Fall: From Page to Stage*.

3 Theatres in London had been temporarily closed several times in the first half of the seventeenth century, but on previous occasions this had been in response to outbreaks of the plague. When the hostilities of the first Civil War ended in 1642 the theatres were closed again – this time for political reasons. They stayed closed for 18 years; and by 1644 the Globe itself had been demolished.

4 The quotation is from Anthony Munday's *A Second and Third Blast of Retreat from Plays and Theatres* (London 1580). His language seems of his time, but his argument is still used: 'Are they not notoriously known to be those men in their life abroad as they are on the stage: roisters, brawlers, ill-dealers, boasters, lovers, loiterers, ruffians? So that they are always exercised in playing their parts, and practicing wickedness; making that an art, to the end they might the better gesture it in their parts. For who can better play the ruffian than a very ruffian?' (in Pollard 2003: 80–81).

5 'In 1993, when there were fewer than 45,000 prisoners, 53 per cent were being reconvicted within two years. In 2004, 65 per cent of those leaving prison were reconvicted' (*The Independent*, 20 July 2008).

   The figures for juvenile crime were far worse: 'Despite the fact that most offenders say they want to get away from crime, reoffending rates average 70% for those given community penalties and 76% for those sent into custody. These rates are even higher for the worst offenders, reaching 96% in the case of those with between seven and ten previous convictions' (*The Guardian*, Tuesday 17 June 2008).

Chapter 6

Telling the Self or Performing Another: The Exploration of Identity through Storytelling, Role and Analogy in West Hill, HMP Winchester

Kate Massey-Chase

In this chapter I will examine the potential impact of theatre and storytelling on the incarcerated identity, where the group identity is magnified and individual identity suppressed. I shall discuss the intrinsic links between narrative and the construction of our identity and explore how autobiographical storytelling can provide not only an opportunity for prisoners to assert their individual identity, but can also act as a vehicle for self-reflection. I will then consider the functions of role and the embodiment of a character, discussing the consequent opportunity to both explore different viewpoints and to reflect on themes and issues within a fictitious context, with an aesthetic detachment that facilitates an opportunity to critique and evaluate the prisoner's own life. I shall reflect on my involvement in three productions with Playing for Time Theatre Company (in 2008, 2009 and 2010) and six storytelling workshops Professor Tim Prentki and I conducted in the autumn of 2009, working with male prisoners in West Hill, HMP Winchester. Throughout, I hope to communicate some of the reasons behind my strong conviction that the use of drama in prisons provides not only a unique learning opportunity, but also a life-affirming and enjoyable journey.

The incarcerated identity

> Our personality is what it is, but also what it is becoming.
>
> (Boal 1995: 39)

The word 'identity' is a term commonly used across individual, national and cultural discourses, yet is so large in scope and fluid in meaning that it can be one many find hard to define. As a term, it has historically taken on profound political significance, particularly since the 1960s, when black, feminist, gay and lesbian liberation movements came to the fore, and with them the birth of 'identity politics' (Weeks 1990: 88). In the fight for the subaltern to have a meaningful and political voice, many marginalised groups – often at the intersections of systemic oppression – struggled to assert their own identity, against a Eurocentric, patriarchal, heteronormative society. Yet – although imbued with political currency, fought for, questioned and struggled with – the term 'identity' is still one fraught with ambiguity, hard to tie down and laden with complexity. The scope for an analysis of the incarcerated identity, therefore, is as boundless as the differences between each individual; every answer to the question 'what does it mean to be a prisoner?' will be different. We can, however, cautiously look for commonalities and explore the patterns that present themselves through each self-definition.

One of the most obvious, and potentially damaging, effects of being imprisoned is the corollary of a reduced personal identity. As Daun Kendig explains:

> [the] stripping of self identity [...] occurs through a series of administrative and security procedures that symbolically appropriate personal identity, while underscoring the individual's loss of rights [...]. This stripping of identity promotes a uniformity, anonymity, invisibility, and silence.
>
> (1993: 198)

As part of the loss of liberty decided as punishment by the courts, the destruction of the prisoner's individual identity includes the removal of their personal belongings, adherence to the prison regime and a mandatory 'uniform'; in HMP Winchester this is the infamous grey tracksuit: shapeless, plain and erasing individuality, epitomising the transformation from an individual to part of a collective.

As the prisoners' individuality is reduced, symbiotically their group identity is enhanced. Separation from the familiar can begin to deconstruct their sense of self; as Prisoner A. told me, during the storytelling workshops in 2009, '[y]our whole identity seems to be altered by this whole culture'. He said: 'Before you know it you'll be using prison language, dressing the same way other prisoners do; you'll even start to think the same way other prisoners do'. He described falling into the lexicon of prison language, using different words, exclusive to prison; although he did not even know what some of them meant (such as 'drop me out, guv'), he described how he found himself using them, despite making 'a conscious decision to try and avoid them'. He said: 'You find yourself getting dragged into the language thing, and then the behaviour ...'. He compared this process to crowd behaviour at a football match or the novel *Lord of the Flies*. The importance of the infiltration of prison language into the subject's everyday parlance is a significant example of how the influence of the prison environment is manifest, and also alters the individual subject's self. If it is 'in and through language that man constitutes himself as a *subject*, because language alone establishes the concept of "ego" in reality, in *its* reality' (Benveniste in Eakin 1999: 21), then this takes on an even greater significance. Deconstructionists suggest that 'subjectivity itself is textual' (Hall 2004: 128); if so, then the very language we use alters our subjectivity.

We understand the world, and our subjective positioning within it, by contrast; however, in a prison environment, the Other against which you contextualise your own identity is comprised of other prisoners and prison staff. This could contribute to further establishing an individual's identity as 'a prisoner'. Neurobiological research suggests that humans possess 'mirror neurons' that subconsciously impel them to mirror the actions of those around them: '[due to] the mirror neurons, humans repeat and imitate a great many body states, expressions and actions of others unconsciously' (Tselikas 2009: 25). This is a specific, neurological example of how our environment may affect our behaviour, as we reflect the behaviour of those around us; for people in prison this will be other prisoners and staff in the prison. Prisoner A. also told me how removal from society, his family and friends, and his loss of citizenship had impacted upon his sense of self, as he said, '[y]ou rely a lot of your own identity on the people that are closest to you' – your friends and family help define how you see yourself and how you feel about yourself. Consequently, if the people around us can impact not only upon our behaviour, but also on how we locate ourselves and our self-definition, this poses an important question when an individual is detained inside a prison: if the people around us have been a key factor in the formation of our identity, is the danger in prison that those people who we see as helping define us are replaced by those 'inside'? If we mirror those around us, what happens if other prisoners and prison officers become those we imitate/reflect? Surely then the impact of incarceration on an individual's identity takes on not only a personal significance regarding self-perception, but also holds the very real implication of changes to cognitive processing and behavioural change.

As Prisoner A. said to me during the 2009 storytelling workshops: 'Prison is all about being in someone else's control'. This begins, he described, with the court proceedings: 'Every day there would be a new thing that would make you feel more helpless'; he described the powerlessness he felt – '[y]ou just have to sit there and accept it' – as 'other people [...] decided my fate'. This lack of control was exacerbated by the injustice this prisoner described he felt, as he told us that he believed he was innocent and had been wrongly convicted. Regardless, however, of the culpability of the individual, for all prisoners a similar process occurs where they often lose their home, finances, job, even – as Prisoner A. protested – his pets. This sense of loss is intensified by a lack of control:

> Inside the walls nothing is certain, nothing can be taken for granted except the arbitrary exercise of absolute power [...] the prison rules are meant to keep you ignorant, keep you guessing, ensure your vulnerability.
>
> (Wideman, in Kendig 1993: 199)

This could be paralleled with Seligman and Maier's investigations in 1967 into 'learned helplessness', where anxiety and decreased motivation is caused by a lack of control, leading to behavioural differences, as there is 'a random relationship between an individual's actions and [the] outcomes' (Peterson, Maier and Seligman 1993: 8). Additionally, lack of logic or explanation behind what could seem an arbitrary exercise of power can have a cognitive impact. Human beings seek to make sense of the world around them, and if they are kept guessing and vulnerable to inexplicable changes of a temporal nature (e.g. surprise interruptions to their daily routine), then this can lead to a heightened state of anxiety, frustration, feelings of helplessness and depression.

How then can we begin a process of rehabilitation, if the identity of the individual is at best confused and struggling, and, at worst, aligned psychologically and behaviourally, with the identity of 'a prisoner'? This is where, I suggest, drama can have a positive impact on the reassertion of the individual identity, in the face of affiliation and assimilation with a negative label, group identity and altered subjectivity.

Incarceration could be seen as 'a ritual of retribution marked by phases of separation, transition, and re-incorporation' (Kendig 1993: 198). This analysis draws its phases from Arnold van Gennep's historical and cross-cultural study of ceremonies marking an individual's life crises, an observation of important life passages and their attendant rituals, divided into three stages. The final stage is one in which a person 'integrates the self with the new role or status', yet 'Victor Turner (1969) describes the transitional or liminal phase [preceding this] as a limbo between a past state and a coming one, a period of ambiguity, of nonstatus, and of unanchored identity' (Schouten 1991: 421). It is in this stage of unanchored identity that I feel intervention is most important, not only to ease the anxiety of a liminal status, but also to intervene before the possibility that the subject will integrate him/herself as 'a prisoner/criminal', with the institutionalisation, negative reinforcement and dehumanisation that can result.

Kendig argues that we can begin to reclaim the world and self through drama: although 'the incarceration process functions as a rite of passage deconstructing the prisoner's image of himself and the world [...] the performance process can work as a complementary rite helping him to reclaim and transform those representations' (1993: 197). Kendig suggests intervention can take advantage of 'the chaos of the transitional phase', offering the prisoners an opportunity to experiment with alternative images and representations of both himself and the world around him, a chance to regain and reclaim control of how he himself and others perceive him (1993: 199). She explains:

> [...] prisoners immersed in the chaos of their penal transition are especially open to the improvisation that occurs in performance transition since these exercises help the men to experiment with new images of the self and the world. In doing so they begin to reclaim control over those images and creatively transform them. The process dramatically demonstrates how performance functions as a way of reflecting upon and discovering meaning in experience, and a way of acting upon and transforming the world and self.
>
> (1993: 197)

Consequently, we can see how the use of drama in prisons provides a unique opportunity to reassert the individual self, in the chaos of the liminal status of a prisoner. In her investigations, Kendig describes one prisoner explaining to her:

> Those who lose *everything* through prison *must* replace lost things [...] in order to be whole – or anything close to whole. Trouble is – finding replacements for the missing segments is a limited task [...]. In order to transcend the prison experience, I had to reach outside of the system.
>
> (1993: 199, emphasis in original)

I suggest the way in which prisoners can reach outside the system, and outside the label of a group identity, is to reclaim their own identity through drama, specifically through the process of storytelling, particularly autobiographical narratives. Through telling their own story, the prisoner has an opportunity to reflect on his life so far and what has brought him to where he is today. Donald Hall suggests: through 'textualizing my selfhood …[we] at least open up for discussion and revision the responsibility that … [we] bring to those subject position(ing)s' (2004: 129) the terms under which we position and describe our self. The act of choosing words to portray our selfhood necessitates a consideration of how we see our self, how others see us and how we feel about this. But in addition to taking responsibility and opening up for discussion our textualised self, autobiographical storytelling also provides the opportunity to revisit and share experiences; this could potentially be a motivating force and counteract a position of learned helplessness. Rather than a number or surname, clad in a shapeless grey tracksuit, the prisoner becomes an individual, with a unique history, beliefs and desires. This is an opportunity to reassert their own identity.

Narrative, storytelling and selfhood

Identity is a life story.

(McAdams 1993: 5)

The power of self-constructed narratives has been recognised as epistemologically and psychologically crucial to the construction of our own identity (Kerby 1991: 1; Eakin 1999: 99; Bruner in McAdams 1993: 29). Indeed '[i]t might be said that each of us constructs and lives a "narrative" and that this narrative is us, our identities' (Sacks 1985: 110). The stories that we tell about ourselves, and hear others tell about us, are fundamental to the construction of our identity. For a prisoner, during their time inside, these stories are likely to be founded in their criminal behaviour, with inescapable and frequent reminders that they are a criminal. If narrative and identity are inextricably linked, and 'the process of making up one's own story is a process of making up one's self' (Benson 2001: 49), then how we construct and relate our own narrative, influenced by the stories we hear others impose upon us, will have a significant impact not only on our sense of self (how we feel about and perceive our self), but also on our embodied self as an 'I' (our sense of identity, how we present ourselves and how we relate to the world around us).

With autobiographical performance, the emphasis moves to the act of telling and the performative aspects of this process: it is not simply the story that is important, but its manifestation, its utterance. If 'it is literally true that the basis of subjectivity is in the exercise of language' (Benveniste in Eakin 1999: 21), then speaking this story aloud becomes of increased importance. Deirdre Heddon describes autobiographical performance as an opportunity for 'marginalised subjects' to 'talk back' and 'engage with the pressing matters of the present which relate to equality, to justice, to citizenship, to human rights' (2008: 2–3). Within the context of the criminal justice system, human rights are a complex and contentious issue. Although the law states that people in prison are subject to certain restrictions to their human rights, it does not condone that they are restricted more than necessary: their punishment is the loss of their liberty, not to be subject to personal degradation. Although prisoners lose their right to liberty (Article 5 of the European Convention on Human Rights), out of the need for the proper administration of justice in a democracy, there are certain rights that cannot be restricted, for example they must not be subject to torture or inhuman or degrading treatment or punishment (Article 3). Political and media attitudes to those 'behind the door', however, often differ from this, as can be seen in popular tabloid newspapers, which frequently use animalistic and dehumanising descriptors, arguably both reflecting and influencing public opinion. The opportunity for prisoners to perform autobiographical narratives to an audience is therefore also significant as:

> Performing the personal in public might allow a connection between the performer and the spectator, encouraging the formation of a community or prompting discussion, dialogue and debate.
>
> (Heddon 2008: 157)

This allows the voice and views of marginalised subjects to be heard and also provides an opportunity to prompt a dialogue between prisoners and those outside, thus promoting an awareness of why some people end up enmeshed in the criminal justice system, caught in the cycle of reoffending, and 'putting a face to what is often the faceless idea of "the prisoner"' (Ryder 2010).

In his play *Prison?* – toured around community venues and performed at the Edinburgh Fringe Festival in 2007 – ex-prisoner Charlie Ryder provides a useful case study to illustrate this dialogue between the public and the prisoner, the personal and the political. In *Prison?* Ryder shares with his audience, through a variety of dramatic techniques, his own experiences of the criminal justice system and being 'inside'. Reflecting on the process of relating his story, Ryder says:

> In my eight months in prison I experienced bullying, violence and abuse. The play allowed me to work through that abuse. As a result it has restored my humanity and dignity, making me a more loving, peaceful and compassionate person.
>
> (Ryder 2010)

Ryder went on to work with The Forgiveness Project, an organisation that explores forgiveness and restorative justice through real people's narratives. The example of Ryder's autobiographical performance not only highlights the potential for sharing otherwise silent narratives with the community, in a way that can be revealing and enlightening, but also demonstrates how the sharing of autobiographical narratives can provide an opportunity for self-reflection.

> If you want to know me, then you must know my story, for my story defines who I am. And if *I* want to know *myself*, to gain insight into the meaning of my own life, then I, too, must come to know my own story.
>
> (McAdams 1993: 11, emphasis in original)

The act of telling an audience our story can be a vehicle for self-examination and an opportunity to gain insight into our own lives. Delivering storytelling workshops with Professor Tim Prentki in 2009, I believe I saw this process in action. Through working on life-maps with the men, and watching them present important stories from their own lives back to the group, I observed and discussed with them this process of self-reflection. One prisoner, Prisoner B., told me (a few months later, and hence after an opportunity for further reflection) that he had really valued the opportunity to think about and tell stories from his life, as it gave him the opportunity to express himself in a way he would not be able to do 'back on the wing'. He said:

It gave me the chance to dig a bit deeper, and to look at the – how was it Tim said it? – the 'colour' of the stories and that, [to] really look at stuff in detail […]. It was good to share stories, like my son being born. I love that story; it's a special one.

Prisoner B. had valued the chance to share one of the defining stories from his life, in an opportunity to express part of his identity (as a father), which was not related to his offending behaviour. This also gave him an opportunity to reflect on which experiences from his life were most important to him, which moments he most valued and why. We can hope that this might encourage him to want to make choices in the future that would lead to similar positive moments.

Interestingly, Leigh Gilmore uses a direct comparison with prison in her reflections on self-representation in autobiography, suggesting '[t]he self who reflects on his or her life is not wholly unlike the self bound to confess or the self in prison, if one imagines self-representation as a kind of self-monitoring' (2001: 20). The act of telling our own story necessitates the act of reflecting on that narrative, and demands self-selection on which parts we decide to disclose. This can instigate reflection both on what we choose to tell and how we choose to tell it, and also provide the opportunity to analyse our life as a continuous journey, rather than reflecting on events in isolation. Through this it may be possible to identify patterns in our behaviour, and whether there is a dominant narrative that drives us.

If we are aware that we understand the world and ourself through narrative, and do not see 'identity' as a fixed and inflexible state, then this has the potential to give us some control over our perceptions of the world, as autonomous subjects who can mould the stories we tell of ourselves. However, what happens if someone has bound themself in an unhelpful, negative or damaging narrative? Perhaps then it will not be a story that they want to share with an audience. What happens if the beliefs we have about ourselves, based on the stories we tell ourselves about ourselves, fix us in an identity that prohibits us from achieving our personal aspirations and dreams? Many prisoners could be seen to be in this situation, trapped in an unhelpful narrative cycle, particularly those caught in the cycle of repeated reoffending. If this is the case, although autobiographical performance could provide an opportunity for self-reflection, the subject may not be able to see beyond the narrative that they feel limits them; they may be reluctant to share their story. Working with Playing for Time on the 2008 production of Brian Woolland's play *Stand or Fall*, one of my strongest memories is of one of the men (Prisoner C.) telling us in the debriefing session at the end of the project: 'I've never done anything in my life that has made anyone proud of me. All I've done is be in prison or doing something to get me in prison'. For Prisoner C., along with many of the other men I have worked with, it seems a fair extrapolation that they might describe their dominant narrative as 'a prisoner/criminal', and this may well not be one they wish to share, celebrate or perform to an audience.

A possible means of re-working an unhelpful narrative is through Narrative Therapy. I am defining the term 'unhelpful' here to mean one that the participant feels is unhelpful to them in meeting their preferred goals and ambitions, although a by-product of this may be a move away from anti-social or criminal behaviour, which is 'helpful' to society, through potentially reduced rates of recidivism. 'Narrative plays an important role in many forms of psychotherapy' (Daniel 2009: 301), and is key to narrative therapy, a systemic therapy, rooted in social constructionism, which recognises that we are both defined and constrained by language: 'language does not merely describe but actively generates the very state of affairs being described' (Richert 2003: 189). Narrative therapy suggests that 'experiences and the self are storied into culturally acceptable and valued narratives that hold currency in one's community and society' (McLean and Pratt 2006: 715), but that this is not always helpful to the individual. Consequently, it looks for moments in the subject's life where something different has happened and they have not conformed to their cultivated dominant narrative; they then help the client develop a new story by rewriting the macro-narrative. As '[i]dentity narratives generate identity judgements' (Eakin 1999: 141), this process can liberate the subject, and enable them to move forward in a more positive way.

Autobiographical performance could also be used as a method to rewrite a more liberating narrative; as Heddon suggests: 'Performing stories about ourselves might enable us to imagine different selves, to determine different scripts than the ones that seem to trap us' (2008: 157). This may be because '[a]utobiographical performance brings to the fore the "self" as a performed role, rather than an essentialised or naturalised identity' (2008: 39). This potentially enables the subject to observe how the self can be constructed, and deconstructed, and consequently provides a means of liberation from the constraints of viewing one's identity as stable, innate and unchangeable.

Heddon's suggestion of the possibility of imagining 'different selves' prompts an important question: for the incarcerated subject, would exploring possible alternative selves be a more helpful focus? And, thus: could it be more useful to examine other 'possible selves' through role, metaphor and character, rather than autobiographical performance (which could be seen to focus more on the past than on the future)? The term 'possible selves' was proposed and developed by Markus and Nurius in 1986 as a way of denoting 'those elements of the self-concept that represent what individuals could become, would like to become, or are afraid of becoming' (Oyserman and Markus 1990: 112); a more in-depth discussion of this can be found in Chapter 9, in Dr Ann Henry's investigation into future possible selves, dispositional empathy and cognitive closure.

Figure 1: General Haigh surveys the battlefield, *Oh What a Lovely War*, 2006.

Figure 2: Soldiers survey the battlefield, *Oh What a Lovely War*, 2006.

Figure 3: Ice cream seller sings, 'Hitchy-Koo' (Claire), *Oh What a Lovely War*, 2006.

Figure 4: 'Sister Suisie Sewing Shirts', (Katie), *Oh What a Lovely War*, 2006.

Figure 5: Dogpile awaits orders, *Ubu the King*, 2007.

Figure 6: Prince Billikins, the Jester and Ubu's soldiers await orders, *Ubu the King*, 2007.

Figure 7: The Jester eavesdrops, *Ubu the King*, 2007.

Figure 8: Queen Rosamund (Faye), and Prince Billikins discuss escape, *Ubu the King*, 2007.

Figure 9: Facing up to consequences, *Stand or Fall*, 2008.

Figure 10: Arabella (Kate), and Slen (Vinnie), read the Mission Newsletter, *Stand or Fall*, 2008.

Figure 11: Jumping the airshaft, *Stand or Fall*, 2008.

Figure 12: Slen (Vinnie) refuses to jump, *Stand or Fall*, 2008.

Figure 13: Sarah (Antonia), out riding in the park,
Stand or Fall, 2008.

Figure 14: 'Hey Big Spender', *The Convict's Opera*, 2009.

Figure 15: Klestakoff (Richie) dines at the Inn, *The Government Inspector,* 2010.

Figure 16: Bribing Klestakoff (Richie), *The Government Inspector*, 2010.

Figure 17: Klestakoff (Richie) woos Maria (Gina), *The Government Inspector*, 2010.

Figure 18: The Judge bribes Klestakoff (Richie), *The Government Inspector*, 2010.

Figure 19: A Faustian Choice, *Soul Traders*, 2011.

Figure 20: Heaven or Hell?, *Soul Traders*, 2011.

Figure 21: Celebrating the sale of Danny Frowst's Soul, Gina (Ella), Waiters (Alex, Gina, Lyndsey), *Soul Traders*, 2011.

Figure 22: Jangley, (Minister of Justice), considers his position, *The Accidental Impostor*, 2012.

Figure 23: The scandal breaks – Reporter, (Ella), *The Accidental Impostor*, 2012.

Figure 24: Ensemble, *Our Country's Good*, 2013.

Figure 25: Shitty Meg harasses Lieutenant Ralph Clark (Liam – understudy), *Our Country's Good*, 2013.

Figure 26: James 'Ketch' Freeman discusses acting with Lieutenant Ralph Clark (Liam – understudy), *Our Country's Good*, 2013.

Figure 27: Mary Brenham (Darcie) and Liz Morden (Charlie), berate Ketch, *Our Country's Good*, 2013.

Figure 28: Harry Brewer (Scott) and Duckling (Lu) go rowing, *Our Country's Good*, 2013.

Figure 29: Harry Brewer (Scott), remembers the dead, *Our Country's Good,* 2013.

Figure 30: Punishment, *Our Country's Good,* 2013.

Figure 31: Dabby Bryant (Mollee), contemplates escape, *Our Country's Good*, 2013.

Figure 32: Recruitment, *The Fight in the Dog*, 2014.
© All photography by Toby Farrow (Hide the Shark).

In a challenging article on discourse in theatre and prisons, James Thompson argues that '[w]e needed to move beyond the easy politics of "giving voice"' (2001: 2), suggesting – from his experiences working at Strangeways prison – that '[m]etaphor created different resonances, connections and memories that the literal could not' (2001: 3). Working with the metaphorical or allegorical also makes the work 'one-step removed', a technique used by Geese Theatre (Baim, Brookes and Mountford 2002: 30). This helps defuse the problem of the overlap between prison theatre and prison therapy, as it has less emphasis on the strictly personal. Elektra Tselikas suggests: '[W]hen theatre is blurred with psychology or counselling it loses its artistic potential and its transformative power for groups and individuals' (2009: 21). When reflecting on her performances of the lives of famous historical women, Sue Jennings recalls that she 'needed some distance from the stories in order to come closer to them, the ultimate paradox of theatre' (2009: 10). She suggests:

> It is not a conscious working out of experiences, rather it is a surprise encounter [with an intuitive connection with a role or text] that enables insight and understanding at a deeper level of the self. This gives the possibility of movement and change.
>
> (2009: 1)

It is this idea of the function of metaphor, character and role that I will next explore, particularly the idea that playing a fictional character, which resonates personally, can provide an affective understanding, not simply of the fictional world inhabited in the play, but also the participant's lived reality.

Exploring the potentiality of the self through analogy and role

> Some borrowed words, a few extra rags, and suddenly you're not scum.
> (Jeffreys, *The Convict's Opera*, Part One, Act 1, Scene 10: 28)

Although the term 'role' can have many meanings, I shall limit this discussion to the analysis of 'role' as a performed character in a piece of theatre, although I shall also discuss how exploration of the idea of 'role' – and the possible roles we can play in our everyday interactions – can help to develop transferable skills that can be drawn on in the outside world. Robert J. Landy discusses how we all play a number of different roles on a day-to-day basis, and argues that a 'full understanding of role implies an understanding of the essentially dramatic aspects of everyday existence' (1993: 7). He also suggests that personal 'well-being depends upon an individual's capacity to manage a complex and often contradictory set of roles' (1993: 8–9).

Working on theatre pieces with Playing for Time, the nine-week production process involves an initial foundation in drama skills, including discussions around role, character and status. When I co-directed *The Government Inspector* in 2010, we looked at the status of characters in the play, and the group discussed the implications of embodying high/low status characters. We explored different physicalities and discussed how changing the way that a character stands, walks and holds themself, and the body language and gestures they use, changes the status they appear to have. We reflected that it did not matter how you felt: if you held your head high, you appeared to be more confident and more powerful. One of the men remarked, '[h]aving learnt all this, I can't wait to get back in court', and many of the men said that they now simply walk around the landings with a little more confidence in themselves. This may be because 'power posing' (holding our posture in an open, tall, strong position) for just two minutes can also affect the levels of testosterone and cortisol in the brain, and so also changes our body chemistry (Carney, Cuddy and Yap 2010: 1363). In the fifth week of rehearsals, one of the men told me that he already felt more secure in his day-to-day interactions since he had joined the drama project; he said:

> I know it sounds silly, but already I'm able to talk to my probation officer and that with, you know, more confidence. Last week I saw her and I just chatted about, well, *nothing* – but for ages. Whereas, like, before I wouldn't say nothing at all.
>
> (Prisoner D. 2010)

This not only demonstrates some of the transferable skills drama projects can accrue – such as increased confidence and communication skills – but also shows how an exploration of the physicality of characters with high and low status can develop an understanding of 'the essentially dramatic aspects of everyday existence'.

Elizabeth Fine distinguishes two types of performance: 'primary' and 'secondary'. Primary performance is 'simply behaviour, the performance of social roles and interactions'. Secondary performance, such as drama, 'imitates and in the process often comments upon primary forms'. Consequently, 'secondary performances become ways of learning, teaching, and in some cases changing primary performance' (Fine in Kendig 1993: 200). The relationship between primary and secondary performance was dynamically and pertinently explored in Playing for Time's production of *The Convict's Opera* (2009). The play, by Stephen Jeffreys, follows the literal and emotional journey of a group of convicts on a transportation ship bound for Australia in the eighteenth century, who are trying to put on John Gay's play, *The Beggar's Opera*. Throughout the voyage, the characters not only learn their parts but also learn about themselves, as the practice of putting on their play becomes a life-affirming process for them all; the arsonist chooses not to set fire to the boat, the lonely vicar finds himself linked to humanity for the first time and the character playing the play's hero learns to become a 'hero' himself. Putting on the play in HMP Winchester added another dimension to the meta-narrative, as of course the men playing prisoners putting on a play were themselves prisoners putting on a play. The narrative of *The Convict's Opera* itself demonstrates the process of secondary performance influencing primary performance, yet seeing real prisoners perform the roles actively provided an opportunity to see this dynamic at play, as we, as a cast, were able to observe the personal journey each of us went on throughout the rehearsal process. A poignant illustration of this occurred whilst watching one of the men rehearse a speech about how doing the play (*The Beggar's Opera*) aboard the ship had made him more confident. Throughout the rehearsal weeks we watched him deliver this speech with more and more confidence; for him there was a rising veracity to the lines he delivered: he too was growing in confidence. Lines from *The Convict's Opera*, such as: 'Got shown some kindness (Part One, Act 2, Scene 2), it is 'a glimpse of freedom' (Part Two, Act 2, Scene 10), 'we have [...] a common purpose' (Part One, Act 1, Scene 8) and 'this is the best of all I ever did' (Part Two, Act 2, Scene 10) are sentiments I have heard expressed repeatedly by many of the prisoners over my three years working in West Hill, HMP Winchester.

During Playing for Time's 2008 project, *Stand or Fall*, I learnt that discussion of characters and role was a useful tool when talking to the men if the subject of our conversations entered territory that we were not allowed to discuss with them, for example if they began divulging information that was deeply personal or related to their offending behaviour. As the play we were rehearsing was common, safe ground, I learnt to use discussion of themes and issues in the play as a way of exploring issues with the men in an appropriate and objective manner. For example, when I was talking with one of the men, Prisoner C., who was playing a character called Gunner Smithy, he started to tell me, during a character development exercise, more about himself and his experiences – particularly ones involving abandonment, rejection and violence – that he had difficulty dealing with. By sensitively returning the topic to his character, asking quite simple questions – for example: 'Do you think Gunner would have experienced anything similar in his life, as a railway navvy in the nineteenth century?' – I was able to return the conversation to the project (and not discuss emotional difficulties or trauma I was ill-equipped and unqualified to deal with), yet still allow him the opportunity to work through his ideas from a different stance. I remember him replying: 'I think Gunner would have been a bit of a loner; he wouldn't like to be tied down' and we were able to discuss his ideas about why this might be, with focus and more objectivity. The tool of analogy and the frame of a fictional character enabled us to explore complex and sometimes difficult themes, whilst maintaining focus on the action of the play. In their handbook of practice, Geese Theatre suggest: 'Generally speaking, working at one step removed is safer than the personal level of work because the distance allows participants to acknowledge their connections to the material at a pace they can regulate themselves' (Baim et al. 2002: 30). This distancing technique is also more inclusive, as, if the story the activities are focussed around is fictitious, it is not based on one person's story and hence not just one person in the group will feel they have ownership of it; instead the whole group can draw out aspects of the narrative that they feel personally resonate with them. This technique also helps the facilitators ensure that the participants 'feel able to work at a productive and psychologically safe level' (Baim et al. 2002: 30), and helps maintain the professional boundaries so important in this area of work.

Geese suggest that roles should be seen as 'dynamic and evolving functions of a central self that can consciously choose what role to play and how to play it', arguing that '[h]aving conscious choice leads to the creative possibility that we can conduct ourselves differently than we have done in the past' (Baim et al. 2002: 20). In this way, through exploring the potential roles we can play and adding this to our repertoire of strategies for dealing with different situations, we can see how Augusto Boal's proposal resonates: 'the stage [...] becomes a rehearsal space for real life' (1995: 44). We can thus learn from our experiments in the fictitious world of theatre, to better prepare ourselves for life outside the rehearsal room.

Trying out other characters and roles becomes a means for exploring our own identity. One of the prisoners I worked with on *The Government Inspector* (Prisoner E.) once said to me: 'Because I'm playing Ossip I can go on stage. Whereas I couldn't if it was me. Which is funny because when I'm playing Ossip, I'm also playing me'. He reflected that he incorporated aspects of his own personality into how he was performing his character in the play, to give it a higher level of authenticity, but that because he was playing a character – pretending to be someone else – he had the confidence to go on stage and perform in a way he would otherwise never have dreamt of doing. Tselikas suggests: 'Players are often surprised by the power of the expressive capacity of their body, of the strength of their voices once they forget about who they think they are and what they think they are able to do, once they concentrate on the action of the play' (2009: 22). Indeed, it is 'because the characters are fictional that we can push to limits and involvements which we would not ordinarily dare to approach' (Wilshire 1982: 25).

Prisoner E.'s feelings about playing his character, and the integration of himself into the fictional role, also relates to Boal's theory of metaxis: 'the state of belonging completely and simultaneously to two different, autonomous worlds: the image of reality and the reality of the image' (Boal 1995: 43). In *Theatre of the Oppressed* (1985), Boal argues that 'at its most effective, theatre places audiences on both the inside and the outside of a virtual world, and it is this duality that leads to significant reflective experiences' (Taylor 2003: 3). This echoes Prisoner E.'s reflections that he could be the character – inside the 'virtual world' – at the same time both as being himself, and observing himself in his performance. This sometimes led to frustration in the rehearsal process as he struggled to perfect articulating the feelings of the character he was playing as truthfully as possible, at the same time as bearing in mind the aesthetics of the performance and his interaction with other characters, including details such as where he should be standing at a particular time. He endeavoured to convey the reality of the fictional character, but also with an awareness that this could only exist within his own reality: the reality of the present. He was, in fact, struggling with the state of metaxis: negotiating a dialogue between the real and the fictional worlds.

Through literature, theatre and other art forms, we can access the thoughts and emotions of others and can consequently see how we, ourselves, relate to the world around us, helping us feel less isolated. Finding a part in a play that reminds us of ourselves, or indeed finding a character that encapsulates who we would like to be like, provides a forum in which we can question how our life fits with our values, and perhaps illustrates the possibility for change. In *Stand or Fall*, the main character, Slen Maguire, makes a positive, pro-social and life-affirming choice, despite the difficulties of peer pressure and potentially adverse consequences. Yet the character could easily be seen not simply to represent one man, in one historical moment, but a cipher for anyone at a turning point in their life, facing a decision with serious ramifications. As Brian Woolland discusses in Chapter 5, he spent a number of weeks workshopping themes and ideas with some of the men in West Hill; consequently he was better able to write a play that thematically resonated with the men, and built on some of the stories they had shared. The story did not belong to one of them in the sense that it was biographical, but rather it belonged to all of them: they had been part of the process of its conception, and the ideas in it related to issues they themselves had faced. This is Boal's 'theatre of the first person plural' (1995: 45) in practice. *Stand or Fall* acted as a vessel for the stories of many of the men, transported into a different historical moment, yet exploring themes and concerns that resonated with their own lives.

Metaphor and myth can deepen our understanding of our shared humanity and also encourage empathy. Through embodying another character, an actor is quite literally putting him/herself in someone else's shoes. As one of the men involved in Playing for Time's production of *Our Country's Good* said, reflecting on his experience of being in the play, '[y]ou can learn a lot about yourself and the people around you'. We can, therefore, see another of the skills that well-facilitated drama can offer in this context, and many would argue that for some offenders – particularly those who have committed violent crimes – a greater understanding of how others may feel in a number of different contexts is fundamental to their rehabilitation.

Not only can one learn empathy through embodying another character, but there are further benefits to the physical embodiment and enactment of a character on stage, as performing a role is an important bodily and psychological experience. Antonio Damasio's research, in 2003, shows the neurobiological roots of feelings and their consequent potential for transformation through physical action (Tselikas 2009: 15). He explains that when experiencing something emotionally the body itself is not detached from this process, as when experiencing 'feelings […] there is [also] a dynamic engagement of the body' (Damasio 2003: 92). Consequently, as 'images enter our minds through the sensory experiences of the body' (Tselikas 2009: 23), it is possible to change these images through physical embodiment of character. If 'the body perceives the world and reacts to what has been mapped in the brain's regions through the body's experiences' (Tselikas 2009: 23), then working physically can help 'bypass existing brain body maps related to certain feelings and create new influences on the existing body maps, thus transforming them as well as the original feelings' (Tselikas 2009: 25). Consequently, we can see that the physical embodiment of characters in prison theatre can be a potentially transformative experience on a deeper level that can be immediately observed, as working physically enables the performer to develop a deeper engagement with the learning experience.

It can thus be argued that there is a great deal of utility in, and benefit to, the physical, dramatic exploration of role and analogy within a prison theatre context. The distancing effect of fiction facilitates perspective-taking, giving participants the opportunity to analyse complex themes and issues 'one step removed' and with an aesthetic detachment. Drama can be used as a vehicle for self-examination and to explore other ways of being, in a safe and secure environment. Moreover, participants can exceed what they thought were their own capabilities, and find new strengths, passions and engagements, using their bodies in new ways and learning from their achievements.

Conclusion

> After the show I smiled for, like, five hours. I couldn't stop grinning to myself. I've never had a natural high like that before… It's the best thing I've ever done.
>
> (Prisoner F., after The Government Inspector)

Since the first show in 2003, until the last in 2014, every year twelve to fifteen undergraduate students have given nine weeks of their lives to work with the men in West Hill, committing physically, intellectually and emotionally to the process of putting on a play with a group of prisoners. They leave the process drained and often tearful, yet supporting each other and declaring: 'I will never forget this experience', '[o]ne of the best things I will ever do in my life – amazing!' and 'I hope that you will carry this experience with you for many years to come – I know that I will'. Audience members leave productions in tears. The men, in the aftermath, are still blinking from the lights, the applause and the swelling of emotion.

Throughout this chapter, I have discussed many of the potential benefits of using drama with people on the 'inside'. I suggest prisoners can reach outside the system, beyond the label of a group identity, and reclaim their own identity through the process of telling/performing their own story. This can provide an opportunity for self-reflection, to revisit and share experiences, and to reassert their individual selfhood. I have also examined the utility of exploring other potential selves through role, analogy and character, taking the focus to the future, rather than the past. I suggest that working 'one step removed' gives participants the opportunity to analyse complex themes and issues with greater objectivity and an aesthetic detachment. I believe drama can be used as a vehicle for self-examination, and that the physical embodiment of a character can be an enlightening process. In theatre, the applause the participants receive at the end – particularly from friends and family who have shared in their success – can instil a greater sense of self-worth, and give them confidence in abilities previously undiscovered.

It would be naïve to think that one drama project will be able to outweigh the extreme consequences of social and economic disadvantage, poor mental health, alienation and lack of supportive social infrastructures that so strongly correlate with offending behaviour. Yet, if in the nine weeks we work with them just one of the participants leaves the project with a little more self-worth, a little more confidence, and a feeling of pride in a public achievement they had never previously believed they could have accomplished, then I cannot help but fervently believe these projects are worthwhile.

References

Baim, C., Brookes, S. and Mountford, A. (2002), *The Geese Theatre Handbook*, Winchester: Waterside Press.

Benson, C. (2001), *The Cultural Psychology of Self: Place, Morality and Art in Human Worlds*, London and New York: Routledge.

Boal, A. (1995), *The Rainbow of Desire: The Boal Method of Theatre and Therapy* (trans. A. Jackson), London and New York: Routledge.

Carney, D. R., Cuddy, A. J. C. and Yap, A. J. (2010), 'Power posing – Brief nonverbal displays affect neuroendocrine levels and risk tolerance', *Psychological Science*, 21:10, pp. 1363–68.

Damasio, A. (2003), *Looking for Spinoza: Joy, Sorrow, and the Feeling Brain*, Orlando: Harcourt.

Daniel, S. I. F. (2009), 'The developmental roots of narrative expression in therapy: Contributions from attachment theory and research', *Psychotherapy Theory, Research, Practice, Training*, 46:3, pp. 301–16.

Eakin, P. J. (1999), *How Our Lives Become Stories: Making Selves*, London: Cornell University Press.

Gilmore, L. (2001), *The Limits of Autobiography: Trauma and Testimony*, London: Ithaca University Press.

Hall, D. E. (2004), *Subjectivity*, London and New York: Routledge.

Heddon, D. (2008), *Autobiography and Performance*, Basingstoke: Palgrave Macmillan.

Jeffreys, S. (2009), *The Convict's Opera*, London: Nick Hern.

Jennings, S. (2009), *Dramatherapy and Social Theatre: Necessary dialogues*, Hove: Routledge.

Kendig, D. G. (1993), 'Acting on conviction: Reclaiming the world and the self through performance', *Anthropology Quarterly*, 66:4, Controversy: Hegemony and the Anthropological Encounter, pp. 197–202.

Kerby, A. P. (1991), *Narrative and the Self*, Bloomington: Indiana University Press.

Landy, R. J. (1993), *Persona and Performance: The Meaning of Role in Drama, Therapy, and Everyday Life*, London: Jessica Kingsley.

McAdams, D. P. (1993), *The Stories We Live By: Personal Myths and the Making of the Self*, New York and London: The Guilford Press.

McLean, K. C. and Pratt, M. W. (2006), 'Life's little (and big) lessons: Identity statuses and meaning-making in the turning point narratives of emerging adults', *Developmental Psychology*, 42:4, pp. 714–22.

Oyserman, D. and Markus, H. (1990), 'Possible selves and delinquency', *Journal of Personality & Social Psychology*, 59:1, pp. 112–25.

Peterson, C., Maier, S. F. and Seligman, M. E. P. (1993), *Learned Helplessness: A Theory for the Age of Personal Control*, Oxford: Oxford University Press.

Richert, A. J. (2003), 'Living stories, telling stories, changing stories: Experiential use of the relationship in narrative therapy', *Journal of Psychotherapy Integration*, 13:2, pp. 188–210.

Ryder, C. (2010), 'The road to forgiveness', Unpublished speech, accessed via email.

Sacks, O. (1985), *The Man Who Mistook His Wife for a Hat and Other Clinical Tales*, New York: Harper.

Schouten, J. W. (1991), 'Selves in transition: Symbolic consumption in personal rites of passage and identity reconstruction', *The Journal of Consumer Research*, 17:4, pp. 412–25.

Taylor, P. (2003), *Applied Theatre: Creating Transformative Encounters in the Community*, Portsmouth: Heinemann.

Thompson, J. (2001), 'Making a break for it: Discourse and theatre in prisons', *Applied Theatre Researcher*, No.2, Article 5.

Tselikas, E. (2009), 'Social theatre: An exercise in trusting the art', in S. Jennings (ed.), *Dramatherapy and Social Theatre: Necessary dialogues*, Hove: Routledge.

Weeks, J. (1990), 'The value of difference', in J. Rutherford (ed.), *Identity: Community, Culture, Difference*, London: Lawrence & Wishart.

Wilshire, B. (1982), *Role Playing and Identity: The Limits of Theatre as Metaphor*, Indiana University Press.

Chapter 7

Lessons from the Prison: The Space between Two Worlds

Annie McKean

T he participation of undergraduate students has been central to Playing for Time Theatre Company's model of practice. It is predicated on working with two groups of people who will undertake a learning journey together, based on reciprocity. Students are recruited to the projects as volunteers and take on the role of mentors, supporting prisoners with aspects of performance, including line-learning, self-presentation, choreography, devising and research into the context of each play. The students are engaged in their own education and the development of their theatre practice. Yet most have little knowledge of the criminal justice system. Conversely, many of the prisoners may be 'experts' in the criminal justice system, but do not necessarily know a great deal about theatre. This chapter will examine the different expectations, motivations and experiences of students who have taken part over eleven years and will explore the ways in which student volunteering has been integral to Playing for Time's work.

Students have different reasons for joining these projects, as will be discussed throughout the chapter, including challenging their thinking about the role and functions of prisons, believing that theatre in community contexts can be transformative, wanting to volunteer, and thinking it might inform future career choices. Some also want to be involved in a production with high performance values, directed by a professional, or feel excited by an unknown context and think it will make for good stories. In the case of two students, personal experiences with the criminal justice system had led them to think that taking part might help them process those experiences in some way, perhaps as a form of closure or catharsis.

The invitation to volunteer and take part in the project is issued in early October and students from across the whole university are invited to attend the first recruitment meeting. The majority of students who engage in the work are drama or performing arts students; however, students studying psychology, social work and criminology have also taken part. Students with multidisciplinary backgrounds can offer support to each other to acquire new knowledge and develop an understanding of the context. This is vital, as to undertake work in secure institutions without understanding the complexities of the political and ideological functions of such institutions is to enter the space unprepared and therefore potentially vulnerable.

Challenging perceptions

Through our work we aim to challenge stereotypes and preconceptions, from both sides of the gate. Prisoners have often said that they thought students were lazy and watched daytime television. Prisoner M. wrote to the Dean of the Faculty of Arts in 2006 saying:

> I'm a prisoner at Winchester prison who was involved in the production of *Oh What a Lovely War* alongside students from your faculty. I would like to say to you that they were a pleasure to work alongside and were a credit to you and your University. Before I had the opportunity to work with these students, my opinion of students was pretty dim, classing all students as the same, however my opinion has changed. Could you please extend my thanks to all the young ladies who helped me over the last eight or nine weeks, when I was rehearsing and performing. I felt like I was not in prison, and for that I will always be grateful to them.
>
> (personal correspondence, 28 April 2006)

Whilst the primary aim of each project is to work with and support the prisoners, there is no doubt that the students who volunteer each year benefit from the work in terms of social and personal development, and this is integral to the process. Students become immersed in a very particular social reality. Here they need to learn not just about an institution that is new to them, with all its complexity of politics and ideology, but also about themselves. As a society, our knowledge and perceptions of crime and the criminal justice system can be warped by a hegemony which is politically useful to those in power, and the students involved in the work do not exist outside of these forces. Working with prisoners can challenge these superficial views and enable students to understand how prejudice is constructed and becomes part of a discourse that serves to demonise and present prisoners as less than human. Reflecting on his experience of taking part, one student said:

> Stereotypes fell apart. I learnt not to judge people by their cover, to respect them for their achievement. I learnt to be open minded.
>
> (Phil, in Jones and Manley 2007)

Here we can see how the projects might contribute to the development of students' emotional maturity. Students have to exercise responsibility by working in a very particular and challenging environment that requires empathy and understanding. Encountering people from different backgrounds can help them develop knowledge about aspects of society previously unknown to them.

A number of students are very young, many barely out of their teens. Yet they often display extraordinary levels of maturity and capability. The third-year student, who took over directing the 2007 production when the director had to withdraw from the project for a period of time for personal reasons, reflected on his experience:

There were large parts of me that worried that I wouldn't be able to step up to the mark and go in and direct twelve prisoners.... You've got prisoners ranging from twenty to up to fifty-something and for them to stand and listen to me and do exactly as I ask them to and place their trust in me, I had to lose some inhibitions, some self-consciousness and try to believe I could actually do it.

(Nick, in Jones and Manley 2007)

The students have consistently risen to the complex and variable challenges facing them, within a model of learning that could not happen in a lecture theatre.

Volunteering and altruism

The fact that the students work as volunteers has an impact on the prisoners, who often assume that they are being paid to be there. They are sometimes baffled as to why someone would choose to give up their time and spend it in a prison. There is no doubt that prisoners' respect for the students is enhanced by knowing that they are volunteering their time, time which could be spent earning money or doing their university work.

Students engaging in work as volunteers are focusing on intrinsic values (which relate to relations with family, community and non-materialistic belief systems, rather than extrinsic, relating to the acquisition of wealth and reputation), which are perhaps also underpinned by concepts of altruism. Music offers a definition of altruism as exhibited by 'one whose *ultimate* aim is to further another's well-being' (2014: 34). The students have often cited this aim as a key motivator to undertake this work. Altruism can also be described as the desire to engage in an activity without expectation of some kind of reward. However, this is a reciprocal relationship: the students give freely of their time but also get something back. There is no doubt that undertaking this kind of work increases their social and cultural capital and enables them to have a deeper understanding of the criminal justice system.

When the project is difficult, with individual prisoners exhibiting challenging behaviour, students can find it hard to feel the rewards they expected from the experience or feel that their presence in the rehearsal room has made any kind of difference. It can be quite late in the process, sometimes only after the first performance, that a prisoner will comment on how the experience has made them feel and will start to behave differently. Like the prisoners, students also have to see the project through to its conclusion in order to fully appreciate the benefits of doing the work.

Trying to understand, and even listen to, experiences that are very different to their own can sometimes be distressing for students. Occasionally, a prisoner will tell the student mentoring them stories about early life experiences, including physical and psychological abuse in childhood, which can be difficult for them to respond to. Students should not be seen by prisoners as counsellors or therapists. This may be exacerbated by the lack of a comprehensive counselling system or psychological services in this Category C Prison. In order to support students who have to respond to these kinds of encounters there are debriefing sessions, after rehearsals, which are designed to help students process what has happened. These are important forums where students can support each other, be supported by the staff team, and also reflect on the learning that has taken place from these interactions.

Working with professionals and informing future career choices

As well as the motives listed above, many students have additionally sought other benefits from taking part, such as the experience of working with professional theatre workers. Some students have been offered work experience in the creative industries as a result of working closely with theatre professionals on these projects. Some have felt that the experience has enabled them to consider wider career options. Indeed, a significant number of graduates have ended up working professionally in areas related to the criminal justice system as a result of undertaking this work during their undergraduate years. As applied and community-based drama and theatre practices are embedded in the drama degree at the university, many students already have an emerging understanding of the ways in which drama and theatre can be used to create interventions in work with marginalised groups in society. Their experiences have led them to work, for example, within psychology teams in high secure prisons, in the probation service, in prison education departments and with young offenders.

One graduate, reflecting on her career choice, wrote to me saying:

> I came to study drama at university thinking I would go into Events Management but now I am working with the psychology team in a Category A prison delivering programmes designed to enable violent offenders to address their offending behaviour patterns. I am planning to train as a Drama Therapist. I would never have done any of this without the experience of working on the prison plays.
>
> (Charmaine, personal correspondence, 2006)

Others have gone on to postgraduate study in related areas of applied theatre; many of these students had undertaken in-depth studies of aspects of the work as part of their undergraduate dissertations and in doing so had furthered their understanding of related areas of theory and practice.

A voyeuristic experience?

In the 2008 production of Brian Woolland's play *Stand or Fall*, two female characters, out riding in the park, comment on the navvies working on the railway line just beyond the boundaries of their father's land.

SARAH:	I only want to look at them from a distance.
ARABELLA:	As if they were animals in the zoological gardens?
SARAH:	Mother took us to the zoological gardens at Belle Vue.
	They have dangerous beasts there. She said it was educational.

(Scene 4, 2014: 11)

Woolland's play was informed by workshops with male prisoners. As he says in the introduction to the play script:

I wanted to create a fictional world, with metaphorical resonances to the men's own situations.

(2014: v)

Students undertaking work in the prison for the first time are aware they are walking into an environment characterised by containment. Their first instinct may be to see the prisoners as the 'dangerous beasts' they are often depicted as in the popular press. Jonny reflected on how he viewed going into the prison for the first time:

You can't deny that there is this curiosity there and you know you're kind of up for it. You want to meet that kind of challenge…of walking through that threshold for the first time.

(Jones and Manley 2007)

The anticipation of working in an ostensibly dangerous environment is reinforced by the security talk given by the prison's security manager before going in for the first time. Students are asked to read a briefing paper on what will happen if any of them are taken hostage by a prisoner or prisoners. They are not allowed to keep the paper and are instructed not to talk about this to anyone. Heritage comments that 'life in prison is always seen through the peepholes of our cultural imagination' (2004: 190). This imagination is fuelled by exposure to images of prisons in the media and popular culture.

Students are asked to conduct themselves with discretion and not to discuss what they are doing with people outside the prison. Confidentiality is one of the key principles underpinning the mentoring process that students are introduced to as part of their preparation for the work and is essential if trust between the two groups is to develop. They are asked not to talk about what they are doing on social media sites and also to be discreet in public places. For example, the pub opposite the university's main student village is frequented by prison officers and prison staff not in uniform, and it is crucial they are not overheard discussing the project.

It would be unethical for students to use the experience as a vehicle for supporting other agendas that may become exploitative or self-serving. For example, a student studying creative writing or journalism may believe that working in the prison will provide them with salacious material for their writing. It is almost impossible to ascertain fully why students have chosen to join the project. A lack of experience or emotional immaturity may mean that they are not fully aware of why they have chosen to undertake the work, or indeed they may choose not to disclose their reasons.

Closure or catharsis?

The issue of whether people are helping themselves by 'helping' others is ever present in this kind of work. Work on theatre projects with prisoners is designed to support them, in a variety of ways, to transcend barriers that prevent them from achieving their previously unrealised potential. When prisoners achieve high levels of success in the work there is no doubt that students will also share in the 'buzz' that follows. Their own feelings of well-being are enhanced and they, like the prisoners, feel good about themselves. However, attempts to use the project to process their own experiences of the criminal justice system can be highly problematic. In the documentary, *Lessons from the Prison*, one student shared some of what had happened to her:

> A while ago I went to court myself, not as a perpetrator but as a victim and I had really not prepared myself for the impact of being in an environment like that knowing that the person who had committed a crime against me was obviously in prison. It just really started to get to me in a way that I hadn't.… I thought I could somehow work through it. You know, on a very personal level it was a small part of the reason why I went in there and it really upset me that it was getting in the way of my enthusiasm and wanting to see the project through to the end because it has been so important to me and it felt like such a great opportunity. I really battled with myself to make that decision to leave the project … I just said I've got to go.… It's not very nice when you realise you've got to back down, but I know I did the right thing.
>
> (Jones and Manley 2007)

The student did later come back into the prison, and support the production externally, through working on the box office. In her third year, she worked in HMP Coldingley to support the development of a Youth Crime Diversion programme, by introducing drama strategies and more dialogical processes with prisoners who were working with young offenders and young people at risk of offending behaviour. When she graduated she was asked to help set up a Youth Crime Diversion scheme at HMP Send. I have cited her experience because it provides an insight into the many and varied journeys students can go on, and how the impact of their experiences in the prison can play out in unexpected ways in the short and long term. Like a building block or jigsaw puzzle, the learning from their experiences in the prison is not always experienced in a linear way.

Gender politics

Every year, there are a larger number of female students than male recruited to the project. In 2006, the group was all female. These students must navigate the hypermasculine culture of the prison. This extends to the officers. Students have reported that they experienced more casual misogyny and sexism from uniformed staff than the prisoners they worked with, who are generally more guarded and respectful.

Before a project starts, prisoners are briefed on maintaining respectful and professional relationships with the students. Likewise, students are briefed on how they must present themselves. Very occasionally, female students have found it difficult to respond to the request not to present themselves in a 'sexualised' manner, in terms of clothing and make-up. Many of the male prisoners have often been locked up for some time, and we endeavour to create an atmosphere that is as professional – and as least sexually charged – as possible.

Other than from the officers, the most overt sexism the female students experience is from prisoners in other parts of the prison, who look down through their windows or out from the exercise yard. Walking through the prison complex to the rehearsal space, the students get accustomed to lewd shouts from the windows of the cells they pass; at this moment they are the ones keenly observed from out of sight. Power dynamics shift and waver, as the politics of sex and space collide. The prisoners with whom they work on the projects are apologetic for their fellow inmates' behaviour, yet their protectiveness can betray benevolent sexism or highly gendered attitudes to social roles. Many of the female students had not worked with or been around a large group of adult men, and compared and contrasted older men in the group with men in their lives, such as fathers, uncles and even grandfathers. It is impossible – and it would be irresponsible – to ignore the sexual politics of the context, sometimes rising to the surface, sometimes a barely noticeable undercurrent.

Preparations for crossing the threshold

Foucault described prison as a transitional space, providing a bridge between the worlds of 'crime and the return to right and virtue [...] "the space between two worlds" the place for individual transformation' (1991: 123). Students must negotiate the space between their world and the world they are about to enter, one often as remote from their life experiences to date as they could imagine. The prison, as a transitional space, will engage them in examinations of the complexities and contradictions embedded in this work. They will each be transformed in some way, as we all are when we step out of our own world and into another.

In prisons, roles are defined, enacted and performances are scrutinised. Lopez describes prisons as 'a high-stakes performance space [...] a theatre of incarceration' (2003: 25).

The audience that the students will be playing to is complex, consisting of prison staff, the production team and prisoners, and they are constantly observed. Kerryn Davies, a drama graduate from the university who worked as the prison's drama tutor for three years, reflected on the 'strict rules which you have to abide by, you know, it's not just a dress rehearsal. If things go wrong there are actual consequences, it's a really steep learning curve for the students' (Jones and Manley 2007).

Before they are allowed into this performative space they have to 'audition' by successfully completing complex background checks and are also asked to take part in a number of workshops, where they use role play to explore scenarios focusing on safeguarding and professional boundaries, including how to respond to a disclosure, discovering illegal activity or attempts at manipulation. This offers the whole project team the opportunity to examine scenarios from a number of different perspectives and to discuss differing outcomes. Debates will inevitably ensue as to the extent to which the team need to understand and respect the prison's primary objective of maintaining security, within the framework of how the rules of the prison operate for all civilians and prison staff, without colluding with oppressive practices. Analysing different scenarios allows staff and students to engage with competing narratives: those of prisoners, prison officers, prison managers and the artists attempting to work within the visible and invisible boundaries that make up the institution. Thompson reminds us that we are always visitors, invited into the prison (2003: 20) and as such can also be asked to leave. The feeling of walking a tightrope between different ideological perspectives in the institution is ever present and needs to be embedded in everyone's thinking.

Mentoring

The process of each student working with a prisoner in a mentoring role is a model that has been in place since the first project when, as discussed in Chapter 3, students were paired up with women prisoners as understudies. It very quickly became apparent that students formed a very positive working relationship with their partner. To keep the boundaries clear, an external goal, the prisoner's artistic journey and the development of their drama literacy, is at the centre of the mentoring relationship. The student's role is that of a facilitator and not one of counsellor or therapist. They are working to guide their mentee and to support them to achieve their full potential in the production. To this end, when asked to work in pairs, the director will often give the pairs a very specific task related to what is happening in the rehearsal space or reflect on aspects of a workshop or rehearsal. This can then be fed back into a plenary session with the whole group. Most of the students have experience of working on theatre productions. Yet, any implied hierarchical structure of a mentoring relationship – where one transmits knowledge or experience to the benefit of the other – is redundant here, as students have much to learn about the experience and technicalities of being in a prison and, indeed, how theatre practice is delivered in this particular context.

Our mentoring model has been refined and supported over the years through a number of different workshops, run before students go into the prison for the first time. In order to develop an effective relationship, students need to develop their self-knowledge, self-management and management of relationships. They are asked to consider their motivations for working in the prison, their strengths and weaknesses, their understanding of the term 'professional boundaries', and how they might deal with certain challenges, such as managing their emotions. They are also asked to consider how verbal and non-verbal cues could lead to misunderstandings between students and prisoners. Further principles related to good practice in mentoring are also examined. These are based on a person-centred approach and include active listening, genuine interest, respect for personal choice, establishing trust and rapport within professional boundaries and non-judgemental attitudes. The whole group work together for at least ten days before any decisions are made as to which prisoner a student will be paired with. This is informed by information from the prison staff and observation of the students in the workshops.

In order that students can find ways of reflecting upon and processing what they are experiencing it is also suggested that they keep a reflective diary covering aspects of Gibbs' Reflective Cycle including:

- Description
- Feelings
- Analysis
- Conclusions

(1988 and 1998)

The entries can be informed by questions such as:

- What have I been involved in this week?
- What has made me feel good?
- What has concerned me?
- What am I curious about?
- What feelings and emotions have I experienced this week?
- What have I noticed about myself?
- What have I noticed about the other students?
- What have I noticed about the prisoners?
- Are there any actions I need to take or things to do differently?
- Are there any issues I need to raise?

Entries in diaries can be used to inform end of session discussions about the work. These preparations for crossing the threshold into the prison heighten the students' awareness of what is ahead of them, but can also create anxiety. Thinking about the various briefings and workshops, a student on the 2006 project said:

> It's so daunting to hear all the rules before you go in…. Even so… I do think you can underestimate how careful you have to be when you are in there.
>
> (Katie, in Jones and Manley 2007)

Uppermost in most students' minds is the concern over professional boundaries. The security manager's briefing usually contains the warning: 'Be friendly, but don't be their friend'. Students commented some weeks later about how these words made them feel:

> The hardest part was how to interact around them because drama can be very touchy feely… You want to form relationships with people because that is what you are used to doing.
>
> (Donna and Claire, in Jones and Manley 2007)

The prison is an intensely claustrophobic environment where comments and actions can be blown out of all proportion and rumours are rife. Students need to find a balance in their interactions with prisoners that will lead to a positive and professional working relationship. Again, it is not until they start to work with the prisoners that they can begin to deal with these difficult, but potentially rewarding, interactions.

Negotiating this terrain begins on the first day of the project when the students assemble outside the gatehouse before entering through the pedestrian entrance of the prison. The journey they are about to undertake is mediated by multiple layers of self-presentation and one that is highly performative. Elliott, writing about the work of Erving Goffman, suggests that Goffman distinguishes between the public and private self in terms of context-specific performance:

> Public identity is performed for an audience, and the private self knows that such performances are essential to identity and to the maintenance of respect and trust in routine social interaction.
>
> (2007: 37–38)

It is important that students are always aware of the need to present themselves consistently; they need to internalise the rules of the establishment and the views of those in power within it if the performance of their role is to be convincing.

Inside the gatehouse: The eye of the panopticon

Before entering the prison students must wear the 'costume' that is appropriate for their role: scrubbed clean of any makeup and wearing Playing for Time polo shirts and baggy trousers, students attempt to give as low-key a performance as possible. They have their script and stage directions: they have already been instructed to be quiet and to conduct themselves with reserve; surveillance cameras and microphones in the gatehouse record their every move. Students have talked about leaving behind aspects of their belief systems and opinions. These include concerns about the effectiveness of the criminal justice system and beliefs about social justice that do not conform to the values of an institution that is deeply conservative and often repressive. The theatrical mask they must wear is one of submission and conformity to the system; their performance must communicate normative and compliant behaviour. As Donna said:

> You have to leave what you are and some of what you are about at the gate because that part of you is not invited inside.
>
> (Jones and Manley 2007)

They enter the gatehouse, line up and present themselves, when called, at the glass barrier to show their ID. Depending on who is behind the glass, there will either be a friendly smile or a neutral expression which may disguise the hostility that, even after eleven years, is clearly felt by some of the staff. This small, confined space is one that marks the boundary between the outside and the rest of the prison complex. As Heritage says:

> The prison gate is a transitional space marked by rituals that seek to distance the world that is left behind from the world that is entered.
>
> (2003: 192)

It is the first of a series of experiences that will serve to heighten the strangeness and insecurity of the environment they are walking into.

The panopticon performs – a presentation of power

On the first day of the project the group, staff and students are taken to the Main Prison Visits Hall where their bags are taken from them and searched with meticulous thoroughness. A 'pat down' body search is also conducted; it is not just the prisoners who suffer the ritual of authoritarian rule and its subsequent humiliations. This experience is designed to emphasise to the whole team where they are, what is expected of them and most importantly who is in charge. The sense of being an invited 'visitor', perhaps under sufferance, is palpable. Some years there is a 'drug dog' in attendance. Unless the officer with the dog is alert, women can suffer the unwanted attention of the dog. A woman in a prison is most likely to be indelicately sniffed by the dog when she has her period. Arguments and complaints to security staff about the ritual humiliation of staff and students when this happens fall on deaf ears; the explanation is that it is just the way the dogs behave.

Ironically, much later in the project, searches dwindle until during the final weeks of rehearsals and the production week itself; the vast array of things being brought in appear to overwhelm the authorities and little is investigated with any real energy or enthusiasm. In 2011, polystyrene boxes of dry ice were brought in daily during the production week. Not once were these boxes searched. It is hard to know whether we had exhausted the system's capacity to maintain strict security rules or that we were now trusted beyond any shadow of doubt. However, such inconsistencies within the system do not create a sense of security; we remain in fear of what might happen should we transgress or should something that has been accepted for years suddenly become unacceptable. Every visit to the prison feels like an improvisation because the rules are constantly changing depending on who is on duty. This continual feeling of insecurity enhances the state of anxiety created by the pressure and stress of working in this environment.

The journey through the prison complex involves the unlocking and locking of many gates and many boundaries must be negotiated. The senses are assaulted daily, the smell of overcooked vegetables emanating from the kitchens, rat poison boxes everywhere, even the occasional rat. The bitter wind that swirls across the open space of this hilltop complex is funnelled by the towering wings of the Category B, Victorian Prison. We walk past exercise yards, past men with heads down or staring blankly as the group pass by; the group is watched by prisoners and the officers guarding them. Refuse hangs from razor wire, thrown from cell windows, and blows around the paths between buildings.

Inside the rehearsal room – a place of security and insecurity

As has been noted elsewhere, the space that is used for rehearsals and performances is a Nissen hut, which serves as the West Hill prison gymnasium. Once the prisoners arrive they and the students engage in a workshop process of theatre games and exercises that are designed to break down barriers between the two groups. Bethan Clark, who had a seven year relationship with Playing for Time, directing shows in the prison, commented on the ways in which students and prisoners work together:

At the start of the project you've got two separate groups. You've the students and then you've got a group of guys from West Hill. It's a complete unknown for them, so what you've got to do is to get them to work together as one group and give them all the skills that they need to be able to put on a performance at the end and to a high standard. So the first three weeks we don't work on the text at all. We work on drama exercises, physical exercises, character exercises, and throughout all the exercises they are building confidence; they're working as a team and also being pushed.

(Jones and Manley 2011)

Once they gain in confidence, the students are encouraged to lead some of this work themselves. In some years, students have co-directed the plays. They have been audited for skills and experience in the pre-project workshops and where possible they will contribute by running elements of the rehearsal process, such as choreography, teaching songs and directing some of the scenes. The creative encounters between students and prisoners allow students to develop understanding and empathy with prisoners, and vice versa, and to work in ways that are socially inclusive.

> It is in the act of creativity that empowerment lies, and through sharing creativity that understanding and social inclusiveness are promoted.
>
> (Matarasso 1997: 84)

Although this might feel like a normal process of workshops and rehearsals, the students will continue to be aware that their behaviour is observed, as is that of the prisoners. The students, having internalised security briefings, must now work out what maintaining professional boundaries actually means and police their own behaviour accordingly. Although this has never happened, students know that if they cross a line they may be asked to leave the project. If their behaviour was linked with a prisoner's behaviour, then that prisoner would also have to leave the project. Should that happen, whilst undoubtedly being upset, the student would resume their normal life. For the prisoner, already removed from their normal life, this could feel devastating. A fine balance must therefore be maintained between establishing a supportive and professional relationship and maintaining the boundaries of that relationship. This is difficult in the hothouse environment of a prison, where the smallest remark or glance can be misinterpreted. It can be one of the greatest challenges of the project for the participating students, as Bippa describes:

> The most challenging thing for me in the process, other than the security checks, was being aware of our actions, because anything that we did would not only affect us but the prisoners as well. For example, this would be not getting emotional, especially because of the environment we were in. I think that I did struggle with my emotions, particularly during the week of the production.
>
> (evaluative questionnaire, 2013)

On one occasion only has an accusation been made about inappropriate behaviour between students and prisoners. In 2006, on his way to the morning meeting with the Number 1 Governor, the West Hill Governor said to me in passing, 'I'll see you later; one of your students was seen kissing a prisoner yesterday'. Two days passed before anything further was done, leaving the whole staff team in a state of anxiety. Later it turned out that a prison officer had seen the project's researcher, a member of the staff team, putting her hand on a prisoner's arm to reassure him as he struggled with words in the script he was holding. It is possible to imagine what motivated the officer concerned to turn such an innocent action into something that could have brought the work to an end. There are some who believe that this kind of work is inappropriate for prisoners and who will look for reasons to undermine the project by making accusations, which could result in everyone being asked to leave the premises. In any other context, a 'storm in a teacup', but in a prison such events create anxiety and reinforce the sense that at any moment the full force of institutional wrath will be brought to bear on the project and the work cancelled. That sense of treading carefully between the shards of glass (see Chapter 1) is ever present.

Despite these potential difficulties the two groups, prisoners and students, are encouraged to spend time socialising with each other. The informal breaks in rehearsals are the times where they can begin to get to know each other. Permission to bring in tea, coffee and biscuits is therefore sought very early on. These are the times when stereotypes can be challenged, barriers broken down and a counter-narrative can be constructed, which challenges dominant discourses about prisoners and their lives. The time spent working in mentor pairs is also important and builds bonds between the two groups. In the 2011 documentary, which was screened before each performance of *Soul Traders*, several prisoners commented on this relationship:

> Alex ... he watches me every minute, keeps prompting when I go wrong. He's been helping me out ... and I feel gratitude for the things he's done for me....
>
> (Prisoner R., in Jones and Manley 2011)

> ... and he says, like, you can do this or you can sing this or you can say this and he's really good at pushing me and helping me with what I can achieve.
>
> (Prisoner L., in Jones and Manley 2011)

Students can also find 'the well-kept secret [...] that prisoners are the most motivated of students' (Moller 2003: 56), when they discover that some of the prisoners will have gone away and learnt their lines well ahead of the undergraduates who have speaking roles. They find very quickly that the relationship with prisoners is reciprocal; prisoners are also often more than willing to share talents that have, like them, been locked away, such as writing poetry, drawing and singing. Students also discover that prisoners survive the system by developing a sense of humour which enables them to transcend life in the institution; many prisoners are charming and witty, and have well developed interpersonal skills. These encounters and experiences serve to dispel some of the myths and stereotypes concerning the characteristics of people that end up in prison.

Leaving the panopticon

Students often comment on how difficult it is to leave the prison complex each day when they know that they are leaving the prisoners inside. This feeling is particularly acute towards the end of the project and during the production week. Wherever a theatrical experience has taken place, close ties will have been established and the feeling of deflation when it is over is often very strong. In the prison, where it seems everything is experienced with greater intensity, this feeling is even more acute. A number of students reflected on how the ending of the project affected them:

> When it was over, it's really quite sad. I went into a bit of a dip for about a week; I didn't know what to do with myself. You don't realise 'til you're out of it how much effort you have put in, how hard you have worked. It's also sad leaving the guys, leaving them inside…I don't think I could ever have comprehended before how hard it would be to finish a project like this.
>
> (Catherine, post-production feedback, 2014)

> After the performance week I felt really down and upset due to how many bonds were created throughout the process and how these had to be cut at the very end.
>
> (Kay, evaluative questionnaire, 2013)

Immediately after the end of a project, students return to the university for three weeks of assessments before going home for the rest of the summer. Staff and some students will go back into the prison for evaluation sessions but there is no 'exit strategy' for prisoners that can bridge the gap between the intensity and joy of a successful project and the return to the everyday tedium of the prison regime (see Chapters 10 and 11). Students are aware of this as they prepare to return to their lives of university, work and home.

The end of any theatre project is often experienced as a form of loss. In the same way that prisoners have talked about the natural 'high' that they have experienced, at the end of a performance there is also that feeling of a 'coming down'. Andrea, who was a social work student, reflected that she came out in tears and 'never thought it would be so emotional leaving!' (Evaluative questionnaire 2013). For the first few years of delivering these theatre projects in HMP Winchester, students were briefed to try to keep their emotions in check. They were told there could be no physical contact apart from a hand shake after each performance and at the end of the final debriefing session on the last day of the project. However, in recent years, at the end of the final session with prisoners, staff and students, the whole group have said goodbye and hugged each other. The presence of the same prison officer throughout the nine-week duration of the project has actually made it easier to transgress strict rules concerning physical contact. This moment of physical contact is a disruption of the highly contained and controlled environment of the prison, a powerful and important way to reassert the humanity of all involved in the work. The momentary breaking of the rules, however, also has to be seen in the context of an eleven-year partnership, during which time high standards of professional behaviour have been maintained. Somehow, over the years, I think that prison officers involved in the projects have observed the ways in which the work has given the prisoners a sense of humanity, something which has been lost during their experiences of life in secure institutions. The final taboo of touching is lifted, momentarily, in the last moments of validation and celebration of achievement, transcending the harsh environment of the prison.

In order to conform to security rules within the prison system, it is not possible to maintain relationships with prisoners once the projects are completed. There are practical considerations related to the safety of staff and students and future work in the institution that underpin this ruling. Strict rules therefore have to be maintained regarding further contact with prisoners. Were a member of staff or student to form a relationship with a prisoner upon release, that person would not be allowed back into the prison, as they would be deemed to be a security risk. Like so many of the restrictions this theatre work is framed within, the cessation of the close working relationship with prisoners is problematic. We have had to internalise the strict rules of the establishment, many of which contradict the core beliefs and values of artists. However, to break the rules would be to put the future of this work in jeopardy; this is something that has to be fully understood by the participating students.

Despite these restrictions, with the full knowledge of the prison's security manager, we ran a campus-based drama group for five years. This group, Over the Wall Theatre Company, recruited people who were loosely described as 'overcoming disadvantage' (see Chapter 12). In this way, it was possible to maintain a working relationship with any ex-prisoner who was released into the area and who wanted to continue with work in drama and theatre. Students who had been involved in the prison projects worked as volunteers to support the group.

Conclusion

Over the years of student involvement in this work, there have been some exceptional and extraordinarily committed students who have taken part in projects in each year of their undergraduate programme. Many of these students have shown high levels of maturity, understanding and insight concerning the work in this challenging context. All students have to be individually accountable to the rest of the team and be responsible for themselves in order to contribute to the cohesion and success of the project. There have been rare occasions when a student has been overwhelmed by the context and has had to withdraw. Sometimes students have to struggle to maintain a persona, which is only part of who they feel they are.

Although the initial pre-project workshops act as a screening and selection process, there have been a couple of students in the eleven years of this work who have seemed fairly unsuited to work in a prison environment because they have had personal issues that have made it difficult for them to control their emotions and behave in an appropriate manner. Despite this, it has still been possible to observe the impact the work has had on these individuals. By the end of a project, their views have radically altered and many have undergone a process of maturation that most likely would not have happened if they had only been working with their peer group in the university or in a conventional theatre context. Overall, the experience has been beneficial and, in some cases, life-changing for the participating students. They have shown signs of enhanced maturity, a highly developed sense of commitment and responsibility, and a greater ability to manage themselves in difficult contexts.

Students have spoken about the ways in which taking part in these projects has enabled them to reflect on their own lives:

> To work in such a context makes you aware of the freedom and opportunities you have. You encounter different people from different backgrounds and that generates reflections and makes you appreciate what you have.
>
> (Donna, in Jones and Manley 2007)

Students have said that taking part in the projects incentivised them to work harder at their university studies. As Donna says above, the prism of the prison experience makes students intensely aware of the paucity of the existence of some of the prisoners' lives and the richness of their own experiences and opportunities. Maria said:

> We take for granted being raised right and maybe if some of them, somewhere along the line, had someone to support them, maybe they wouldn't have ended up that way.
>
> (post-production feedback, 2014)

These young people, starting to face adult life away from family, are given the opportunity to examine aspects of the wider world, thrown into relief by the extreme context of a prison. Additionally, they learn how to respond to and behave in different and strange settings. They meet people from diverse social backgrounds, people whose lives have not been as fortunate as their own. When prisoners tell their stories they are offering a challenge to the status of prisoners as 'the other'.

In other ways, these projects offer students the opportunity to enrich and widen their experiences as part of a process of development and transition into adult life. University life for most undergraduates entails a series of new experiences, heightened by – for many – the realities of being away from home for the first time. Away from the old routines and dynamics of family life, most students face a process in which they start to define themselves in the roles that will shape their social self and construct their adult identity. As Andrea says: 'Achievement is a very powerful thing; it can change someone's life for the better' (Evaluative questionnaire 2013). This is true for the prisoners and the students. Taking part in a prison theatre project offers a unique learning experience, both in terms of self-development and also in broadening their understanding of social and political issues.

I am going to leave the last word to Mollee who took part in the last three shows in West Hill:

I cried because I knew I wouldn't ever see them again…. It's also when you see the way the emotion hits them … I remember looking at Scott, last year, this 37 year old man who for nine weeks took so much from the project but never really showed masses of emotion; there were tears running down his cheeks and that really hit home and I thought 'that's the power … that's the power of this kind of project'. I gave him a hug and he was sobbing on my shoulder saying, '[t]his project has changed me, it has changed the way I think about things'. That is what my tears are for; they are tears of joy because it has hit home for them but it's also tears of sadness because now we're stopping it…. For me it is seeing the emotion in the guys and M___, the penny dropping on the Monday. You know, M___, when we said bye, he gave me a hug and he said, 'I'm sorry for being such a shit and I wish I had woken up a few weeks ago'. You know for me, those words, they're such gold, for me, that's what the whole project is all about.

(post-production feedback, 2014)

References

Elliott, A. (2007), *Concepts of the Self*, Key Concepts Series, 2nd ed., Revised and Updated, Cambridge: Polity Press.

Foucault, M. (1991), *Discipline and Punish: The Birth of the Prison*, London: Penguin.

Gibbs, G. (1998), *Learning by Doing: A Guide to Teaching and Learning Methods*, Oxford: Further Educational Unit, Oxford Polytechnic.

Heritage, P. (2004), 'Real social ties? The ins and outs of making theatre in Brazilian prisons', in M. Balfour (ed.), *Theatre in Prison: Theory and Practice*, Bristol: Intellect, pp. 190–92.

Jones, L., and Manley S., (2007), *Lessons from the Prison: The Student Experience*, Documentary Film, United Kingdom: LaunchPad Productions.

——— (2011), *Soul Traders*, Documentary Film, United Kingdom: LaunchPad Productions.

Lopez, T. A. (2003), 'Emotional contraband: Prison as metaphor and meaning in U.S. Latina Drama', in T. Fahy and K. King (eds), *Captive Audiences: Prison and Captivity in Contemporary Theatre*, London: Routledge, pp. 25–40.

Matarasso, F. (1997), *Use or Ornament? The Social Impact of Participation in the Arts*, Stroud: Comedia.

Moller, L. (2003), 'A day in the life of a prison theatre programme', *The Drama Review*, 47:1, pp. 49–73.

Music, G. (2014), *The Good Life: Wellbeing and the New Science of Altruism, Selfishness and Immorality*, London: Routledge.

Thompson, J. (2003), *Applied Theatre: Bewilderment and Beyond*, Bern: Peter Lang.

Woolland, B. (2014), *Stand or Fall*, Oxford: Oxford University Press.

Chapter 8

Our Country's Good by Timberlake Wertenbaker: Creating Liberatory Spaces? Reflections on Process and Performance

Marianne Sharp

In his now well-established essay entitled 'Rough theatre' (2008), David Greig describes his experience, in 2001, of witnessing a theatre performance by a young actor in a bullet-hole riddled garage, on a 'steep terrace of houses high above a valley' in the small Palestinian village of Beit Jala, close to Bethlehem. He describes seeing, across the valley, the three tanks, parked at the edge of the Israeli settlement of Giloh, 'with their guns pointed squarely over Beit Jala' (2008: 209). Greig describes the powerfully visceral sensations he experienced in witnessing this performance of 'rough theatre', by a group of young theatre artists called INAD, and suggests that the existence of this small piece of art in the brutal environment in which they existed enabled the young people to question and reflect upon their situation. He suggests that what he experienced was a 'profoundly political moment' occurring in relation to the environment, rather than the content of the performance itself. Greig argues that:

> The simple theatrical conjuring of a different world laid like a ghost image over a visible and threatening 'real' world somehow offered up the idea that – because the imagination made one thing possible – the imagination could make all things possible.
>
> (2008: 210)

How far this moment was 'profoundly political' *only* for Greig, as a foreign visitor unused to the realities of life in the West Bank, is debatable: the harsh realities of the environment in which these young theatre-makers are forced to operate remains. Perhaps the profundity occurred because moments like these highlight the absolute human compulsion to create art whether or not the threat of death is starkly present, and in the United Kingdom we infrequently encounter such stakes in our own artistic practices. I am interested in Greig's account with regard to my own reflections on the process of directing theatre work in prisons, because of the sharply observed comparison he offers up to the reader in response to his experience. He notes how INAD's theatre logo on the door of the garage-theatre had bullet holes in it, and goes on to describe how on his return to London, he noticed the Royal Court's logo (new at the time) also looked as though it had bullet holes in it. Further, he noted how, not unlike the interior of INAD's theatre space, the new interior of the Royal Court contained deliberately 'distressed' materials and an unfinished look including bare brick-work and exposed plaster. Greig suggests that the unfinished look of the theatre space at the Royal Court is in keeping with its 'political history and intent' and that the design features 'indicate the spontaneity of performance and the integrity of process over finish' (2008: 211). The comparison, however, sparks a question that is at the heart of my interest in Greig's account: he asks what might be 'the difference between the politics of creating self-conscious theatre amongst real bullet holes and the creation of self-consciously political theatre amidst a bullet hole look [?]' (2008: 211). Further, he asks 'whether this difference has anything to teach us about the creation of genuinely liberatory theatre spaces [?]' (2008: 211). I want to explore this idea in relation to my experience of adapting and directing Wertenbaker's *Our Country's Good* for Playing for Time's 2013 production in West Hill, HMP Winchester.

I am not suggesting for a moment that Greig's experience in the West Bank can, or should, be mapped explicitly on to the very different living and working conditions of a prison, which is, dependent on your perspective, a less threatening environment in which to exist than that of a conflict zone, but rather that his question highlights something vital about the power of theatre in direct relation to the realities of the environment in which it exists. Further, it prompts a consideration of the relationship of the environment to the ways in which the bodies and identities of the performers are experienced both within and beside the fictional world of the play. In what ways, and for whom, the experience of making work in HMP Winchester might create 'genuinely liberatory theatre spaces' was very much the element at stake in my experience of the process of working on this project: particularly in light of the themes at work in Wertenbaker's play.

Based on Thomas Keneally's 1987 novel *The Playmaker*, *Our Country's Good* is a play about the power of theatre. Set during the passage of the first fleet of convict ships to Botany Bay in Australia, it draws on historical fact and tells the story of the staging of a production of Farquhar's *The Recruiting Officer* by a company formed of prisoners, led by Lieutenant Ralph Clark. The themes of this play are heightened when staged in the context of a contemporary prison: we are watching a group of prisoners, in a prison, putting on a play about a group of prisoners putting on a play, in a penal colony. This process of staging the play-within-the-play in *Our Country's Good* highlights the performed nature of the operations of power in the social systems in which it is produced. It does this, in part, by raising questions about identity in the context of the nature/nurture debate:

TENCH: We are talking about criminals, often hardened criminals. They have a habit of vice and crime. Many criminals seem to have been born that way. It is in their nature.

PHILLIP: Rousseau would say that we have made them that way, Watkin: 'Man is born free and everywhere he is in chains'.

(Act 1, Scene 6, 'The Officers discuss the Merits of the Theatre' 2009: 18)

It also does this, in part, by staging sections of rehearsal that enable the audience to experience a fictionalised theatre-production-process and observe the results on the participants:

DABBY: I think *The Recruiting Officer* is a silly play. I want to be in a play with more interesting people in it.
MARY: I like playing Silvia. She's bold, she breaks rules out of love for her Captain and she's not ashamed.
DABBY: She hasn't been born poor, she hasn't had to survive, and her father's a Justice of the Peace. I want to play myself.
ARSCOTT: I don't want to play myself. When I say Kite's lines I forget everything else. I forget the judge said I'm going to have to spend the rest of my natural life in this place getting beaten and working like a slave [...]. I don't have to think about Kable, I don't have to remember the things I've done, when I speak Kite's lines I don't hate anymore. I'm Kite. I'm in Shrewsbury.

(Act 2, Scene 7, 'The Meaning of Plays', 2009: 73–74)

Arguments are made by Captain Arthur Phillip, the governor of the colony, that express the possibility that education and art might affect us in ways that have more to do with imagination and becoming than a harsh, fixed reality might offer:

PHILLIP: The theatre is an expression of civilisation. [...]. The convicts will be speaking a refined, literate language and expressing sentiments of a delicacy they are not used to. It will remind them that there is more to life than crime, punishment. And we, this colony of a few hundred will be watching this together, for a few hours we will no longer be despised prisoners and hated gaolers. We will laugh, we may be moved, we may even think a little. [...].
TENCH: I'm not sure it's a good idea having the convicts laugh at officers, Arthur.

(Act 1, Scene 6, 2009: 21)

Captain Tench's line here pre-empts the anxiety noted by Major Ross later in the scene: 'Order will become disorder. The theatre leads to threatening theory [...]' (Act 1, Scene 6, 2009: 25). This anxiety is produced when identities that might be assumed to be fixed are seen as potentially unfixed. Colette Conroy, in the context of discussing the ways in which 'the body' is, or indeed and arguably 'all bodies' are, a potential distraction from, or threat to, 'the coherence of the artistic structure' in play-based theatre, points out that

[t]heatre is founded upon a tension between being engrossed in the physical world of the room where the performance takes place and being engrossed in the fictional world of the play.

(2010: 37–38)

She further suggests that this threat occurs if we, as audience members, start to doubt that a given action is intentional (2010: 38). *Our Country's Good* exposes the possibility of theatre to reveal something about the identities of those in the society that engage in the play-making and watching process. What is at stake firstly within the play itself is the potential overspill from the tension that Conroy describes here: there is a necessity in *Our Country's Good* for some of the officers to explicitly resist being 'engrossed' in the world of the play and hence lose their clarity about who belongs where in the social strata. Reading Tench's words in light of Conroy's suggestion, for Tench it is vital that he remembers exactly which 'room' we are in. This anxiety, of course, mimics that of Plato in *The Republic*, where he would keep theatre out of his ideal city, because when we risk the possibility of being moved to feel any kind of emotion based on our engagement with something that is not 'real', we risk making poor judgements that might have actual consequences (Plato 2007). These circumstances are mirrored in the actualities of the context of prison theatre. The second thing at stake in the foundational aspects of dramatic narrative in the theatre, that Conroy describes here, is the risk of the fiction being interrupted by the presence of the real bodies of the performers in a way that causes the audience to doubt the intentions of the artists. Should this occur, the integrity of the fiction is broken. *Our Country's Good* exploits this tension by layering an interplay of fiction and reality into the narrative of the drama. Hence in the doubled context that is afforded to the audience of Playing for Time's work within the walls of a contemporary prison, the identity divisions of our own society are potentially brought into sharp relief for participants and audience members through the process and performances of this project. We cannot fail to recognise that the fictional 'world' of the play *is*, to a certain extent, 'the physical world of the room where the performance takes place' (Conroy 2010: 38). *Our Country's Good* contains the clear message that theatre has the power to transform the experience of individuals and to provide a space of imagination in which, through the process of role playing, it becomes evident that individual identities are more fluid than those who derive value from their own socially or politically powerful status might wish.

In this sense, *Our Country's Good* is making a similar argument to Greig's for the power of 'rough theatre', through which 'the simple theatrical conjuring of a different world laid like a ghost image over a visible and threatening "real world", might [offer] up the idea that – because the imagination made one thing possible – the imagination could make all things possible' (2008: 210). The scenario Greig describes is an environment where bodies are subject to constant threat, there is a sense of being watched, and there are certain bodies that must remain/exist only in certain demarcated areas. In *Our Country's Good*, there is a different kind of constant threat to those involved in the penal colony that arrives in Botany Bay – beatings, starvation, disease, death. There are demarcated areas where certain kinds of individuals should, or should not operate (officers' camp, prisoners' camp) and the colony and its officers are invaders, colonisers of a territory, a 'new' land. As in the scenario Greig describes, it is clear that the brutal conditions to which the convicts in the play are subjected exist and remain as a constant threat in spite of the illumination that is provided by the theatrics.

In *Our Country's Good*, there is a further threat looming, that of the devastation that the colonisers will wreak on the Aboriginal population of the colonised area: this is made manifest by the presence of the Aboriginal character, who sits outside the action as an observer and omen of what is to come beyond and around the action of the play. I had to make the difficult, and somewhat uncomfortable, choice to cut this character – vital in Wertenbaker's play – from our production.[1] Due to time constraints on the length of the production imposed by the operational needs of the prison, and the brief I was given, the priority had to be keeping the scenes and sections of the play that would best reflect the environment in which we were working. The presence of the Aboriginal character speaks to the devastation and violence at the root of colonial mentality, and the relationship between the officers and convicts of the penal colony and the wider national environment in which the penal colony exists. On one level it might be the case that where we were staging a production that was 'about' the environment, both immediate and national of our own surroundings, the audience – as representatives of the community and, in part, nation, beyond the walls of Winchester prison – were the uncanny replacement for the Aboriginal figure, though their presence clearly does not speak to quite the same questions in quite the same way.

The question of the relationship of the presence of the outside, 'invited' but public audience, to the production process and performance is a curious one in Playing for Time's work. In my role as director, this relationship was something of which I was constantly aware, and – unusually – towards which I felt oddly hostile throughout the process. Reflecting back on Greig's anecdote about INAD, what seemed powerful in this context was the lack of audience, and Greig's recognition of the significance of the act of making theatre – in spite of the insanity of the context – for the participants of the work. Similarly, in *Our Country's Good*, the learning and personal transformations that we are encouraged to recognise as occurring through the process of theatre-making happen exactly there: in the process. The audience who enter the prison to see Playing for Time's work have no sense of the detail, or struggles, or challenges that occur throughout the course of the project: that is the nature of production, that you hide the means of it – even in contexts where the means of it are an explicit component of the narrative or performed 'world' of the production, for example in certain kinds of post-dramatic performance work. In that sense, the majority of audience members do not see the reality of what it means to make theatre in a secure environment: they see the relatively polished result of a disciplined process. We disguise the reality of the prison gymnasium in which we perform, and we bring in set, floor-cloth, lighting and costumes to transform the reality of the environment into the fiction of something rather more middle class and palatable. In this sense, we are creating the opposite of the Royal Court's 'bullet-hole look', and with the fiction of our theatrics, manufacturing a strange mask of normality for our 'rough' theatre.

My sense – that grows out of a certain feeling of protectiveness towards the cast in this particular context – is that in spite of their actual journey through the prison gates to get to the performance venue, the external audience needs the fiction that we are in a 'safe' environment and that we are watching prisoners 'do well', and do 'something good'. The politics implicit in such assumptions make me anxious, because they risk reinforcing the status of prisoners as 'other', and the production becomes a performance of colonised bodies acting out their adherence to middle-class notions of theatre as something that 'good' people do. The 'didn't they do well, for prisoners' response to work in this context is the one I dread. One of the reasons, however, that Playing for Time has continued to produce large-scale productions in this way, is because of the dynamic that is produced by the bringing together of a number of different communities in the context of these productions.

Involved in the process, there is the production team 'community', consisting of those employed to deliver the project; the student 'community', who volunteer to participate in the project; the 'community' of prison staff including education tutor(s), and officers/security staff and the prison governor(s), who are more, or less, supportive of the work dependent on their individual perspectives on the value of arts practices in secure environments; and the diverse 'community' of prisoners, including prisoners not involved directly in the project who come to see the work. These groups are all represented in some way in the demographic of the audience. In addition, friends and family members of the participating prisoners are invited, as are local dignitaries (the mayor), and there is the extension of the invitation to apply for tickets to members of the public from the local area who have heard about the work over the years that the projects have been running. The project is an intervention into the prison environment and one of the objectives – inevitably hard to measure – is attitudinal changes within the prison, where the participating prisoners must continue to exist, at least for a time, beyond the completion of the project. The presence of the diverse audience body is part of the dynamic that potentially enables some shifts in perception by all of the 'communities' involved to occur, on a range of levels. In the regular prison environment, prison officers watch prisoners. In the event of the performances, officers watch other audience members watching the prison governor, watching prisoners and students play prisoners and officers and the governor; families of the prisoners watch officers watching prisoners and students playing prisoners and officers; prisoners watch themselves watching prisoners and students being watched by officers and students and their own families etc. Translating Greig's real description into a metaphor here, in other words, the production of the 'bullet-hole look' that masks the 'real bullet-holes' in this environment is, perhaps, a necessary fiction. For me, the 'real bullet-holes', which exist in the process and production of staging *Our Country's Good* in HMP Winchester, are the realities of the violent divide between the communities that come together in the performances of Playing for Time's work: at the end of the production, we all go our separate ways, and some of us are locked up again.

Working methods

My task, then, as director, seemed to call for a way of working that specifically navigated the presence of these diverse communities and, through a combination of the play content, the staging and the context, might create the possibility for some members of those diverse communities to experience 'genuinely liberatory' moments in their encounter with the work in this particular theatre space.

My questions were:

1. How successfully might adapted aspects of ensemble principles and practices drawn from the ensemble work of certain established artists/companies function as training tools for a diverse non-professional cast in a prison context?
2. How far would working with these practices develop a sense of community within the cast – a disparate group at the outset of the project – and how would this sense of community translate into the creation of 'genuinely liberatory [...] spaces' in performance (Greig 2008: 211)?
3. How/in what ways, and for whom, were identities 'mark[ed] or change[d]' (Schechner 2002: 37) through the process and performance?

I regularly work with ensemble training practices in my own teaching and directing practice. The word ensemble denotes 'togetherness'. Prison life separates individuals in prison from the outside world, and within the prison, from each other. I do not intend to discuss the morality of these distinctions here. Some of the exercises I work with are basic ensemble training tools derived from the work of Polish theatre company, Gardzienice. I learned these some years ago in a series of workshops with Paul Allain, who trained with the company, so I acknowledge the lineage here, though I have not trained directly with that company. The company works a lot with song and with the principle of 'mutuality' in which the basic unit in the theatre is two performers, not one, so there is an emphasis on the mutual reliance of performers built in to the working process from the 'warm-up' stage of rehearsals right through to performance (see Staniewski/Hodge 2003). This seemed to be an appropriate starting point for introducing the two communities that formed the cast: the group of prisoners and the group of students.

I have also undertaken training in ensemble improvisation with Rachel Rosenthal (1927–2015) in two of her signature DbD (Doing-by-Doing) workshops and in workshops with her current ensemble company (see www.rachelrosenthal.org). Rosenthal's practice similarly relies on a heightened sensitivity in self/other relationships in the listening, sensing and seeing of the other participants in the work. Differently to my work on this play in HMP Winchester in 2005, I drew on my experience in these practices for the 2013 rehearsal process for *Our Country's Good*, with the intention of our work sharing an ethics of practice rather than, necessarily, aesthetic results with the work of these artists/companies. This was coupled with the aim of developing a working method, with the non-professional cast of prisoners and undergraduate students, that would enable the very diverse and disparate group who signed up for the project to cohere as a company with a shared way of working and mutual sense of reliance that would translate effectively into performance. Part of this choice was about seeking to create a piece of work that did not fall into the common 'traps' of applied theatre project performances that are well-intentioned but lack sufficient attention to the aesthetic aspects of the work and part of it was to enable the prisoner cast to experience the quality of the mutual reliance and 'flow' that can occur when you genuinely listen and respond to others within the work. Mihaly Csikszentmihalyi's several-decades'-worth of research on notions of 'flow', or what he terms 'optimal experience', was gathered in his classic work, *Flow* (2002), first published in the United States in 1990. Csikszentmihalyi's interest evolved from questioning what aspects of human activity form the basis of the experience of happiness. He describes flow, or 'the optimal state of inner-experience' as 'one in which there is *order in consciousness*. This happens when psychic energy – or attention – is invested in realistic goals, and when skills match the opportunities for action' (2002: 6, emphasis in original). Csikszentmihalyi's description here offers insight into why, for me, it is vital to work, in part, with performer training practices in the context of applied theatre projects (indeed, for me, in all theatre projects in which an untrained cast are the primary performers). The cast need to be provided with a mutually understood and shared set of skills so that they are not left exposed in the event of the meeting with the theatre audience. This point may seem obvious, but there are many theatre exercises that simply involve playing games, for example, and these, whilst they may function as enjoyable 'ice-breakers' and help to develop a valuable sense of play, for the most part do not provide an untrained cast with the necessary tools to navigate the complex and potentially exposing experience of performing to an audience and delivering a clarity of meaning in the moment of performance. Csikszentmihalyi goes on to suggest that '[t]he pursuit of a goal brings order in awareness because a person must concentrate attention on the task at hand and momentarily forget everything else' (2002: 6), as in Arscott's description in Act 2, Scene 7, described earlier. Further, it was our hope that the cast would recognise the significance of the identity politics at work in the act of their choosing to participate in the staging of this particular text in the context of their current existence as prisoners. These ways of working, however, require focus, discipline and a willingness to employ a fully embodied 'listening' to others, and arriving at the point where that 'listening' can occur was, for me, the challenge. How might it be possible to develop a sense of discipline within the company in a way that the group, and the individuals within it, might take ownership of it rather than have it enacted upon them, in the way that, for the prisoners especially, discipline was enacted upon them in their daily experience in a regimented manner?

Helen Nicholson has noted an uncomfortableness that I share, in the context of applied drama: claims that this form of work is socially transformative (2005: 12). Nicholson asks: 'If the motive is individual or personal transformation, is this something which is done *to* the participants, *with* them, or *by* them? Whose values and interests does the transformation serve?' (2005: 12). The poetics at work in the relationships between the participants in this project, the rehearsal and performance form(s) employed and play-content therein situate the work, overall, on a sharp edge between the 'inculcat[ion of] messages of obedience' through the artistic process and the consciousness-raising and 'mobilis[ation of] active citizens' that might be argued to be the ideal objective of the work (Prentki and Preston 2009: 13–21). Nicholson describes her preference for the term 'transportation', as distinguished in Richard Schechner's writings on the topic (see Schechner 2003) because transportation denotes 'performers [being] "taken somewhere", actors are even temporarily transformed, but they are more or less returned to their starting places at the end of the drama or performance' (Schechner in Nicholson 2005: 12). This idea of transportation is a helpful way of thinking about the processes that might be occurring between prisoners, students and diverse audience groups in the journey that they go on together during the performances of *Our Country's Good* within the prison walls: not least because unlike the convicts in Wertenbaker's play who were literally transported to another world during their passage to Australia, our performers and audience members literally return to their respective starting places (inside or outside of the prison walls) at the end of the performance. The going 'somewhere', which Nicholson and Schechner discuss, for me conjures up the image of a portal: something that opens up in the dimension in which we exist to take us through to another reality, even if only in our imagination.

We began every rehearsal with a warm-up that might last up to an hour and half. Like the practices on which I was drawing, the 'warm-up' is not separate from the 'work'. The exercises that formed this part of the rehearsals were, for me, vital in beginning to build the sense of community amongst the cast. In spite of the task ahead and the time constraints, we did variations on the routine described below in every single rehearsal, so that the cast became used, very quickly, to operating in the performance space together as if they were performing. The structure began with the group in a circle – so we were all visible to each other – and we went through a gentle physical routine that worked the whole body from head to toe, incorporating exercises with the hands and feet to develop awareness of our whole body as the expressive 'tool' of the actor. We then moved to breath work. During the breathing sequence I incorporated breathing exercises drawn from the body-voice work of Zygmunt Molik, exercises that heighten awareness of the relationship between the body and breath. Molik was a member of the laboratory theatre of Jerzy Grotowski for 25 years, with whom I undertook training workshops in Poland and the United Kingdom (the link here with the practices of the Gardzience company is through their director, Wlodzimierz Staniewski, who worked intensively with Grotowski through his 'para-theatre' phase). As an example, one of the breathing exercises we did involved slowing down the breath by breathing in through one nostril for a count of four; holding the breath for a count of four; and breathing out through the other nostril for a count of four. This exercise parallels breath-work in various yoga practices. Slowing the breath and focusing on following the breath in this way calms the body and helps with feeling 'present', thereby heightening our receptiveness to others. Following breath-work we moved to humming. We learnt a relatively well-known folk-song, 'The Water is Wide', during the first rehearsal. We learnt it in two-part harmony and we hummed it through several times and sang it every day during rehearsals. Once we moved to singing, we 'walked the song' through the space, working with awareness of space and bodies moving through space as we sang. This developed listening and spatial awareness amongst the group, but was, in itself, a powerful communal experience in which to participate: it became a kind of ritual for the group. Moving together and singing together in this way creates soothing sound vibrations that permeate through all of the bodies in the room. The words of the song are as follows:

The Water is Wide
I cannot get o'er
And neither have I wings to fly
Give me a boat that will carry two
And both shall row, my love and I

For me, the sense of separation across water, the wish to travel and to find or re-find love, and the poignant simplicity of this wish in the context of both the play and the real conditions of the prison environment – where one is separated from loved ones and exists in conditions that are designed to isolate – helped to create a context in which the rest of the rehearsal could evolve. The opening of the production was the same song-action that we had repeated every day in rehearsals, which spanned a two-month period (three days per week in the first month, five days per week in the second month). It connected the company in a ritual act that would create a 'bridge' both in rehearsal and in the performances from the gymnasium in West Hill to the world of the play. My hope was that because when we got to the performances, the cast were used to enacting this ritual, it would enable them to stay focused on each other, and the action of moving and singing, rather than on the audience and on their anxieties about performing.

From the song work, we moved into exercises that build concentration and mutual reliance. These were simple exercises, common to many theatre training forms, but they were structured in a similar way to the way Rosenthal structures exercises on the first day of her DbD experience (see Rosenthal 2010) and they were designed to take the group from a point of focus on one other individual into larger group improvisational structures. We worked often with mirroring exercises, with pairs being asked to start again if it became clear that one person was leading and the other following, so that pairs could practise trying to work in sync with each other, rather than falling into leader-follower patterns. We moved from mirroring into sculpting exercises (what Rosenthal calls 'Dolls' and 'Dolls at a Distance') eventually working up to giving and receiving movement impulses in partner-work and working with whole group 'flocking' exercises (up to 30 people at a time moving in synchronised formations). Like the song-work, these actions kept the cast in a constant state of concentration on the others in the company. Returning to Csikszentmihalyi, he offers two terms that '[describe] states of social pathology [that] apply also to conditions that make flow difficult to experience: *anomie* and *alienation*' (2002: 86, emphasis in original). The first, '*anomie*', or 'lack of rules', is French sociologist Emile Durkheim's name for 'a condition in society in which the norms of behaviour [...] become muddled' (2002: 86). The second, 'alienation', is 'a condition in which people are constrained by the social system to act in ways that go against their goals' (2002: 86). Csikszentmihalyi states that:

> [T]hese two obstacles to flow [...] are functionally equivalent to the two personal pathologies, attentional disorders and self-centeredness. At both levels, the individual and the collective, what prevents flow from occurring is either the fragmentation of attentional processes (as in *anomie* and attentional disorders), or their excessive rigidity (as in alienation and self-centredness). At the individual level *anomie* corresponds to anxiety, while alienation corresponds to boredom.
>
> (2002: 86)

In the context of the performances, this daily practice of focusing on others produces less anxiety and self-consciousness than if the performer only has to think about remembering their own lines, for example. The result is often a heightened sense of absorption, on the part of the performers, in the action and their relationship to others on stage, and this is almost always engaging to watch. Boredom is avoided because the performers are constantly working on a task, even where they are present in a non-speaking capacity.

Once the play was cast (between two and three weeks into the nine-week process) we began to build aspects of character work, including speech-work, into the warm-up section and into the improvisations. Cast members developed sequences of repeatable, small gestures (which might also include a way of walking) and improvised with their sequences. We added in some exercises drawn from Stanislavski's work, in particular 'circles of attention', to heighten the awareness of the group with regard to the choices they might make about where to look, at whom, with what effect in a given scene. The larger group of 30 was broken down into three groups of ten, and each smaller group improvised with a set of options: walking, freezing, stopping and running through your sequence of gestures, stopping and saying a line of your character, stopping and improvising with a sequence of three different circles of attention. There was therefore a limited set of tools with which to improvise, but like the mirroring exercise in pairs, the whole group of ten must do the same action, or type of action (including speech options) at the same time, without me being able to see a leader. The groups became quite good at this over the course of the rehearsal process. This idea was translated into certain scenes by putting one or two choreographic improvisation rules in place for certain characters: if character 'a' was in one corner of the space, character 'b' needed to be in the opposite corner; if 'a' crossed the space, 'b' had to balance out that movement by moving simultaneously and switching places.

Once we had run through one of a number of variations of the overall sequence described here, we would begin scene work. During the entirety of the rehearsal process, my focus was on the dynamic in the space between the cast members, and the ensuing spatial relationships – in a choreographic sense – between them and the three audience seating banks. I prioritised these elements over doing detailed scene work, and would often delegate to the cast to work on the detail of their speech emphasis and tone in small groups, having multiple scenes rehearsing at the same time. When I worked with the performers in a given scene, I would focus on the dynamic between them, the choreographic rules for that scene, and tried to keep their attention on how to follow the action and dialogue within a given scene, even if they were not speaking. The emphasis, for me, was on giving the cast rules, shapes and actions in a given scene so that they would be, in some way, occupied at all times in a game that involved focusing on other people's actions, asking them (as in Rosenthal's practice): where are you needed in this picture? In this way – though to experienced ensemble performers these strategies may seem obvious – the cast fell into a form of mutual reliance on each other, but in a way that demanded a high level of concentration. Wertenbaker's text was one layer of meaning in the performances, but there was a physical 'underscore' at work in scenes, over which the text was laid. Of course there was a relationship between action and word, but the choreography in each scene meant that the performers were constantly working through tasks and layering the dialogue over those tasks. The effect of this, generally, is that the performers become so intent on performing the tasks in a given scene that they, effectively, 'forget' to 'act', in the heightened sense of the term, and are rather absorbed in the enactment of the task. One of the student cast members commented to me, in a post-project reflective discussion, that he had been surprised by how hard he had found himself working as a non-speaking member of the ensemble whose presence in the performance space was focused on supporting the mood or a scene or transition, or actions of others, for the duration of the production, so my hope was that it was possible for all members of the cast to experience moments of 'flow', both on an individual and collective level.

Process: Challenges and discoveries

Our cast of fifteen undergraduate students and fifteen prisoners (fourteen by production week as one cast member was released shortly before the end of the process) constituted a group about three times larger than necessary for staging *Our Country's Good*: usually actors double-up on several of the roles in the play. The project is run on a basis of inclusion however, so all prisoners and all students who signed up for the project were included in the cast. The ensemble approach to working and the incorporation of song (there are no songs in *Our Country's Good*, but we worked with four) enabled us to create sequences within the performance that involved everybody. The prisoners were given priority in the casting so all of the male-speaking roles in the production were taken by prisoners, though the audiences were not necessarily aware that this was the case.

One of the interesting occurrences was the shift in the relationships between the prisoner cast through the process. Most of the prisoners had not acted in, nor seen, much (if any) theatre prior to this project. There were exceptions to this, but there was an incredibly diverse range of participants both in age and social and educational backgrounds: some participants had real challenges with literacy levels, some were simply very wary of each other, bullying was occurring, some struggled to take themselves or the process seriously and battled confidence issues – these were some of the early challenges. The student cast were also on a huge learning curve as for the majority it was their first experience of entering a secure environment and both groups had to negotiate their preconceived notions of what constituted a 'prisoner' and what constituted a 'student'. Participation in the rehearsal process required discipline, commitment, a willingness to explore the unknown and a willingness to learn and engage with techniques and processes that were new to most of the participants, including students, prisoners and some of the production team. By the end of the process several prisoners noted, in group feedback sessions, how their attitudes towards other prisoners had shifted within the company and how they would now engage with people with whom they were unwilling to communicate prior to the experience of the process.

Many of the student cast equally underwent a change in attitude and understanding of both what 'kinds' of people find their way into the prison system, and a change in their understanding of what their own presence in the project signified. The mentoring system used by Playing for Time, discussed by Annie McKean in Chapter 7, for example, is often regarded by the students as them 'helping' the prisoner cast. In this instance (and in previous projects I have experienced) there was a point in the process where many of the prisoner cast began working harder than some members of the student cast, and often the mentoring was, on a level, working both ways. One of the prisoner cast members enjoyed helping one of the student understudies learn his lines. The particular student understudying the largest male role (Second Lieutenant Ralph Clark) had, in part via the insistence of the prisoner with whom he was paired for mentoring and unbeknownst to me, learnt all of his part. We had no time to rehearse the understudies, so when the prisoner playing Ralph Clark had to appear in court with a day's notice on the opening performance date, the understudy had to step in for that night. I told the student in question that he could perform with the script, and trusted him to deliver the text well. To my utter delight, and with only the dress rehearsal to run through his part with the cast, he covered the first night without needing the script and gave an excellent performance. The student was very capable, so this achievement is very much a testament to his own commitment to the project. However, the ensemble process and the two-way exchange that occurred as part of the mentoring process between prisoners and students seemed to have enabled this change of cast on the first night to seamlessly occur without throwing off-balance either the individuals concerned, or the whole company.

In Act 1, Scene 6: 'The Authorities Discuss the Merits of the Theatre', the prisoner-cast were all present and engaged in playing out the central debate of the play, which centres around whether or not the prisoners in the Botany Bay penal colony should be allowed to stage a play. The arguments for and against the value of this activity are debated in detail, as noted earlier in this chapter, and mirror the ongoing question of what prisoners in contemporary British prisons should or should not be allowed to do whilst serving a sentence.

ROSS: And you say you want those contumelious convicts to act in this play. The convicts!

(Act 1, Scene 6, 2009: 17)

ROSS: This is a convict colony, the prisoners are here to be punished and we're here to make sure they get punished.

(2009: 18)

TENCH: If you want to teach the convicts something, teach them to farm, to build houses, teach them a sense of respect for property, teach them thrift so they don't eat a week's rations in one night, but above all, teach them how to work, not how to sit around laughing at a comedy.

(2009: 22)

During our production week there was an issue raised in the national news that spoke directly to this question, so the production felt timely. Midway through the process I had a discussion session with the prisoner cast, outside of the formal rehearsals, about the significance of this scene and during this we questioned what it meant for them to be playing officers and raising these questions for a public audience. During this discussion some of the prisoners recognised the potential ways in which staging the play spoke to questions about their own social identity, and we discussed what it might mean to own these questions as we staged the play. For example, one of the prisoners noted that his brother had made clear to him that he didn't think the group should be doing a play in the prison. The brother had expressed that he felt the prisoners were there to be punished, and that they should not be engaged in activities that might be perceived to be fun: a view commonly expressed in media debates about prisoners and what activities are appropriate or not for those incarcerated.

Scene 6 is not easy to perform. Though the debate is clear, the dialogue is complex and littered with historical and literary references. In addition, we staged our production with audience on three sides (this was as close as we could get in the prison gymnasium to the shape of Greek amphitheatres in which, as noted in Scene 6, the Greeks believed it was a citizen's duty to watch plays) so the cast had to learn how to operate with 360-degree awareness and work appropriately with audience sight-lines in this formation. This arrangement also meant that all participants at the performance, cast and audience, were visible to each other. For me, the 'flow' achieved by the prisoners in this scene, evident in the responsiveness to each other in their movement through the space and the quality of listening occurring in the dialogue, was where the results of the rehearsal methods were most evident. The self-reflexivity apparent through the clarity of the enactment of this scene was one of the places in the production where, to return to Greig's 'rough theatre', I think the 'different world laid like a ghost image over a visible and threatening "real" world', was not just 'mak[ing] things possible', but was offering up a kind of contradiction that was, perhaps, making 'the fabric of "reality" [...] tear' and enabling those willing to 'see, behind it, the real world with its rifts and crevices [...] indignant and distorted' (Greig 2008: 220). One of the fascinating moments, for me, in the performance week, was watching the Number 1 Governor of the prison watching the prisoner playing Captain Arthur Phillip (the governor of the prison colony) stating: 'Some of these men will have finished their sentence in a few years. They will become members of society again, and help create a new society in this colony. Should we not encourage them now to think in a free and responsible manner?' (Act 1, Scene 6, 2009: 21).

Working with improvisatory structures prior to scene work meant that when we came to choreograph larger group sequences, for example with the whole cast, though these were challenging, the group already knew how to function in the space together and how to listen to each other. As an example, at the end of the show there was a dance involving a sequence of specific actions. There is no dance at the end of *Our Country's Good*, but we chose to finish with this because it was a way of engaging the whole cast in an action that we felt summarised the ways in which we had worked together across the process. It was a celebratory act of our achievement together as a company. This sequence involved the entire cast (29 in the final event) and was devised by the whole cast across one rehearsal session with the intention that the group could take ownership of the material. During the session I divided the company up into four groups. Each group were given a set of six actions plus each group was given one additional action that was different to each of the other groups. In their groups they were asked to create a movement sequence/short dance together from this set of actions. We then placed two groups at a time in the space together running through their sequences and structured some whole group movements around this to take this sequence into the final song. Whilst I think ending our production in this way was not, per se, in keeping with Wertenbaker's intentions for the final moments of *Our Country's Good*, it did demonstrate something of the coming together of the student and prisoner communities in the course of the project process, possibly more so in the creation of this sequence in rehearsal – in which the groups cooperated within and amongst themselves remarkably easily – than was necessarily clear in the same way in performance.

Shifting identities

In the month following the performance week I went to two education sessions in West Hill to engage in some evaluative discussions with the prisoner cast about their experiences of the whole project. I worked with Richard Schechner's identification of the seven functions of performances (see Schechner 2002: 37) and we worked through each one and discussed if, how and where each 'function' related to the prisoner's experiences of our work together. The functions are:

1. To entertain.
2. To make something that is beautiful.
3. To mark or change identity.
4. To make or foster community.
5. To heal.
6. To teach, persuade or convince.
7. To deal with the sacred and/or the demonic.

The prisoners found connections between the work we had undertaken together and each of the functions in some way. There were three main points that arose from the discussion. One point centred around feelings of pride and achievement that seemed to be related to audience responses to the work. Two cast members compared the unexpected 'high' that they had experienced after the performances to their encounters with substance abuse. They both expressed that the performance 'high' had been more exciting because it was marked with a sense of pride and that this was a revelation and a discovery for them and a form of pride that they would want to experience again.

A second point centred around the men's sense of how their relationships with each other had shifted. They brought up the issue of stereotyping in prison environments and mentioned their stereotyping of each other, of the students and the ways in which they assumed the audiences would be stereotyping them prior to seeing the show. We talked through the different ways in which the process we had undergone might allow for some intervention into these stereotypes. Although the men found connections between their experience of the process and all of Schechner's functions, many of the points they raised focused around how they perceived themselves and how (they felt) others perceived them. The performances took place in the prison gymnasium in West Hill, HMP Winchester. There was a short amount of time between the end of the performance and the moment when the audience and prisoner cast are separated and escorted, by security staff, from the gymnasium when the two groups are able to converse briefly in the performance area. Several of the men shared comments that they had received directly from audience members after one or more of the performances and it transpired that a number of them had been engaged in conversations where the audience member had assumed that they were from the university. They had been asked questions such as which part of the university were they from? Or what degree subject were they studying? The audience were not aware, when they saw the performance, which male members of the cast were students and which were prisoners and had clearly misidentified several of the prisoners as students, or as a tutor in one case. Equally, some of the male students in the cast were asked what they had done to be 'in here', and were misrecognised as prisoners. Whilst a couple of the prisoner cast acknowledged that they had then been rather embarrassed to explain that they were 'from in here', some also expressed surprise and a sense of relief in the recognition that, whilst their usual experience is that of being criticised for their actions, it was possible to be seen by others as 'being good' and achieving. In a company discussion the morning after the first performance, one of the prisoner cast expressed: 'We're in here for crimes. Nine times out of ten we're criticised for what we do, and we're – you know – the lowest of the low. But for that time, we [were] as good as the public. We were accepted' (Prisoner S., *Our Country's Good*, post-performance recorded discussion, 2013). Another cast member noted: 'I'm just glad they [audience] saw us as people, rather than 'criminals' for a change. It's just nice to be recognised as a person' (Prisoner A., post-performance recorded discussion, 2013). This experience, though anecdotal, demonstrates that in the quality of the performances given, it was not always clear or easy to distinguish prisoners from other males from the university. My hope is that those members of the audience who engaged in such dialogues may have recognised the implications of their questions, or their surprise when faced with the reality that people inside the prison may not be so different from people outside the prison. I am not suggesting, necessarily, that audience members who clearly misidentified prisoners and students came into the prison with an especially narrow concept with regard to prisoner or student identity, but that here were certain moments that offered up an opportunity to recognise prejudices that might be more broadly embedded in our culture and thinking.

The third point that arose from the discussion was that two of the men raised the issue of how their experiences in the respective social contexts in which they existed when outside of the prison meant that in the past they would have been embarrassed to be involved in an artistic activity. They suggested this was because it would be regarded as 'unmanly' in their social circles. Both of these prisoners said that the project process had caused them to face up to some of their own 'issues'. They further noted that in the future they would consider getting involved in creative activities and how, because they could feel grounded in their own reasons for wanting to do that, they suggested that they would not care so much about peer pressure to conform. Others noted that they felt the overall experience was 'confidence-building', and one prisoner responded that on release: 'I think I'm going to end up taking my kids to [see] theatre, to get them involved' (Prisoner M., post-performance recorded discussion 2013). Responses from the prisoner cast were almost exclusively positive, though one participant noted that he had found it difficult after the project ended to not be able to maintain any of the social bonds created across the cast and production team through the process. The question of how to follow up on such intensive project experiences remains and needs further consideration, but it seemed to be helpful that the two follow-up sessions enabled a space at least for these experiences to be articulated and discussed amongst those present.

The prison governor, and various members of prison staff, expressed their surprise, after the event, at how engaged the prisoner-group were in the production. The governor, who was supportive of the project going ahead, noted to us how he had come to the performance in a frustrated mood, because he was feeling that it would be dull and perhaps not the best use of his time. His response after seeing the production was that he had been 'blown away'. He expressed that he had never witnessed the men from the cast-group engaging in any activity with the level of commitment to the project and each other that he had witnessed in the performance. I don't know, beyond our time in the prison, how far his recognition and that of other prison staff might have produced an attitudinal change towards the men in the production. What was clear, though, was that some shift in perception of the prisoners in the project had occurred, even if only in a small way.

In the sense that the project process and production was a sharp learning curve for all participants, the integration that occurs between student cast, prisoner cast, production team, prison staff and, in the final event, audience, is something that can, perhaps, speak to the ideal relationship between a society and its prison population. It seems clear that, on a small level, some form of 'transportation' did occur for many of the participants. In certain moments in the production, the layerings of fiction and reality in the 'tension between being engrossed in the physical world of the room where the performance takes place and being engrossed in the fictional world of the play' (Conroy 2010: 37–38) enabled the 'the fabric of "reality" […to] tear', and enabled those willing to 'see, behind it, the real world with its rifts and crevices […] indignant and distorted' (Greig 2008: 220). The hope through this occurrence is that, aside from the changes in understanding of any stereotyped idea of 'prisoner' that the student cast, production team and audience might experience, the small attitudinal changes from prisoners and staff within the prison will, in certain instances, last beyond the limitations of this project, and at best may enable the recognition from some that the roles taken on in the day-to-day running of such institutions are also a performance – however socially necessary that performance may be in certain cases. These shifting attitudes to self and others that occurred through the process and staging of *Our Country's Good* can potentially contribute to the 'liberatory' discovery of other worlds of experience and ways of being that exist beyond the confines of whatever 'worlds' and ways of being have led to individuals becoming either 'despised prisoners' or 'hated gaolers' (Act 1, Scene 6, 2009: 21). As Prisoner J. noted: 'Through this process we could understand each other better, in a way that we may not otherwise have known if we hadn't had that opportunity of experience' (post-performance recorded discussion, 2013).

References

Allain, P. (1997), *Gardzienice: Polish Theatre in Transition*, London and New York: Routledge.

Campo, G. with Molik, Z. (2010), *Zygmunt Molik's Voice and Bodywork: The Legacy of Jerzy Grotowski*, London and New York: Routledge.

Conroy, C. (2010), *Theatre & the Body*, Basingstoke: Palgrave Macmillan.

Csikszentmihalyi, M. (2002), *Flow*, London, Sydney, Auckland and Johannesburg: Rider.

Greig, D. (2008), 'Rough theatre', in Rebecca d'Monte and Graham Saunders (eds.), *Cool Britannia? British Political Drama in the 90s*, Basingstoke: Palgrave Macmillan, pp. 208–21.

Nicholson, H. (2005), *Applied Drama: The Gift of Theatre*, Basingstoke and New York: Palgrave Macmillan.

Plato (2007), *The Republic*, Classics 3rd ed., London: Penguin.

Prentki T. and Preston, S. (eds) (2009), *The Applied Theatre Reader*, London and New York: Routledge.

Rosenthal, R. (2010), *The DbD Experience: Chance Knows What It's Doing!* London and New York: Routledge.

Schechner, R. (2002), *Performance Studies*, London and New York: Routledge.

—— (2003), 'Performers and spectators transported and transformed', in P. Auslander (ed.), *Performance: Critical Concepts in Literary and Cultural Studies*, vol. 1, London: Routledge.

Staniewski, W. with Hodge, A. (2013), *Hidden Territories: The Theatre of Gardzienice*, London and New York: Routledge.

Wertenbaker, T. (2009 [1988]), *Our Country's Good*, in B. Naismith (ed.), London: Methuen Drama.

Note

1 I would like to thank Timberlake Wertenbaker, who fully recognised the particular needs of our project in HMP Winchester, and very kindly gave permission for me to edit down *Our Country's Good* for Playing for Time's production. Wertenbaker's play is still under copyright, and this was the first time she has given anyone permission to cut the play. *Our Country's Good* is an intricately constructed work and much of the editing I did was in trimming words and sentences (with the exception of cutting the Aboriginal character) as it was impossible to remove any scenes without losing vital plot points or valuable layers from the dramaturgy.

Chapter 9

The Drama of Change: A Comparative Study of University Students' and Prisoners' Dispositional Empathy, Need for Closure and Future Possible Selves

Ann Henry

Reducing recidivism – what works?

This chapter uses empirical data to explore whether drama has a positive and/or viable role to play (pun intended) in reducing recidivism – not as an alternative to accredited evidence-based prison programmes led by psychologists working within HM Prison Service, but offered alongside them. According to Farrington:

> recidivism among adult offenders is usually measured by reconviction. The Home Office Offender Group Reconviction Scale 2 (OGRS2) uses static information, such as criminal history and demographic data, to predict the likelihood of an offender being reconvicted within two years of a community sentence or discharge from custody.
>
> (2003: 15)

In 2013, McGuire completed 100 meta-analyses (systematic reviews) of individually focused treatment outcome studies on reducing criminal recidivism and/or anti-social behaviour published in the period 1985–2013. McGuire concluded that rehabilitative rather than punitive strategies were more likely to bring about behavioural changes amongst offenders.

What is in this chapter?

This chapter discusses psychological data from a prison-based drama project and explores the potential of drama to motivate and/or bring about change in how prisoners and drama students see themselves and others. The chapter contextualises my involvement in the drama research and summarises findings from psychological measures of 'dispositional empathy', 'need for closure', and 'future possible selves' of prisoners and drama students. Dispositional empathy is multi-dimensional in nature (Davis in Chopik, O'Brien and Konrath 2016). According to Chopik et al. it 'comprises distinct emotional (tendencies to feel concern and compassion for others) and cognitive components (tendencies to imagine different viewpoints beyond one's own)' (2016: 1). Need for closure is defined as 'the desire for a definite answer on some topic, *any* answer as opposed to confusion and ambiguity' (Kruglanski 1989 in Kruglanski et al. 1993: 861). Oyserman and Markus (1990b: 141) define future possible selves as 'the individual's self-relevant expectations for the future. They include what a person hopes to become, expects to become, and fears that he or she might become'. They argue that achieving a balance between expected and feared selves is an important aspect of motivation. A balance would occur if the expected possible self (e.g. I will get a good job) is offset by feared possible selves in the same domain (e.g. I could be unemployed and on the street).

A brief overview of the psychological theories underpinning the prison-based drama research is provided, as well as the strengths and limitations of the theories, methods and findings. This chapter also attempts to contextualise and integrate the research and findings within a broader literature. In particular, I've drawn upon the 'Good Lives Model' (GLM, Ward and Stewart 2003), which takes a holistic view regarding how to motivate offenders to change. In particular, the GLM focuses on non-offending elements linking to the hopes and aspirations of offenders. The GLM model contrasts (as well as complements and coexists) with a more traditional forensic psychological approach focusing on the nature of the offence/crime(s), guilt, remorse and discourses of risk.

The final section discusses the findings and relevance of prison drama work to forensic psychology. In particular, I briefly discuss the potential of drama workshops and productions to help understand the role of future possible selves, emotional empathy and the need for cognitive closure. I conclude by locating this research within a broader research context highlighting that drama work in prisons provides an exciting and important opportunity for a holistic and integrated approach to offender rehabilitation and reducing recidivism. The chapter concludes by acknowledging the challenges of this type of research, but highlights the positive reformatory potential of drama projects both within and outside of a prison context.

I feel a strong sense of privilege to have been part of the drama production in the prison. Whilst involved with the drama rehearsals and performances, I began to think about Ward's GLM (Ward and Stewart 2003), which argues strongly for a holistic understanding of offenders. Taking part in the drama production allowed me to be less judgemental towards the prisoners. This meant that I no longer saw prisoners as one-dimensional beings (offenders) solely constructed by their crimes. Instead, I saw them in a more humane and compassionate light, based on how they behaved towards others during drama rehearsals, performances and my research interviews. Being involved with the prison drama project was uplifting for prisoners and students alike. During and after each of the drama performances, there was a shared and palpable sense of optimism and hope by all. I felt honoured to share these experiences.

A brief glimpse into the world of forensic psychology

Forensic psychologists can facilitate cognitive-behavioural programmes to tackle offending behaviour (McGuire 2008). Such programmes focus on interpersonal, as well as cognitive skills training to enhance an offender's ability to communicate and interact with others and their ability to solve problems. Interpersonal skills training can sometimes involve using role play to help create real life situations within a prison context (McGuire 2008). However, the powerful influence of role playing is not new within psychology, as was dramatically demonstrated by Zimbardo in the Stanford Prison experiment in 1972 (cited in Gazzaniga and Heatherton 2006).

McMurran (2007) provides a comprehensive review of the issues and challenges of trying to motivate offenders to change their offending behaviour. McMurran (2007) and Lopez Viets, Walker and Miller (2007) argue, amongst other things, that motivation is an interpersonal phenomenon. As such it is something 'that occurs and changes within the context of human relationships' (Lopez Viets et al. 2007: 17). Thompson supports this view as he explores the importance of such interpersonal relationships in regard to the effectiveness of participatory theatre in offender treatment initiatives. He argues that 'the use of theatre exercises, games, role-plays and dramatic metaphor as part of offender rehabilitation programmes [...] are a valuable part in these programmes and that they play a useful role in the motivation of participants' (Thompson 2007: 103).

Despite the evidence to show that participatory theatre can help motivate offenders to change, it is unlikely that you will find psychologists using this method within a prison context. Instead, it is more likely that UK-based prison psychologists will offer a range of Ministry of Justice accredited programmes aimed at targeting and reducing offending behaviour such as Enhanced Thinking Skills (ETS) and Controlling Anger and Learning to Manage It (CALM). According to the Ministry of Justice, there are currently 47 different accredited programmes in prison (MOJ 2014).

Across the country, some prisoners have access to creative arts activities/interventions, but this is often sporadic and not a part of their regular programme. Geese Theatre Company's Re-Connect programme, for example, facilitates 'offenders to consider and explore issues connected with their release and reconnecting with a life outside prison using theatre performance, experiential exercises, skills practice role-plays, and metaphors such as the masks' (Harkins et al. 2010 1). Geese Theatre Company do project-based work, and in 2015–16 they worked with 680 adults. In the UK criminal justice system, they are the best known company in a rehabilitation context using theatre methodologies, but still only reach a small percentage of prisoners.

Having a good life – what is the Good Lives Model (GLM)?

Not surprisingly, the majority of mainstream forensic psychology research within prison and/or the community focuses on offending behaviour and the level of risk to others. However, the Good Lives Model (GLM), proposed by Ward and Stewart (2003), aims to reduce recidivism by engaging and motivating offenders to change in order to achieve activities or experiences that benefit them (Barnao, Ward and Robertson: 2015). Tony Ward and his colleagues in New Zealand have provided a different perspective towards rehabilitating offenders. The GLM was originally used with sex offenders, but has also been used successfully with other types of offenders in the United Kingdom and across the world. Barnao, Robertson and Ward state that 'the Good Lives Model is a strength-based approach to offender rehabilitation that is concerned with assisting offenders to achieve their goals as well as managing their risk for reoffending' (2010: 203).

Current forensic psychological theories and research, especially the GLM, help with understanding offending behaviour and how to reduce recidivism by motivating offenders to change. According to the 2016 Ministry of Justice report on reoffending rates:

> Adult offenders had a proven reoffending rate of 24.7%, representing a small decrease of 0.7 percentage points compared to the previous 12 months and a fall of 2.2 percentage points since 2003, this rate has been fairly flat since 2004 fluctuating between 24.5% and 25.5%.
>
> (MOJ 2016)

What are future possible selves and how might they be relevant to prisoners?

Forensic psychology theories can help us to understand offending behaviour and recidivism. However, other psychological research on future possible selves provides opportunity to cross-fertilise with forensic psychology research. Dunkel and Kerpelman (2006) provide an overview of research on possible selves, which has been used with a number of topics such as gender, therapy, motherhood, health, stress, and enhancing student motivation.

Historically, the motivational aspect of future possible selves is underpinned by the writings of James ([1890] 1963). His early work highlighted the importance of different domains of possible selves and how these might provide the motivation for behaviour (Brinthaupt and Lipka 1992). Research in the 1970s and 1980s adopted a broader socio-cognitive approach to the self and explored how the self-system might be involved with self-regulatory processes (Duval and Wicklund 1972; Carver and Scheier 1981; Markus and Sentis in Brinthaupt and Lipka 1992). This led the way for research exploring how possible selves might be linked to how we think about our goals, aspirations and fears (Markus and Nurius 1986; Markus and Wurf 1987). Thus, possible selves also serve an evaluative and interpretative function for the current view of self. The current self is given meaning by virtue of the motivational and regulatory aspect of future possible selves, such as the 'expected' and 'feared' selves. Thus, the concept of future possible selves provides a useful mechanism for understanding how some people might develop a delinquent self, whilst others do not.

The first study to explore links between delinquency and possible selves was undertaken by Oyserman and Markus (1990). They found that highly delinquent youths described their 'expected' future selves in more negative ways such as 'depressed', 'alone' or 'junkie'. These youths described their 'feared' selves as involving crime and/or drugs. In contrast, the officially non-delinquent youths generated more achievement-orientated 'expected' selves in terms of academic success and their 'feared' selves focused on failing in school. They concluded that adolescents are more vulnerable to delinquent activities when they have fewer positive 'expected' selves in conventional domains (i.e. school achievement) and/or when their positive 'expected' selves (i.e. being employed) do not balance with a 'feared' self in the same domain (i.e. being unemployed). Relatively little research has been done with prisoners regarding the potential motivating role of future possible selves. However, Meek (2007) explored the role of possible selves in regard to young fathers in prisons and found that future 'feared for selves' as bad fathers was a motivating factor in avoiding reconvictions.

A multidimensional approach to emotional empathy and the need for cognitive closure

In considering future possible selves, an interesting question concerns whether taking part in drama can bring about changes in the level of empathy of prisoners. Palmer (2003) provides a short review of research showing that offenders show less empathy than non-offenders (Chandler 1973, Kaplan and Arbuthnot 1985 in Palmer 2003). Palmer highlights research showing that offenders are often reported as lacking in the ability to see issues from other people's perspective. Davis (1980, 1983) devised the Interpersonal Reactivity Index (IRI), which is a measure of dispositional empathy that takes as its starting point the notion that empathy consists of a set of separate but related constructs (see further details in the method section below).

In addition to exploring the role of empathy in regard to motivation for change and future possible selves, another thought-provoking question concerns whether resistance to change is linked to what Kruglanski, Webster and Klem (1993) refer to as 'motivated resistance'. They argue that resistance is linked to how open a person is to persuasion and thus change. Kruglanski et al. (1993) designed the Need for Closure (NFC) scale to measure stable individual differences in the need for (or to avoid) cognitive closure. In regard to the prisoners in this study, their scores on the NFC at the start and end of the project were used to see whether they became more open to ambiguity, and thus increased their potential to change their lives upon release from prison.

Based on the above theoretical bases, both qualitative and quantitative research questions were explored comparing the drama group prisoners, control group prisoners and drama group students. These questions are listed below.

Quantitative research questions focusing on ratings of empathy and cognitive closure:

Q1. *Need for Closure Scale* – *Do the drama group prisoners score differently than control group prisoners and drama group students at Time 1 and/or at Time 2?*
Q2. *Interpersonal Reactivity Index* – *Do the drama group prisoners score differently than control group prisoners and students at Time 1 and/or at Time 2?*

Qualitative research questions focusing on future possible selves and interview data:

Q3. *How do drama group prisoners and drama group students perceive their experiences of taking part in the drama project?*
Q4. *How are descriptions of future possible selves similar and/or different for drama group and control group prisoners and drama group students?*
Q5. *Does taking part in a nine-week prison-based drama project influence prisoners and/or students' perceptions of their future possible selves at Time 1 & Time 2?*

Method

Design

This was an innovative and novel small-scale piece of action research in a Category C prison context. The design of the project was discussed with a senior forensic psychologist, and it was decided to include both quantitative and qualitative measures to provide a more in-depth exploration of the research questions. A multi-method approach was used incorporating both questionnaire and interview data during two time periods over a nine-week period. At the start of the drama project (Time 1), baseline measures were taken, i.e. *Possible Selves Questionnaire (PSQ), IRI* and *NFC and interview questions* (see materials section below for further details).

At Time 2, at the end of the project after completion of the live performances, further interview data were collected and also the NFC, IRI and PSQ measures were repeated. The same quantitative measures were used with the control group prisoners at Time 1 and Time 2. The order of presentation of measures was controlled so that all participants received the PSQ as the first measure. To control for possible order effects of the psychometric measures, half of the participants received the NFC, followed by the IRI and vice-versa for the other half of the participants.

Participants

There were ten students (including the author) and ten prisoners, nine of whom took part in the research. All of the prisoners were male, and there were two male and eight female students who took part in drama research. The ages of the male prisoners ranged from 24 to 70 years and the students from 18 to 51 years. As a comparison group, seven male prisoners were recruited from the prison Education Department (an opportunity sample). Their ages ranged from 28 to 55 years old. However, one of them withdrew from the project prior to Time 2, so only the data from six are included.

Materials

At the start (Time 1) and after the drama production (Time 2), data were collected using the following measures:

1. Need for Closure Scale (NFC, Kruglanski et al. 1993)

It is a self-report scale consisting of 42 items designed to assess stable individual differences in the need for (or to avoid) cognitive closure. It is a bipolar measure that requires respondents to rate the extent to which they agree with statements using a six point Likert scale ranging from 1 (*strongly disagree*) to 6 (*strongly agree*). For example, preference for closure items include: 'I'd rather know bad news than stay in a state of uncertainty', and statements reflecting a desire to avoid closure include: 'I tend to put off making important decisions until the last possible moment'. A composite 'need for closure' score was calculated by adding responses from each item (after reverse scoring for those items reflecting a preference for avoiding closure).

2. Interpersonal Reactivity Index (IRI, Davis 1980, 1983)

The IRI contains a total of 28 items consisting of four seven-item sub-scales, each tapping a separate facet of empathy (*perspective taking, empathic concern, personal distress* and *fantasy*). The perspective taking (PT) scale measures the reported tendency to spontaneously adopt the psychological point of view of others in everyday life ('I sometimes try to understand my friends better by imagining how things look from their perspective'). The empathic concern (EC) scale assesses the tendency to experience feelings of sympathy and compassion for unfortunate others ('I often have tender, concerned feelings for people less fortunate than me'). The personal distress (PD) scale taps the tendency to experience distress and discomfort in response to extreme distress in others ('Being in a tense emotional situation scares me'). The fantasy scale (FS) measures the tendency to imaginatively transpose oneself into fictional situations ('When I am reading an interesting story or novel, I imagine how I would feel if the events in the story were happening to me').

3. Possible Selves Questionnaire (PSQ, Oyserman and Markus 1990)

The Possible Selves Questionnaire consists of an open-ended, self-completion measure relating to two possible future selves (expected and feared self, next year). Participants were asked to list up to four 'expected' and four 'feared' selves that they expect (or fear) being like next year. For each of these selves, they were asked to answer 'yes' or 'no', to indicate if they are currently doing something in order to achieve (or avoid) these future selves. When they answered 'yes', they were asked to write what they are currently doing to attain or avoid (as appropriate) the future expected and feared selves next year. These are referred to as 'strategies' for achieving or avoiding future possible selves (Oyserman and Markus 1990).

Coding of the PSQ
Each of the qualitative descriptions for the 'expected' and 'feared' selves was coded according to Oyserman and Markus' (1990) coding scheme. The coding categories used were: *achievement, interpersonal relationships, personality, physical/health-related, material/ lifestyle* and *negative* (for expected self) and *non-normative* (for feared self) with only the

last category differing between the expected and feared possible selves. Due to lack of space, the balance scores for each of the three groups are not included. Neither are the strategies for achieving future expected selves and avoiding feared selves included in this chapter.

Oyserman and Markus argue that the expected and feared possible selves provide maximum motivational effectiveness when they are in the same domain. Balance means having both a positive and negative aspect of a future goal, for example having an expectation (next year I will be) and a matching concern (next year I want to avoid) that fit together or create a more coherent whole. Two examples of balanced selves and strategies are shown below:

Achievement – next year I expect to be earning money and I want to avoid being in debt.

Interpersonal relationships – next year I expect to spend more time with my son and I want to avoid people that might tempt me into committing more crimes.

4. Semi-structured interviews

Hand-written notes were taken during individual interviews with all participants in the drama production. Due to security restrictions, as well as time and space constraints, the interviews were not audio-recorded. Individual interviews with the control participants took place in a separate building. At Time 1, participants in the drama project were asked open-ended questions such as 'why did you volunteer for the drama project?' and at Time 2, they were asked 'what have been the positive and negative aspects of taking part in the project?' For the control group participants, the questions focused on how things were going with the education course/s they were taking, for example 'Which educational course/s are you taking at the moment and why did you choose that course?' Only interview data from the drama group prisoners and students are presented in this chapter. Data were analysed using inductive thematic analyses (see Braun and Clarke 2006).

Procedure

In order to gain permission to work on the research project in the prison a number of formalities had to be completed several months before the start of the drama project. These included submitting a research application form to the Ministry of Justice and also directly contacting the prison governor and prison forensic psychologist. Ethical approval was received from the Psychology Department at the University of Portsmouth. After a meeting with the prison governor, approval was obtained to undertake the research project alongside the prison drama production.

For the prisoners and students, the data collection took place in a small room attached to the rehearsal/performance space. For the control group prisoners, these data were collected in a quiet room in the education block. All participants completed the measures in the presence of the researcher and they were interviewed individually. All participants were provided with informed consent sheets and informed of their right to refuse or withdraw from the study without any repercussions. Only one prisoner in the drama production refused to take part in the project.

Section 1: Thematic analyses of semi-structured interview data at Time 1 and 2

An inductive thematic analysis was used with the interview data at Time 1 and 2. This approach meant the themes are grounded in the data, rather than a preconceived theoretical framework as suggested by Patton (in Braun and Clarke 2006: 83). At Time 1, the drama group prisoners and students were asked two questions, as shown in Figure 1 below:

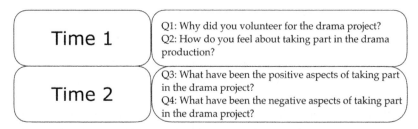

Time 1
Q1: Why did you volunteer for the drama project?
Q2: How do you feel about taking part in the drama production?

Time 2
Q3: What have been the positive aspects of taking part in the drama project?
Q4: What have been the negative aspects of taking part in the drama project?

Figure 1: Interview questions asked of drama group participants (prisoners and students) at Time 1 and 2.

In response to Q1, three themes were generated from the interviews with the drama group prisoners (*Time, Challenge* and *Enjoyment*).

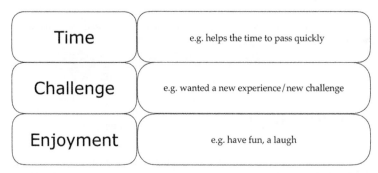

Time   e.g. helps the time to pass quickly

Challenge   e.g. wanted a new experience/new challenge

Enjoyment   e.g. have fun, a laugh

Figure 2: Time 1 Drama group prisoners – Q1. *Why did you volunteer for the drama project?* Three overarching themes were generated.

Both the prisoners and students referred to *challenge* as a key reason for volunteering to take part in the project. However, the drama group students did not mention *time* or *enjoyment* in response to Q1. Instead, the second theme that emerged for the students was *career* as they spoke about career goals, such as wanting to work in applied drama, getting acting experience to add to their CV and the importance of voluntary work as shown in Figure 3.

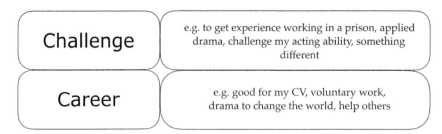

Figure 3: Time 1 Drama group students – Q1. *Why did you volunteer for the drama project?* Two overarching themes were generated.

In response to Q2, the drama group prisoners focused on *anxiety* issues such as feeling nervous, anxious and/or apprehensive, or worries about learning the script. In contrast, the drama students focused more on their *enjoyment* of the project.

The students acknowledged that they were nervous on the first day, but concentrated on how their confidence and efficacy had developed and the positive aspects of learning new things, meeting new people.

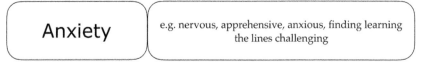

Figure 4: Time 1 Drama group prisoners – Q2. *How do you feel about taking part in the drama production?* One theme was generated in regard to their feelings of 'anxiety'.

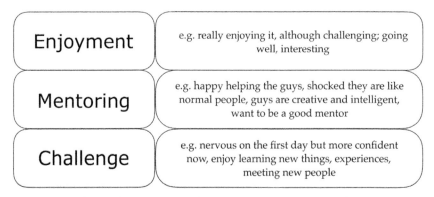

Figure 5: Time 1 Drama group students – Q2. *How do you feel about taking part in the drama production?* Three overarching themes were generated.

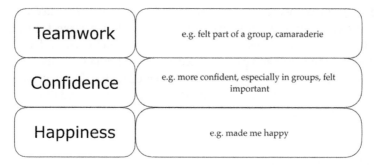

Figure 6: Time 2 Drama group prisoners – Q1. *What have been the positive aspects of taking part in the drama project?*

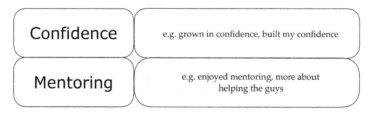

Figure 7: Time 2 Drama group students – Q1. *What have been the positive aspects of taking part in the drama project?*

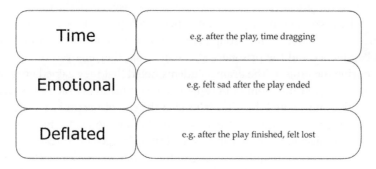

Figure 8: Time 2 Drama group prisoners – Q2. *What have been the negative aspects of taking part in the drama project?*

Interview data at Time 2

Figure 6 shows that there were three themes summarising the positive aspects for the drama group prisoners (*team work, confidence, happiness*). Both groups talked about how the project had made them feel more confident. The drama group students also focused on the positive aspects of *mentoring* the prisoners during the workshops, rehearsals and performances.

In regard to Q2, three themes (*deflated, emotional, time*) were generated from the drama group prisoners concerning the negative aspects of the drama project. In particular, the prisoners talked about how they felt a gap in their daily prison lives now that they no longer had the workshops, rehearsals and performances with the drama students. They felt sad that the project had come to an end, so felt lost. Time seemed to drag for them without learning their scripts, rehearsals and interactions with the drama students and director. There was a sense of grieving in their comments.

Interview data – so what does it mean?

At Time 1, most of the drama group prisoners and students said they volunteered as it was a new opportunity and interesting challenge. The majority of the drama group prisoners had not done any formal training in drama/acting, although one or two had done so at school. The prisoners highlighted that taking part in the drama project would be a good way of passing time and would be fun. In contrast, the students focused more on the useful experience that they could gain and the positive impact on their future career choices in applied drama. However, when asked how they felt about taking part in the drama (such as doing the workshops, rehearsals and learning scripts), the drama group prisoners were more negative than the students as they felt nervous, anxious and apprehensive with little confidence or optimism at that stage of the project. In contrast, the students had more confidence and self-efficacy about their ability to learn and grow from the project. They also enjoyed their mentoring roles and saw no negative aspects of the project.

At Time 2, when asked about the positive and negative aspects, there were some similarities and differences between the drama group prisoners and students. Both groups felt that they had gained confidence and the prisoners also stated that they enjoyed the team work and felt happier during the project. The drama students noted that they gained great satisfaction from their mentoring role by helping and supporting their mentees to achieve success in their acting roles. Both groups noted that they felt sad at the end of the project and said that they would miss working with each other. The prisoners also mentioned feeling a strong sense of deflation after the project had finished and felt that time dragged once again, whereas during the project it had passed more quickly. Some of the students mentioned that they felt tired after the project, especially those who also had part-time jobs in addition to their university work to complete. However, overall both groups agreed that they were glad to have taken part in the project and some of them would like to do so again (if given the opportunity).

Section 2 – Need for Closure (NFC)

NFC data were compared for the drama group prisoners, control group prisoners and drama group students for each of the six sub-scales: *order, predictability, decisiveness, ambiguity, closed mindedness* and *lie scale*. The lie scale is standard procedure in such psychological measures and aims to see whether respondents are consistent in how they respond to similar questions. At Time 1 and 2, no participants scored above 15 on the lie-score scale, meaning that they were completing the measure consistently (so less likely to be lying), thus all data were included in the analyses. A composite 'need for closure' score, referred to as the 'overall' score, was calculated by totalling scores across items (after reverse scoring for those items reflecting a preference for avoiding closure).

The data for Time 1 are presented, then Time 2. An independent samples t-test was used to compare each of these participant groups on the overall NFC score, five sub-scales and lie scale (see above). Figure 9 below shows the following:

- At Time 1, there were two statistically significant differences found in the *overall* and *predictability* NFC scores when comparing the drama group prisoners and students.
- When comparing the control group prisoners and the students, there were three significant differences in the NFC scores for the *overall*, the *predictability* and *order* sub-scales.
- The mean scores for both groups of prisoners were higher on the *predictability* and *overall* scores than for students. The control group prisoners also had a higher order score than the students. However, the effect sizes in this small sample are low (ranging from 1.47–1.87). An effect size of 0.21–0.50 would be needed to indicate moderate effect size.

There were no significant differences in any of the NFC scores for the drama group prisoners and the control group prisoners. Thus, the drama group prisoners and control group

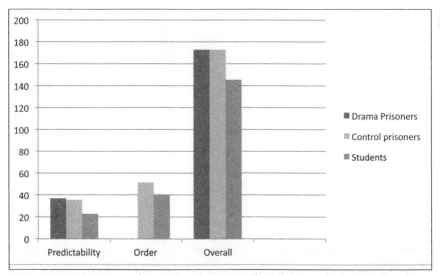

Figure 9: Time 1 comparison of mean scores showing significant differences for the NFC sub-scales.

prisoners both scored higher on *predictability* and the *overall* NFC scores than the drama students. This indicates that both groups of prisoners had a higher need for closure, which indicates that they might feel uncomfortable with change and perhaps limited in their capacity to cope with change. Higher scores on NFCS are related to a stronger desire for stability and permanence (Kruglanski et al. 2007).

Need for Closure at Time 2 – what did we find?

At Time 2, there were four significant differences found for the drama group prisoners and students in the *overall, order, decisiveness* and the *predictability*. There were two significant differences between the control group prisoners and students in the *overall* NFC and the *order* scores.

Thus, at Time 2, the drama group prisoners and control group prisoners continued to score higher on *order* and the *overall* NFC scores than the drama students. The drama group prisoners also scored higher on *predictability* than students (the same as in Time 1). However, at Time 2 (but not Time 1) the drama group prisoners (but not the control group prisoners) also scored higher on *decisiveness* than the students. Perhaps this was due to their reports of feeling more confident in themselves, as noted in the interviews.

As with Time 1, at Time 2 there were no significant differences in any of the NFC scores for the drama group prisoners and the control group prisoners. However, it is interesting to note that at Time 2, the mean *overall* score for the control group prisoners

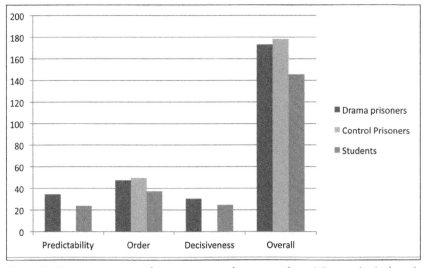

Figure 10: Time 2 – comparison of NFC mean scores showing significant differences for the four of the sub-scales.

increased more than the other two groups. It would be speculation to state why this might be, but a possibility might be that the control group prisoners were becoming more rigid and the drama group prisoners less rigid in their need for closure (e.g. desire for clarity and avoidance of ambiguity). Without additional longitudinal data, it is not possible to be clear whether this was a short-term or long-term effect of taking part in the prison drama.

Need for Closure – what do the findings mean?

Both groups of prisoners scored higher than students on the *overall, order, decisiveness* and *predictability* sub-scales in the NFC, suggesting that they have a higher need for closure than students. Higher scores on NFCS are related to a stronger desire for stability and permanence (Kruglanski et al. 2007). This also suggests that the prisoners might feel uncomfortable with change so perhaps limited in their capacity to cope with change. Although there were no significant differences between the drama group prisoners and control group prisoners in the *overall* sub-scale scores at Time 2, it was interesting to note that the control group prisoners had an increase in their *overall* NFC score at Time 2, compared to Time 1. In contrast, the drama group prisoners' *overall* NFC score remained relatively stable between Time 1 and Time 2 as did the *overall* NFC scores for the drama group students. Thus, we could speculate that the prisoners in the control group became less comfortable with change (than either the drama group prisoners or the students). However, this is not a controlled experiment, so other factors might equally explain this finding such as different experiences between the two groups of prisoners. Hence, future longitudinal studies are needed to avoid speculating about this cross-sectional finding.

How might this relate to prisoner rehabilitation and reducing recidivism?

Further questions could be raised regarding how prisoners' higher scores on some of the Need for Closure sub-scales might impact Ward's Good Lives Model (GLM, Ward and Brown 2004; Ward, Mann and Gannon 2007; Ward and Fortune 2013). The GLM argues that prisoners have the same basic needs as others in society. Ward et al. list the following as important human needs: life (including healthy living and functioning), knowledge, excellence in play and work (including mastery experiences), excellence in agency (i.e. autonomy and self-directedness), inner peace (i.e. freedom from emotional turmoil and stress), friendship (including intimate, romantic and family relationships), community, spirituality (in the broad sense of finding meaning and purpose in life), happiness and creativity (2007: 90). However, higher scores on the NFC scale could suggest that some prisoners might have more rigid cognitive expectations regarding these ten primary human needs. Hence, cognitive rigidity needs to be further explored when assessing a prisoner's risk (to others) as well as when considering prisoners' future possible selves as motivators regarding 'expected' and 'feared' selves.

The next two sections present the findings from the IRI and PSQ, which assess emotional empathy and future possible selves (respectively).

Interpersonal Reactivity Index (IRI, Davis 1980, 1983)

IRI data were compared for the drama group prisoners, control group prisoners and drama group students for each of the four seven-item sub-scales, each tapping a separate facet of empathy (*perspective taking, empathic concern, personal distress* and *fantasy*). An independent sample *t*-test was used to compare each of these participant groups on the four sub-scales (see above).

There were no significant differences at Time 1. However, at Time 2 there were two significant differences found for the drama group prisoners and students on the *fantasy* and the *personal distress* sub-scales of the IRI. There was one significant difference found for the control group prisoners and students on the *personal distress* sub-scale of the IRI.

At Time 2, students scored higher than both groups of prisoners on *fantasy* and *personal distress*. There were no significant differences between the drama group prisoners, control group prisoners and the students on the *perspective-taking* and *empathic concern* sub-scales. These findings suggest that the drama group students have a higher tendency

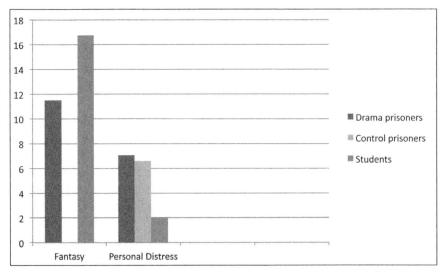

Figure 11: Time 2 – comparison of mean IRI scores for 'Personal Distress' and 'Fantasy' showing significant differences between the three groups of participants.

to experience distress and discomfort in response to extreme distress in others ('being in a tense emotional situation scares me'). Also, unsurprisingly, the drama group students are shown to have a higher ability to imaginatively transpose themselves into fictional situations than the drama or control group prisoners. An enhanced ability to think imaginatively would be expected for this selective group of students who were all studying drama at university.

Section 3: Possible Selves Questionnaire (PSQ)

In this section, both qualitative and descriptive statistical data are presented from the PSQ at Time 1 (start of the drama production) and Time 2 (afterwards). Figure 12 shows the six categories used for coding the PSQ responses at Time 1 and 2. In the PSQ coding manual, there is only one variation between the expected and feared selves in regard to 'negative' or 'non-normative' behaviours.

In response to *who they will be next year?* drama group prisoners did not provide any descriptions relating to *achievement*. In contrast, the control group and drama group students

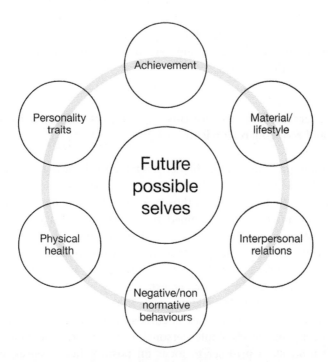

Figure 12: Six coding categories for the future expected and feared selves.

provided two and six descriptions of *achievement* respectively. However, the drama group prisoners provided 22 *material/lifestyle* descriptions, compared to 15 and 13 for the other two groups. These included descriptions such as: where they will be living and that they expect to be working etc. In contrast, the drama group students provided 11 descriptions relating to *personality traits* (e.g. happy with self, confident, hard-working, etc.) compared to only 3 descriptions from the other two groups. All three groups scored similarly in regard to *interpersonal relationships* (family, partners, friends, etc.), *physical health* and *negative/non-normative behaviours*. Drama group prisoners and students both scored 7 and the control group prisoners scored 6.

In response to *'what don't you want to be like next year?'* both the drama group prisoners and control group prisoners did not provide any descriptions in regard to *achievement*, and only 1 was provided by the students. The drama group prisoners provided 10 *material/lifestyle* descriptions compared to 6 and 7 for the other two groups. These included descriptions such as: unemployed, around people that get me into trouble, stuck in a rut. The drama group students provided 17 descriptions relating to *personality traits* (e.g. unhappy, bored, scared, etc.) compared to only 3 descriptions from the other two groups.

For *interpersonal relationships*, the drama group prisoners did not provide any descriptions, whereas the control group provided 4 and the students 3 descriptions. For *physical health*, the control group prisoners provided 4 descriptions compared to 2 for the students and 1 for the drama group prisoners. For *non-normative/risky behaviours*, the drama group prisoners provided 14 descriptions of what they wanted to avoid (broke, being in prison, unemployed, etc.) compared to the 6 provided by the control group prisoners and zero for the students.

Links between interview data, need for closure, interpersonal reactivity index, future possible selves and reducing recidivism?

Based on the findings presented in the chapter, it is not unrealistic to hypothesise that having a high or low need for closure and an ability to empathise with the emotions of others might influence future selves that we expect or those we might fear becoming. When the findings from all four of these methods are combined, they provide a novel and informative way of exploring how positive changes in prisoners might be effective within a short period of time (nine weeks). The evidence here suggests that taking part in the drama production brought about many positive changes in thinking, confidence, feelings and ability to consider the self in the future. These data could be further explored by using more advanced statistical techniques such as multivariate analysis of variance, regression modelling and/or multidimensional scaling. Such statistical methods might be able to show in what way a high need for closure, high levels of interpersonal sensitivity and understandings of others' emotions might motivate a prisoner to focus on positive future selves, whilst avoiding negative future selves.

However, the question of whether a short-term drama production can bring about a longer term positive change in behaviour and/or reduce recidivism cannot be answered by this cross-sectional study. Instead, longitudinal quantitative and qualitative data are required to follow up the prisoners for several months after a drama production.

What are the strengths and limitations of the project?

There are several strengths to this project, including the innovative role of Playing for Time Theatre Company in gaining access to a prison context (as discussed in other chapters). Ministry of Justice access to a prison population for research is notoriously difficult. Thus, undertaking research in a prison context for any amount of time is a rarity and a privilege. Other strengths include the multi-dimensional and cross-disciplinary nature of the theoretical bases of the research questions – drawn from forensic, social and developmental psychology, criminology and the arts. The design of the study incorporated both quantitative and qualitative data at two different time points (at the start and end of the project). These allow a more in-depth exploration of the potential role of the prison drama in bringing about any changes in emotional empathy, need for closure and future possible selves. The findings of the qualitative data provide an insight into the thoughts, feelings and experiences of the drama group prisoners and students. The PSQ data offer an important awareness of how the expected and feared future possible selves might be linked to motivations to change, thus reducing recidivism. This chapter has discussed how the findings might relate to Ward's GLM. Another strength is the inclusion of a control sample group of prisoners from the prison Education Department. This allowed comparisons to be made regarding whether drama group prisoners differed significantly from other prisoners in scores on the NFC and IRI and future possible selves.

Inevitably, there were many limitations and restrictions in regard to the project. This research is more like a pilot project, as the small sample size and low effect sizes from the NFC and IRI mean that the findings (although useful indicators) cannot be generalised to a larger population of prisoners. After completion of the project, restricted access to prisoners and/or their personal data meant that further longitudinal data could not be collected to assess any impact on reducing recidivism.

Conclusion and suggestions for future research

Based on the qualitative and quantitative analyses, the evidence supports the view that taking part in a nine-week drama production can bring about short-term positive change in prisoner's emotional empathy and a reduced need for closure. Thus, taking part in a nine-week drama production can bring about positive cognitive and behavioural changes in a prison context.

In conclusion, drama work in prison (such as that offered by Playing for Time) offers opportunity for prisoners to envisage more positive future selves and develop their ability to empathise with others, and allows them to be more open to personal change. However, this was a small-scale cross-sectional study and so future longitudinal research is needed in order to follow up participants. For example, it would be useful to interview them a year after completing a drama project, as well as having access to their records to see whether they reoffend or not.

In the words of Ward and Fortune:

> [...] turning around a life involving crime is no easy task and requires the provision of relevant and adequate levels of social and psychological resources from the community as well as a determination to change from offenders. It seems pretty obvious to us that it is easier to persuade individuals to seek less harmful lives if they have a reasonable chance at achieving more fulfilling ones.

(2013: 43)

There remains, however, the thorny question of whether society has the willingness to accept and facilitate ex-offenders' motivations to change and/or support their capacity and ability to rehabilitate upon their release back into the community. This will require further future longitudinal research and is beyond the scope of this book.

References

Barnao, M., Robertson, P. and Ward, T. (2010), 'Good Lives Model applied to a forensic population', *Psychiatry, Psychology and Law*, 17:2, pp. 202–17.

Barnao, M., Ward, T. and Casey, S. (2015), 'Taking the good life to the institution: Forensic service users' perceptions of the Good Lives Model', *International Journal of Offender Therapy and Comparative Criminology*, 5, pp. 1–21.

Barnao, M., Ward, T. and Robertson, P. (2015), 'The Good Lives Model: A new paradigm for forensic mental health', *Psychiatry, Psychology and Law*, pp. 1–14.

Braun, V. and Clarke, V. (2006), 'Using thematic analysis in psychology', *Qualitative Research in Psychology*, 3, 2006, pp. 77–101.

Brinthaupt, T. M. and Lipka, R. P. (1992), *The Self: Definitional and Methodological Issues*, Albany: State University of New York Press.

Carver, C.S. and Scheier, M. P, (1981), 'Control theory: A useful framework for personality-social, clinical and health psychology', *Psychological Bulletin*, 92, pp. 111–35.

Chopik, W. J., O'Brien, E. and Konrath, S. H. (2016), 'Differences in empathic concern and perspective taking across 63 countries', *Journal of Cross-Cultural Psychology*, pp. 1–16.

Davis, M. H. (1980), 'A multidimensional approach to individual differences in empathy', *JSAS Catalog of Selected Documents in Psychology*, 10, pp. 2–19.

—— (1983), 'Measuring individual differences in empathy: evidence for a multidimensional approach', *Journal of Personality and Social Psychology*, 44, pp. 113–26.

Dunkel, C. S. and Kerpelman, J. L. (eds) (2006), *Possible Selves: Theory, Research & Applications*, New York: Nova Science Publishers Inc.

Duval, S. and Wicklund, R. A. (1972), *A Theory of Objective Self Awareness*, New York: Academic Press.

Farrington, D. P. (2003), 'Key results from the first forty years of the Cambridge study in delinquent development', in T. P. Thornberry and M. D. Krohn (eds), *Taking Stock of Delinquency*, Longitudinal Research in the Social and Behavioral Sciences: An Interdisciplinary Series, Boston, MA: Springer, pp. 137–83.

Gazzaniga, M. S. and Heatherton, T. F. (2006), *Psychological Science*, 2nd ed., New York: W. W. Norton & Co.

Geese Theatre Company, http://www.geese.co.uk/about. Accessed 25 October 2016.

Harkins, L., Pritchard, C., Haskayne, D., Watson, A. and Beech, A. R. (2010), 'Evaluation of Geese Theatre's re-connect program: addressing resettlement issues in prison', *International Journal of Offender Therapy and Comparative Criminology*, 55:4, pp. 546–66.

Henry, A. J. (1997), 'Short stature and early adolescent self-evaluations', Ph.D. thesis, Southampton: University of Southampton.

—— (2009), 'The role of future possible selves, gender and self-reported delinquency in early adolescence', M.Sc. dissertation, Portsmouth: University of Portsmouth.

James, W. (1963), *The Principles of Psychology*, New York: Holt, Rinehart & Winston.

Kao, G. (2000), 'Group images and possible selves among adolescents: Linking stereotypes to expectations by race and ethnicity', *Sociological Forum*, 15, pp. 407–30.

King, L. (2001), 'The health benefits of writing about life goals', *Personality and Social Psychology Bulletin*, 27, pp. 798–807.

Kruglanski, A. W., Pierro, A., Higgins, E., Tory, E. and Capozza, D. (2007), 'On the move or staying put: Locomotion, need for closure, and reactions to organizational change', *Journal of Applied Social Psychology*, 37:6, pp. 1305–340.

Kruglanski, A. W., Shah, J. Y., Pierro, A. and Manetti, L. (2002), 'When similarity breeds content: Need for closure and the allure of homogenous and self-resembling groups', *Journal of Personality and Social Psychology*, 83:3, pp. 648–62.

Kruglanski, A. W., Webster, D. M. and Klem, A. (1993), 'Motivated resistance and openness to persuasion in the presence or absence of prior information', *Journal of Personality and Social Psychology*, 65:5, pp. 861–76.

Lopez Viets, V., Walker, D. D. and Miller, W. R. (2007), 'What is motivation to change? A scientific analysis', in M. McMurran (ed.), *Motivating Offenders to Change: A Guide to Enhancing Engagement in Therapy*, Chichester: John Wiley & Sons Ltd., pp. 15–30.

Markus, H. and Nurius, P. (1986), 'Possible selves', *American Psychologist*, 41, pp. 954–69.

Markus, H. and Wurf, E. (1987), 'The dynamic self-concept: A social psychological perspective', *Annual Review of Psychology*, 38, pp. 299–337.

McGuire, J. (2008), 'What's the point of sentencing?', in G. Davies, C. Hollin and R. Bull (eds), *Forensic Psychology*, Chichester: John Wiley & Sons Ltd., pp. 265–292.

—— (2013), '"What works" to reduce re-offending 18 years on', in L. A. Craig, L. Dixon and T. A. Gannon (eds), *What Works in Offender Rehabilitation: An Evidence-Based Approach to Assessment and Treatment*, London: John Wiley & Sons, Ltd., pp. 20–49.

McMurran, M. (ed.), (2007), *Motivating Offenders to Change: A Guide to Enhancing Engagement in Therapy*, Chichester: John Wiley & Sons Ltd.

Meek, R. (2007), 'The parenting possible selves of young fathers in prison', *Psychology, Crime & Law*, 13:4, pp. 371–82.

Ministry of Justice (2014), HM Prison Service, 'Offender Behaviour Programmes (OBPs)', July, https://www.justice.gov.uk/offenders/before-after-release/obp. Accessed 29 July 2016.

Ministry of Justice, 'Proven reoffending statistics', *Quarterly Bulletin*, October 2013 to September 2014, England and Wales, *MOJ Statistics Bulletin*, https://www.gov.uk/government/uploads/system/uploads/attachment_data/file/541187/proven-reoffending-2014-q3.pdf. Accessed 28 July 2016.

Oyserman, D. (2009), 'Possible selves coding scheme', University of Michigan, http://www.sitemaker.umich.edu/daphna.oyserman/home. Accessed 28 July 2016.

Oyserman, D. and Markus, H. (1990), 'Possible selves and delinquency', *Journal of Personality & Social Psychology*, 59:1, pp. 112–25.

Oyserman, D. and Markus, H. (1990b) 'Possible selves in balance: Implications for delinquency', *Journal of Social Issues.*, 46:2, pp. 141–157.

Palmer, E. J. (2003), *Offending Behaviour, Moral Reasoning, Criminal Conduct and the Rehabilitation of Offenders*, Devon: Willan Publishing.

Thompson, J. (2007), 'Motivating offenders to change through participatory theatre', in M. McMurran (ed.), *Motivating Offenders to Change: A Guide to Enhancing Engagement in Therapy*, Chichester: John Wiley & Sons Ltd., pp. 103–20.

Towl, G. (ed.) (2007), *Psychology in Prisons*, Leicester: British Psychological Society.

Ward, T. and Brown, M. (2004), 'The good lives model and conceptual issues in offender rehabilitation', *Psychology, Crime and Law*, 10:3, pp. 243–57.

Ward, T. and Fortune, C. (2013), 'The Good Lives Model: Aligning risk reduction with promoting offenders' personal goals', *European Journal of Probation*, 5:2, pp. 29–46.

Ward, T., Mann, R. E. and Gannon, T. A. (2007), 'The Good Lives Model of offender rehabilitation: Clinical implications', *Aggression and Violent Behavior*, 12:1, pp. 87–107.

Ward, T. and Stewart, C. A. (2003), 'The treatment of sex offenders: Risk management and good lives', *Professional Psychology, Research and Practice*, 34, pp. 353–60.

Acknowledgement

Thank you to Dr Adrian Needs (University of Portsmouth) for his involvement with the design and ethical approval of the study.

Chapter 10

Exit Stage Left: Conversation, Creative Writing and Coping with Loss: An Introduction to Scott's Diary

Kass Boucher

In 2013, a group of male prisoners from HMP Winchester took part in a Playing for Time Theatre Company project, a production of Timberlake Wertenbaker's *Our Country's Good*. At the time, I was a tutor in the prison's Education Department, tasked to deliver an NCFE qualification in *Performance Skills Using Acting* alongside the project so the men taking part could work towards an accreditation as they rehearsed. One task I set them was to keep a diary during the rehearsal process to record their own progress as performers. This would not prove to be easy. In this context, it is not just levels of literacy that can be low but self-esteem and confidence too, all of which play their part in making some prisoners very reluctant to undertake writing exercises. That said, great efforts were made and many of the men succeeded in keeping a record of milestones reached during the rehearsal process. One man, however, took the task on in a way I hadn't expected. By the end of the nine-week rehearsal period Scott had filled two exercise books with diary entries. They began as a document of tasks carried out each day but finished as an insight into how Scott felt, not just about the project but also about himself. Honest, self-aware, funny and often poignant, these diary extracts chart a man's journey from prisoner to performer in his own words: from 'the fishbowl to the sea' as Scott put it (Appendix 1).

Reading the diary entries, the impact the project has had on Scott is clear. In the early stages he is already writing about rehearsals as 'something to look forward to' (Scott 2018: 211). As the project progresses he predicts that he will 'write this up as a massive achievement' and towards the end, reflects on its effect on him as a person: 'I believe this process has been a big help in my recovery and my new life' (Scott 2018: 216). Scott was not unique in this respect; many of the men were able to express in their diaries what the project was beginning to mean to them:

I have built up confidence and courage to perform and I have enjoyed coming to drama… it makes me feel so happy.…. The music makes me feel more calm and I find it helps me deal with my anger.

(Prisoner M., rehearsal diary, March 2013)

I have liked singing. It makes me feel happy to sing.

(Prisoner D., rehearsal diary, March 2013)

I've gone from thinking drama was a joke for people with nothing better to do to embracing it and becoming a huge part of my life.

(Prisoner L., rehearsal diary, May 2013)

What made Scott's diary stand out, however, was the way in which it told a story, complete with a protagonist who transformed from someone who 'never had the patience or the desire to become involved in something as deeply serious as this' (Scott 2018: 215), to someone who had discovered a passion for drama and was 'determined to do it outside' (Scott 2018: 216). The diary was, in that respect, a fascinating document in its own right. When we decided to enter the diary for the Koestler Trust Awards, an annual competition for the creative work of the securely detained (Scott won a Bronze Award for Nonfiction Life Writing in 2014), this led to a new development in the evolution of Scott's work, one that would reveal further insights. Editing the diary together led to conversations with Scott during which he reflected further on the drama project; he hadn't realised he would have to learn lines and wear a costume and had become frustrated as he battled to memorise monologues with a poor short-term memory. But Scott had also experienced new sensations, such as the elation felt at the end of each performance that he described as 'the best buzz I have genuinely had' (Scott 2018: 218).

One topic established itself as a recurring theme in both the conversations and the diary extracts: the sadness experienced after the project had ended.

Now I am back in my cell feeling really good and very sad all at the same time…. The play is over and all us inmates are just a load of criminals and it's all gone a bit retrograde.

(Scott 2018: 220)

Once again, Scott was not unique in experiencing mixed emotions at the end of the project:

It was an emotional day for students and prisoners. Taking down the stage and seating felt criminal – no pun intended! We had all come together as a drama family so it was hard to say our goodbyes.

(Prisoner L., rehearsal diary, May 2013)

Many of the men, including Scott, had begun to express concerns and fears about life outside of the project even before the first performance was over. Only three weeks into rehearsals Scott writes that he will be 'gutted when it's over because it will mean life will return to normal' (Scott 2018: 212). At the same time, another man writes, 'I wish we could be in the gym [the rehearsal space] all day instead of going back to our rooms' (Prisoner M., Rehearsal Diary 2013). The same man thinks that there should be a permanent drama course in the prison because 'it is making people feel better about themselves […] making them have great self-esteem […] and confidence' (Prisoner M., Rehearsal Diary 2013). If the men taking part were already anxious about life after the project while still in rehearsals, then what were the implications for their well-being once the project had ended? What support would they require to come to terms with the end of such a powerful experience? And, what could be done to maximize the positive outcomes for the men involved?

The Playing for Time team went back into the prison after the project had ended to see the men for a follow-up session, and used structured exercises to generate feedback from them about the experience. The enthusiasm with which the men greeted both the team, and the opportunity to talk about the performances, was revealing. There was still a lot to talk about it seemed – a conversation to finish, as Scott would later suggest:

> It is abrupt when [the project] ends…. We go back to what we were doing and it's all cut off and done. Humans don't like being cut off. It's like two people on the phone and while one person is speaking the other crashes the phone down.
>
> (Scott, reflections, 2013)

We are reminded, then, that for the prisoners that we work with, the sense of being 'cut off' is both an emotional and stark, physical reality. The loss of connections with other people, even those only recently made, can be felt deeply.

Only a formal longitudinal study can tell us what the long-term effects of such projects are upon the participants, although research exists to suggest that participation in arts activities in prisons has a positive effect on reoffending rates. For example, Merron Mitchell (Vice Principal, Offender Learning, The Manchester College), speaking at the Cred/ability International Conference: *Effective Interventions in Prison Arts* at the Institute of Education on 6 September 2014, stated that 'only 26% of prisoners involved in arts during their sentence reoffend compared to 58% who aren't'. The men involved in this project clearly communicated to us some of the short-term effects, telling us that immediately afterwards, in amongst the pride and happiness felt about what had been achieved, there were also strong feelings of sadness. For some participants this deep sense of loss is akin to a sudden bereavement, exacerbated by the oppressive and claustrophobic nature of the environment. What happens to these feelings of loss if left unaddressed? What impact might these feelings have upon the men without the supportive presence of the Playing for Time team? One man in particular (in response to the question, 'Would you do it again?') wrote, 'the feeling of negativity after the play finished puts me off doing another in-house project' (Anon., Feedback 2013). In a diary entry the day after the final performance Scott himself says, 'All the time we were doing this theatre production us lads were just normal lads and now it's all over we are just untrusted criminals again' (Scott 2018: 220). Even Scott, whose enthusiasm for the project and burgeoning interest in drama is clear from his diary entries, is compelled by his feelings in the immediate aftermath of the project to state, '[I]f the chance came up to do this again, as brilliant, humbling and unbelievably exciting as I found this to be, sadly, I wouldn't do it again' (Scott 2018: 220). Though Scott later reconsidered this view, he did so within the context of a conversation about the lasting effects of the drama project that took place whilst editing his diary. What of the men who are not given the opportunity to have that conversation and reconcile their feelings about their experience? Does the absence of the time, space and support to contextualise their feelings of sadness within the broader, more positive outcomes of their participation consign them to a different emotional journey with a less uplifting ending to the experience?

Previously in his diary, Scott tells us that, as the production week approaches, he has developed 'faith in the team' (Scott 2018: 218). By his own admission, he approached the project with trepidation because it required that he push himself out of his 'comfort zone' to 'do something I normally wouldn't do at all' (Scott 2018: 211). The project had allowed him to risk putting his trust in others and see that 'faith' rewarded. He was not alone. For many of the men this positive experience of working with other people revealed the potential benefits, not just of being accepted themselves but of also accepting others and being part of a team. One such benefit, immediately evident, is a greater sense of well-being. In *Happiness: Lessons from a New Science*, Richard Layard states, '[i]f we really want to be happy, we need some concept of a common good, towards which we all contribute' (2005: 5). One man indeed says that his favourite part of the process was 'working as a whole company' (Anon., Feedback 2013). Another says, '[w]e became a good ensemble which helped me to perform the play as part of the team' (Anon., Feedback 2013). Other men agree that their attitudes towards others have changed and that mixing with other people 'broke down barriers' and allowed them to feel more 'comfortable' talking about 'life and other things' (Anon., Feedback 2013). Layard confirms that '[w]e are inherently social and our happiness depends above all on the quality of our relationships with other people' (2005: 8). In *Drama as Therapy, Theatre as Living*, Phil Jones takes this concept even further and states that '[t]he festive act of people coming together through drama and theatre is seen to have social and psychological importance' (1996: 3).

Jones observes that this is in part because theatre can 'bring people together and [...] deeply affect their feelings, their politics and their ways of living' (1996: 4). In light of the impact that this particular aspect of the work could have on the men in the future it seems important, if not essential, to capitalise on any such personal development and harness it in a positive way, rather than allow it to disappear into obscurity once the project has ended.

In my role as prison tutor, I was able to spend further time with the men after the 2013 project as they completed portfolios for their accreditation. As memories of the project began to fade against the backdrop of daily prison life, thoughts of an exit strategy for the project began to form: an extended process that would give the men space within which to explore and discuss their experience in a supportive environment and provide a 'buffer' between the drama project and life back on the wing. The aim of any such strategy would be to make the transition back into everyday life in prison a smoother one that filled the 'void', as one man called it, left in the wake of the abrupt end of the experience (Anon., Feedback 2013).

In the first three years of Playing for Time's work in HMP Winchester, a drama tutor in the prison had worked with prisoners who took part for two weeks after the production had ended. The tutor ran mini-projects that allowed the participants to make use of the skills they had acquired by, for example, producing in-house documentaries. In the third year of the project, the prison also introduced Safe Ground's 'Family Man' programme,[1] delivered by the drama tutor with prisoners who had taken part in the annual theatre production. This programme also utilised the participants' new skills by using role play, and provided a transition back into the 'outside world'. It was not an explicitly reflective exercise by design and whilst the group would have discussed the project and what they had achieved, this was not the sole focus. By 2013, however, no provision for any post-project work, reflective or otherwise, was in place other than a one off visit from members of the Playing for Time team to gather feedback from the prisoners who had taken part. In the intervening years, getting the prisoners back into work and education (within the prison) as quickly as possible had become of increasing importance to the prison staff. Over the course of time, pressures on staffing and budget cuts, plus changes in policy and delivery of prison services that directly impact the day-to-day prison regime, all played their part in relegating the feelings of the prisoners far down the prison staff's list of priorities in favour of getting things back to 'normal'.[2] For practitioners, in this case the Playing for Time team, the lack of support and resources for a more holistic approach to the prisoners' experience from within the prison regime itself makes attempts to continue to work with them once the project has ended complex and difficult.

Despite the challenges, however, there was clearly a need to provide an opportunity for the prisoners to talk about their thoughts and feelings about the end of the project. Reflecting on the effects of the experience might alleviate some of the sadness recorded by previous participants. In other words, as one man would suggest, it could provide a 'drama detox' (Anon., Feedback 2014). Drawing on my professional background, I felt that the therapeutic benefits of creative writing could provide an exit strategy that would go beyond simply talking about the experience even though conversation would remain an important part of the process. In his article, 'Writing about emotional experiences as a therapeutic process', James Pennebaker states that '[t]he mere expression of a trauma is not sufficient. [...] [G]ains appear to require translating experience into language' (1997: 164).

In this case, the 'trauma' is not the experience of the project itself but rather the removal of that experience from the day-to-day lives of the prisoners: the trauma of loss. The project runs for nine weeks – a long time for prisoners who are living one day at a time. By the final performance, the prisoners have been spending the whole of each day in rehearsal with the Playing for Time team and many feel this loss from their daily routine very deeply.

With this in mind, and remembering that the conversations I had with Scott were initially triggered by his own writing, I felt the aim of the exit strategy – to provide an opportunity for reflection and processing the work – could best be facilitated by translating the experience into the written word. This would allow for an appropriate therapeutic experience, and, therefore, for gains to be made in the way that Pennebaker describes. Whilst the decision to encourage the men to explore their experience via writing was partly instinctive, it was also an approach supported by research into what is referred to as 'expressive writing' (Pennebaker 2009: 264). This is a form of writing in which participants are encouraged to write about their deepest thoughts and feelings in relation to particular events or experiences. As Pennebaker tells us:

> [...] an increasing number of studies have demonstrated that when individuals write about emotional experiences, significant physical and mental health improvements follow. [...] in general, writing about emotional topics is associated with significant reductions in stress.
>
> (1997: 162)

Research into the use of expressive writing in a therapeutic context suggests several key reasons why expressive writing works:

> Not talking or writing about an important event is a form of emotional inhibition that can cause long-term stress [...].

> [...] Expressing or exposing emotional upheaval can result in 'emotional changes' that lessen trauma and reduce anxiety therefore 'helping improve daily functioning'. Writing encourages 'self-regulation' of emotions [...].

> [...] Writing results in 'cognitive changes' that help people 'make sense out of confusing or upsetting events in their lives'.
>
> (Pennebaker 2009: 268–69)

Expressive writing is an art form that encourages autonomy in the writer as it serves as a tool for generating feelings of power and control over the world around us, a benefit that many writers would identify with. As the author Terry Tempest Williams has said, 'I write to imagine things differently and in imagining things differently perhaps the world will change' (2001: 6). However, this is not the only way that writing can be used to empower those that feel disempowered. Megan Hayes describes how:

> [w]riting expressively gives us a sense of relief and is often a helpful reaction to experience. [...] When participants wrote with a chosen positive emotion in mind this appeared to foster a sense of progress in the writing [...] i.e. the writer made plans of action beyond the page.
>
> (Hayes 2015: 1)

By encouraging the men to write soon after the project ends, the drama project becomes the 'positive emotion' in mind when writing. By writing through the lens of this positive experience they are more likely to feel the sense of relief and progress that Hayes describes, thus experiencing some sense of control at a moment of emotional disorientation.

When the opportunity to trial such an exit strategy arose the following year (in 2014, Playing for Time returned to the prison to stage their next production, *The Fight in the Dog* by Rib Davis), I was still in contact with Scott as I continued to work as a tutor in the prison's Education Department. Scott was pleased to be nearing his release date, but sad that it would not allow him to take part in that year's production. I decided to run my idea for an exit strategy past Scott. Did he think it would be a good idea to run some sessions with the men after the project, I asked, allowing them a chance to both talk and perhaps write about it as he had? Scott thought the sessions would be a good idea but wasn't so sure about the writing: 'Personally, I'd love to do something like that [but] some of the lads find writing difficult', he told me (Appendix 1). Scott's insight was well founded. As Morrisroe states 'Poor literacy is prevalent amongst young offenders and the prison population. 48% of offenders in custody have a reading age at or below the expected level of an 11-year-old' (2014: 7).

My experience as a teacher, particularly in the prison environment, meant that differentiating tasks to suit different learning styles and levels of literacy was embedded in my everyday practice. The fact that writing exercises would be more of a challenge for some than others was not, therefore, a reason to discount using them. I would, however, have to be sensitive to the men's individual needs in this respect. The absence of formal assessment would be the key to the success of any writing exercises. This certainly supported the choice of an expressive writing approach. As Pennebaker and Sexton state, '[o]ne of the critical features of the expressive writing paradigm [is] an absence of feedback' as any perceived judgment could encourage a negative model of what is referred to as 'social support', particularly when working with those who already feel judged and inhibited by a lack of literacy skills (2009: 269). I was keen not to judge or assess the writing that the men would produce. However, whilst a lack of judgement may be essential to the success of writing exercises in this context (when the purpose is to offer a form of relief and release in the midst of emotional upheaval), it seemed appropriate to offer a platform for feedback should the men wish to receive it, particularly as positive feedback would almost certainly build their confidence.

Having decided upon an approach, it was also necessary to consider what topics would be used as stimuli for the creative writing workshops. I felt the workshops should exploit the potential of the fictional stimulus, i.e. the play, as engaging with this would provide deeper reflection upon the process. As author and writer-in-residence at HMP Maghaberry, Carlo Gebler stated when speaking about the 'moral benefits' of reading and writing:

When you read or listen to a narrative you leave yourself and become someone else and you see the world through their eyes and feel what they feel. When you finish, you are not the same person you were before. You have learnt something.

(Gebler 2014)

Feedback received from participants in 2013 confirmed that for some men, including Scott, the project had sparked an interest in storytelling and fictional narratives that had not, to date, been awakened. Talking about the play they had performed (*Our Country's Good*), Scott said:

The writing … was brilliant. It draws you in. You think it's real. I had to remind myself it was make believe. I've never read fiction – I don't like it. But, because this was putting me in there it made me think, 'You know what? I could believe this.'

(Scott, reflections, 2013)

Another man, when asked what his favourite part of the process was, said, '… the dress rehearsal because everything became real life' (Prisoner S., feedback, May 2013). Another said, 'I wasn't so much pretending to be the character, but living the character on the stage' (Prisoner J., rehearsal diary, April 2013). Further comments from the men also suggested that the experience of entering a fictional world within the context of a performance had been beneficial to them in other ways relating to their own identity and other personal issues:

[…] it helped me step out of my own shoes and into the character.

(Prisoner L., rehearsal diary, April 2013)

I felt free on stage.

(Anon., feedback, May 2013)

Another said that theatre in prison was a good thing as it provided 'an avenue of expressionism [sic], understanding, feeling and hopefulness…' (Prisoner J., feedback, May 2013).

As 2014's project approached, arrangements were being made for that year's play to be written in response to workshops that the director would run with a small group of prisoners in West Hill, HMP Winchester. The play that evolved was set in 1914, marking the centenary of the outbreak of the First World War. It told the story of a young man who was imprisoned as a conscientious objector. The subject matter had the potential to throw up many interesting issues for debate and discussion. Themes such as faith, patriotism, loyalty, individuality, personal strength and, of course, the nature of imprisonment would inform the men's performances during the production but might also encourage some interesting personal journeys too. The focus of the post-project sessions would, therefore, be the new ideas the men had about themselves, their abilities, their beliefs, principles and potential as a result of taking part in the production. The exit strategy would also aspire to provide a tangible legacy of the project for the men who took part – something to exist beyond their memories, something they could revisit and use to remind them of what they had achieved. This legacy would be their responses to the project, written down and preserved for posterity, in the manner of Scott's diary from the previous year. As Scott observed about how his own diary will function:

To look back on, as a snapshot of a past life… I'd like to read it in fifty years' time, if I'm still knocking about.

(Scott, reflections, 2013)

The first stage of the exit strategy workshops was to give the men the opportunity to share their initial responses to the project. They made positive comments about what they had gained from the experience, often relating to a growth in confidence and a recognition that the project had brought, as one man said, 'different characters off the wing together' (Anon., feedback, 2014). When asked when they felt most empowered during the process, the majority of men cited variations on the theme of being 'on stage' with one saying he 'loved [...] taking on different roles'. He added that he found 'pretending to be someone else for a little while' made him feel better (Prisoner P., feedback, 2014). Jones indeed suggests that 'the taking on of an alternative identity through drama may have a therapeutic element to it' (1996: 5). He goes on to describe how:

> expressing problematical material and emotions through the arts changes the relationship to the problems or feelings. [...] the creation of fictive representations of emotions [is] useful in the healing process of therapy.
>
> (1996: 9)

In this case, the opportunity to explore a fictional world through the eyes of a character had provided the men with the means through which to also explore their own feelings and identities. When asked what characters they identified with and why, responses included: 'Blane ... because he stuck by his beliefs' and 'George ... because he had it hard but was strong' (Anon., feedback, 2014). In Jones's analysis of the use of role play in dramatherapy he comments that an individual's identity is 'constructed through the roles they play in various contexts' (1996: 196). The men, it could therefore be argued, recognised aspects of the fictional characters' psychological make-up that they themselves could identify with. But, how does this entry into a fictional world become an opportunity for personal development? Consider again Gebler's statement on the power of both reading and identifying with fiction: 'You understand, then you articulate what you understand' (Gebler 2014).

By adopting a character and viewing the world from that character's perspective the men were able to explore different identities, making connections between the roles assumed both in their own lives and in the fictitious lives of the characters they were playing. This provided an opportunity to review their attitudes towards others. Layard tells us that empathy and understanding have to be learnt and practiced, particularly if they have been omitted in what he refers to as 'the education of the spirit' in childhood and adolescence (2005: 201). Assuming the perspective of a fictional character affords the opportunity for such an education because, when playing a role, identity becomes a more fluid concept, as Jones explains:

> When involved in drama or in enactment, an identity is shifted. [...] The individual does not respond or act in the way they usually do. They do not consider themselves to have the attributes and qualities normally ascribed to them.
>
> (1996: 202)

By virtue of this process, the participants are, therefore, presented with an opportunity to see the world through a different lens, to learn empathy and understanding that ultimately leads to an improved sense of well-being because, as Layard concludes, 'our happiness depends profoundly on our attitudes [towards others]' (2005: 200).

Identifying this potential for personal development and transformation serves to pull the negative feelings being experienced by the men into sharper focus. As with the previous year, the 'high' experienced after a successful run of performances was quickly followed by the reality that it was over. When asked, 'how did you feel after the performance week?', responses ranged from, 'bored', 'disappointed it had finished' and 'a bit low' to 'sad', 'gutted it's over' and 'depressed' (Anon., feedback, 2014). Noting that for several men the moment during the project when they felt 'most disempowered' was 'at the end' reminded me of the powerful, emotional reaction Scott had had when the project ended the previous year.

In the event, the sessions ran weekly for six weeks, beginning the week immediately after the last performance. The men who had taken part were invited to attend, voluntarily, to talk about their experience. The men were required to return to work and education immediately after the project ended, so the sessions were run at lunchtime to make it as easy as possible for them to attend if they wished. Unfortunately, this meant the sessions also clashed with the only time when the men were able to leave their cells, associate with each other, make telephone calls and use the yard outside to walk, exercise and get fresh air. Being able to run the sessions also depended entirely on staffing on the wing itself, as this dictated whether the men were unlocked during this period in the first place. Before the sessions even started, just two days after the project had ended, two men had already been transferred to other prisons and the logistics of including another man who was housed in a different part of the prison were insurmountable. Of the remaining eight men, four were on a compulsory all-day course for the first session. Despite all these obstacles, over the six weeks, all of these eight men came along to at least one session, with a core group of four attending every session. Of these eight men, it's worth noting that two of them had, by their own admission, been very difficult to work with for the duration of the rehearsals. They had, in what was already a particularly challenging group, been very resistant to all aspects of the process and shown little evidence of enjoying themselves. Their strong personalities had allowed them to both dominate and intimidate the other men and, at times, even the students. I was more than a little surprised when they came to the post-production sessions on the first day. Interestingly, one of them brought with him photographs of his baby daughter to show me and the group, a gesture that generated an impromptu conversation amongst the men about the responsibilities of fatherhood and the difficulties of being a dad 'on the inside'. It felt to me that this was the first time he had demonstrated any evidence of vulnerability or desire to 'belong' to the group. The time taken for him to reach this point was such that it hadn't occurred until after the production had ended. I was, therefore, glad that the post-production sessions had allowed him to have this experience and bond with the other men, albeit briefly, despite the project now being effectively over. The other of these two men would go on to attend several sessions, even missing his lunchtime jog around the yard to do so, and ultimately wrote a short piece about his experience in which he noted: 'I had a rough start but when I got into it I had a great time'. He went on to state: 'My confidence grew with the more performances I did'. He was not the only man for whom the final few performance days offered the first signs of enjoyment and commitment to the project, but I was pleased that the post-production sessions had given him an opportunity to acknowledge that to himself and others.

As the sessions progressed, photographs and audience reviews of the performances were provided for the men to look at and read. Poems were read and discussed and questions such as: 'Is theatre in prisons a good thing?' were posed. Gradually, writing exercises were introduced that allowed the men to explore the impact that the project had had upon them whilst they readjusted to life in prison without the routine they had become used to over the previous weeks of rehearsals. In many cases discussions turned to the future, often because this was the direction in which the men themselves took the conversation.

The material that was produced reflected the individual responses of the men to both the project itself and the follow-up workshops. From letters and character studies to poems that engaged with both the subject matter of the play and plans for the future, each man found a way to express some element of his experience in writing, as Scott did a year earlier. One poem called 'Inappropriate', written by Prisoner J. about the drama project itself, ends with the words: 'Oh how I wish I was doing it now', a sentiment that serves as a reminder that an exit strategy, no matter how carefully constructed and facilitated, can't entirely eliminate the sadness experienced by participants when projects such as these end. Nor, perhaps, should it aspire to, as experiencing and processing that sadness is, arguably, a vital element of moving on from a powerful, transformative event. However, that line also reminds us that providing a platform from which to express that sadness will always be a valuable enterprise, particularly if it allows the participants to utilise new skills and interests they have developed.

With this in mind, it was important to ascertain how the men themselves had responded to the use of writing tasks in the sessions.

When asked for their thoughts on the post-project sessions, the men who took part offered their own comments on the writing experience:

It's really good to express yourself and to write how you feel.
(Prisoner D., feedback questionnaire, June 2014)

I was interested … because it would be nice to show to my son.
(Prisoner L., feedback questionnaire, June 2014)

I enjoyed it because I was writing a poem … I will continue to write on my own.
(Prisoner J., feedback questionnaire, June 2014)

When considering that the men were, with one or two exceptions, initially reluctant to commit any of their thoughts or feelings to paper, that some hadn't written anything on paper for many years and that the majority had never attempted any kind of 'creative' writing before, these comments offer evidence of the benefits of introducing expressive writing into the post-project sessions. Seeing their own writing – about their own experience – on the page allowed the men to consider not just what they had written but how the act of writing made them feel. Engaging with what is felt in response to the act of writing, as opposed to digesting a critique of the writing itself, also promotes independence. Being encouraged to view the process of writing – as opposed to an external critique of the product – as the key component of the exercise allows participants to continue writing without the need for intervention from the practitioner. This does, of course, require the initial guidance and encouragement to be carefully mediated in order not to create a level of dependence unhelpful to the process of moving on. Where this is achieved, an individual then requires only the basic tools of pencil and paper to participate in the physical act of writing on their own, having been given the inspiration and confidence to write in the first place. In an environment where autonomy over one's own experience is in short supply, and where so many activities are supervised to some degree, the relative freedom to write how, where, when and about what one chooses becomes a path to independent and autonomous participation.

The comments from the men who took part in the sessions also suggest what is, perhaps, of most importance to them, and mirrors Scott's assertion that '[h]umans don't like being cut off' (Scott, reflections, 2013). The men were asked for their reasons for coming or what they enjoyed most:

> … interacting with the people who took part … I enjoyed drama and I wanted to carry on talking to others about it.
> (Prisoner J., feedback questionnaire, June 2014)

> Discussing what went well in the play made me feel good.
> (Prisoner D., feedback questionnaire, June 2014)

> Talking things through … reminds you of the fun you had.
> (Prisoner C., feedback questionnaire, June 2014)

As Pennebaker says, '[t]ranslating important psychological events into words is uniquely human' (1997: 165). If we recognise the humanity in each of the men, regardless of personal history and context, it becomes clear that providing time and space for the men to express what has happened to them is not an optional extra for a transformative arts project, but a basic human need that must be fulfilled.

In his diary, after the first performance of *Our Country's Good*, on 30 April 2013, Scott wrote: 'That was truly unbelievable and one of, if not *the*, best nights of my life' (Scott 2018: 218). A year later, Scott reflected again on his own experience:

Once it ended I felt a little empty, almost like I'd reached a dead end. I was afraid that I would never get that feeling again. But, during the process I was asked to keep a record/ diary of the project and being able to explain the experience to others was an unbelievable achievement. It has opened so many doors for me.

(Appendix 1: 208)

With the passage of time it is perhaps inevitable that memories of their time as performers in an ensemble will, to some extent, fade. However, a platform for reflection, self-evaluation, discussion and self-expression after the experience can provide a legacy of the project for those that take part that is both positive and tangible. As Scott says:

[…] because I have written it all down and kept the results I have a part of my life that I'll never forget.

(Appendix 1: 208)

This was a small-scale trial and there was not, unfortunately, a drama project in HMP Winchester in 2015, meaning that it was not possible to expand upon this exit strategy model further at the time. That said, the outcome of the trial in 2014 suggests that there is scope for more exploration of creative writing as a successful exit strategy. It can be distressing for all those involved, participants *and* practitioners, to return to the status quo having experienced the transformative effects of such a project. If a process exists to facilitate the transition from prisoner to performer, then the importance of marking that transition at the end of the process must surely be recognised. As one man who took part in the 2013 drama project said afterwards: 'You need closure. You need the wrap party' (Anon., feedback, 2013).

As this introduction to his diary comes to an end, the last word should go to Scott. Just as his words inspired the idea behind those first post-project writing sessions, so they also reflect something of how the process works, what it can mean and his hopes for his own writing:

Now you can wonder what the atmosphere would be like in your own head even if you weren't there. I suppose that's what good about reading. You can put yourself there even if you weren't there. I hope that's what people get from it anyway.

(Appendix 1: 207)

References

Davis, R. (2014), *The Fight in the Dog*, unpublished.

Gebler, C. (2014), 'Keynote speech', *Cred/ability International Conference: Effective Interventions in Prison Arts*, London: Institute of Education, September 6.

Hayes, M. C. (2015), 'Towards a positive psychology of creative writing', in M. C. Hayes and S. Nicholls (eds), *Creative Writing Lab: Developing Models for Creative Writing in the World*, York: St John University.

Jones, P. (1996), *Drama as Therapy, Theatre as Living*, London: Routledge.

Layard, R. (2005), *Happiness: Lessons from a New Science*, London: Penguin Books.

Mitchell, M., (2014), 'Effective Interventions in Prison Arts', *Cred/ability International Conference*, Institute of Education, London, 6 September.

Morrisroe, J. (2014), *Literacy Changes Lives: A New Perspective on Health, Employment and Crime*, London: National Literacy Trust.

Pennebaker, J. W. (1997), 'Writing about emotional experiences as a therapeutic process', *Psychological Science*, 8:3, pp. 162–66.

Pennebaker, J. W. and Sexton, J. (2009), 'The healing powers of expressive writing', in S. B. Kaufman and J. C. Kaufman (eds), *The Psychology of Creative Writing*, Cambridge: Cambridge University Press, pp. 264–72.

Safeground (2015), *Programmes and Services: Family Man*, http://www.safeground.org.uk/programmes-services/family-man/. Accessed 23 June 2015.

Scott, (2018), 'From the Fishbowl to the Sea: A Nine Week Journey', in McKean, A. and Massey-Chase, K. (eds), *Playing for Time Theatre Company: Perspectives from the Prison*, Bristol: Intellect, pp. 209–223.

Tempest Williams, T. (2001), 'Why I write', in C. Forche and F. Gerard (eds), *Writing Creative Nonfiction: Instructions and Insights from the Teachers of the Associated Writing Programmes*, Ohio: F & W Publications, pp. 6–7.

Notes

1 'Family Man is an intensive group-work programme for men and young men in prison using family relationships as a vehicle for developing skills essential to education, training and employment, while challenging attitudes and thinking and contributing to desistance from crime. The programme utilises drama, fiction, group discussion, games and written portfolio work to support students to develop and maintain their family relationships' (Safeground 2015).

2 See Chapter 2 for further details of the impact of cuts and changes to prison budgets and education provision in the eleven years of staging productions at West Hill, HMP Winchester.

Appendix 1

Scott and I had several conversations in which he reflected upon his experience of the project and the diary entries that he wrote. These are extracts from conversations that took place in October 2013 and April 2014.

Q: What did you think was in store when you signed up to the theatre project?

A: When I joined I thought I would be behind the scenes, I didn't know it would be acting. I was horrified at first but then I thought, 'I can do this!' I did a music concert in the main prison a few years ago and was a lead singer and I remembered that I had enjoyed the applause.

Q: Why did you write so much in your diary?

A: To look back on, as a snapshot of a past life. It was part of the project and I think you might as well do everything. I'd have my tea and then write about what I did that day. When I read it, I see good days and bad days but, even on the bad days, I learnt something.

Q: What do you think about the final edit?

A: Some of it's quite funny. When you read it back like this it looks more 'story' like. There's a lot there. How did I find that much to write? Because it was something I'd never experienced before, a once in a lifetime experience. To experience that in that context with those people, 'cos I'm never coming back here again. I'd like to read it in 50 years' time, if I'm still knocking about. I didn't expect it to end up like this [edited and printed out]. Something good's come out of it.

Q: How does this version compare to the original?

A: It hasn't made it any worse, put it that way. (Laughs). Now, you could wonder what the atmosphere would be like in your own head even if you weren't there. I suppose that's what's good about reading. You can put yourself there, even if you weren't there. I hope that's what people get from it anyway.

Q: How has it felt, reading through what you have written?

A: It brings it all back. The other day I read through the script as well [*Our Country's Good*]. It's surprising how much I remembered. It's nice. You read [the diary] and you think, 'I remember that, I enjoyed that', or 'I must have looked a right tit'.

Q: How do you feel about other people reading it?

A: It's a strange feeling. Everyone's self-critical and I thought, 'Why would anyone want to listen to something I wrote?' I really hope they enjoy it.

Q: In your diary, you said that you would be 'gutted' when the theatre project ended and that you felt 'sad' when it was over. What could be changed to make the end of the project easier on the men that take part?

A: It is abrupt when it ends. It's a bit regimental. We go back to what we were doing and it's all cut off and done. Humans don't like being cut off. It's like two people on the phone and while one person is speaking the other crashes the phone down.

Q: Would you have found it helpful to do something straight afterwards? Perhaps some group writing based on the project?

A: That's a difficult question. A lot of lads go back to their jobs. I would but a lot of the lads had different levels of commitment to the writing. Some of the lads find writing difficult. Personally, I'd love to do something like that.

Q: What should the diary be called?

A: From the Fishbowl to the Sea. Prison is like a fishbowl. In the fishbowl you're trapped but you can see where you want to be. When you first come to prison [they] lock so many doors. [You] feel the walls closing in on you. The theatre is the net that scoops you up and puts you down the toilet. Rehearsal is being flushed down the toilet and being in the sewer (you don't know what's going on, where you are or what's going to happen – it's scary). The sea is performing, being free for a bit. It didn't feel like I was in prison.

(October 2013)

Once it ended I felt a little empty, almost like I'd reached a dead end. I was afraid that I would never get that feeling again. But, during the process I was asked to keep a record/diary of the project and being able to explain the experience to others was an unbelievable achievement. It has opened so many doors for me – it's all a little overwhelming, considering I didn't realize what I was writing at the time.

Also, because I have written it all down and kept the results I have a part of my life that I'll never forget.

(April 2014)

Chapter 11

From the Fishbowl to the Sea: A Nine-Week Journey

Scott

Monday 4 March 2013

I have begun to be a part of the maddest thing I have ever tried and that's become part of a theatre production called *Our Country's Good*. It involves a load of lads from West Hill and students from Winchester University. To be honest, a lot of us from the prison probably have a preconceived idea what the students will be like and no doubt the students the same!

Tuesday 5 March

Today has been our second full day and we also got to meet all the other students from Winchester University. We started with a few stretching exercises and games and stuff. In the afternoon we learnt a song that's going to be in the production and it's quite good. I chose to go into the section of the group to sing the harmony and the rest just sang in the normal way. When it came to putting it all together it sounded really good. I really enjoyed today very much. Tomorrow we're going to be given a copy of the entire script. I think that from tomorrow each day is going to get a lot more challenging.

Wednesday 6 March

Our third day today and it started as it always does with a few stretches and we went through the song we started yesterday. I am really enjoying this drama group and am very glad that I decided to get myself involved in something like this as it gives me the chance to put myself out of my comfort zone and do something I normally wouldn't do at all.

Thursday 7 March

We have been doing quite a lot of acting in today's sessions and it's been really enjoyable. I find all the acting a fun and taxing challenge. When I am given a part to play I try to learn those lines to the best of my ability and aptitude. Doing things like this helps me with my short-term memory and gives me something to look forward to. It also gives me a great sense of achievement at the end of it all. I am learning things like how to read lines and how to remember them the best way. I think that this is definitely something that I would like to carry on once I am released from here as I find each day a challenge in a new and enjoyable way. We also get to meet other people from different walks of life to the lads in here with me!

Tuesday 12 March

Today we did some more script reading and acting, which I am finding easier the more we do it. We were also given the new words to the second song. I was in the harmony group again as I always find that singing style more of a challenge. One thing that I learnt today is that my singing voice is much more versatile than I first believed it to be.

Thursday 14 March

Today didn't start well. First there was no electric and also no heating in the gym where we rehearse. We had a short meeting in the association room while we waited for them to sort things out. Also, today the director, Marianne, took each of us in turn to have a little talk about what kind of role we would like to have. I told Marianne that I would love to take on the role of either Midshipman Harry Brewer or even Robert Sideways, one of the prisoners, because they are both very challenging roles and I would learn a lot along the way if I was to play either of these great characters!

Tuesday 19 March

The week began like every other with all our exercises and stretches. I am really looking forward to every day starting and I will be gutted when it's over because it will mean life will return to normal. The one thing I took on board and learnt this week was that I am rather good at doing harmonies in singing. I enjoyed it very much. It's a bit of a shame there's no solo singing in this because I would love to have volunteered to do something like that. Oh well, maybe next time!

Wednesday 20 March

Today we did a bit of practice acting out one of our scenes and, to be honest, it's not at all as easy as it is made out to be. I learnt a lot of little tips from the other actors like putting our voices out into the room and saying words and sentences in the right way depending on the way they are written; like, are they said in a happy, sad, angry or confused way and also to add a facial expression to that sentence!

Thursday 21 March

We were cast today and I got the part of … Midshipman Harry Brewer and I am so happy and pleased that I got one of the parts I actually asked for. My mentor is Mollee, one of the students, and that is really good as well as she is so helpful, positive and happy. I really am so excited and I cannot wait till the end of April to do these plays. The person that is playing my love interest in this production is a student and that's good too because she is also very happy and helpful.

Tuesday 26 March

This week is mostly going to be taken up by going through all the play songs and, most importantly, the scenes in each of the acts. I am really looking forward to all my parts in the play because from my point of view Harry Brewer has a really big part in this production. My character is a very disturbed individual and I will do my best to portray the disturbed mind of my character, which won't be easy. I can't wait to get out there and get on with it. I am learning more about my character all the time and I have a fantastic mentor. She is really encouraging. I just hope I can help her as much in the next few coming weeks.

Wednesday 27 March

More practising of each scene has been the order of the day. It's nice to see how things are slowly coming together as each day passes and how much of an effort a lot of the lads are putting into this project. My lines are really coming together. I am finding some of them harder than others but I find repetitive reading the easiest way of learning them. Some of the other lads don't read their lines that much and I find myself worrying about the other scenes but that's only a couple of them. Most of them are doing really well though and it's all going to be good, I hope.

Thursday 28 March

We started today with the songs, warm ups and more rehearsals. I have had a real problem with a toothache the last few days but I'm pressing on regardless and doing my best.[1] I am starting to see what all these focusing exercises are all about with the breathing and number games etc. They are helping me get my brain into gear for the start of each day. My mentor has really helped with my monologue and all my other lines and I don't think that I would be as far along with my scenes without her.

Tuesday 2 April

My tooth is really hurting today and I am trying to do everything I can to take my mind off it. Today it's been so bad. I found it hard to concentrate on anything at all. I hope by the end of the week my problem has gone, literally.

Wednesday 3 April

We went over act one, scene one today and it's really coming along great! I think it's great to see all the scenes take shape and slowly come together. Unfortunately, I can still see that there are one or two people that aren't making as much effort as all the rest but, on the whole, the lines are going well.

Thursday 4 April

Today we went through the first scene of act one again and we also did scene six of act one. I also had my tooth out today, so I don't have that mad ache anymore. As each day passes, this production is becoming more and more real. All of our costume measurements are done, tickets are all done and a reporter has been in.[2] It's things like that that drill it home as to how long it is till the first full dress rehearsal and then the first proper performance. I am beginning to get that feeling of nervous tense excitement and it is a very strange feeling. I am learning to control it with the breathing techniques I have learnt at the start of the morning sessions – onwards and upwards!

Monday 8 April

We went through some of our most important scenes today and practised movement and where each character will be in relation to each other during those scenes. Myself and Chris, who plays Ralph, did scene four of act one today, which is called 'The Loneliness of Men'. I also went through scene seven of act two where Harry and Duckling go rowing. I hate the way my character treats Duckling especially as he's meant to love her. Harry is very draconian with Duckling and bullies her, but I think that Duckling also gives him mixed messages and doesn't really tell Harry how she feels until it's too late and he dies. I am really starting to understand the character I am playing and his demons that are tormenting him in his mind. To me it sounds, and kind of feels, like he is always looking for reassurance from others that he isn't going mad. I also believe that he desperately wants to be loved by Duckling and accepted by the officers as a friend.

Tuesday 9 April

Scene one, act one is really becoming learned and meritorious and I am glad that I am part of it. Everyone, or nearly everyone, is really starting to take this seriously. We also did a weird activity that involved making our character relate in some way to an animal that we had chosen. At first I found it hard to find any connection between the two at all. I started to get it after a little while. I found it a bit strange relating an animal to a human in a serious manner but in a very mad way me and my mentor began to get what it was all about. I don't think my mentor gets how much her support in this production means to me. Acting in front of so many people is massively alien to me and her encouragement is largely what's keeping me in this play. I genuinely believe I wouldn't have what it takes to get through this as, believe it or not, confidence doesn't play a big part in my life.

Wednesday 10 April

Act one gets so much better each time we do it and everyone is using their script less which makes it even better. I can't get over how fast each day is going. I have got to know some of the students really well and I consider them friends not just some other actor.

Thursday 11 April

These days of rehearsal are really starting to gather pace and get interesting. Watching each scene as it takes shape and hearing all the songs sound a lot better each time we practise them gives me a lot of pride and shows how much work people have been doing on this production and how much we all (well, nearly all) want this play to go without any hitch at all. I am gonna do my level best to say my lines and act as my character and I just hope that all the effort I am putting into it will show on curtain up night. I hope to God that my mind doesn't go blank and I fall flat on my face. I have never had the patience or the desire to become involved in something as deeply serious as this so I sincerely hope that I can do my part justice and make the whole team and cast proud!

Monday 15 April

Things are really moving along now as we are going through each and every scene one at a time. I sometimes find it hard to believe that we have come so far and have got through as much as we all have – it's brilliant.

The next couple of weeks are going to be taken up by continuous scene rehearsals and portfolio work. A lot of us are putting ourselves well and truly out of our comfort zones but I almost don't want this production to end and I'll be quite sad once it's all over. One thing that does worry me is my mind deserting me on curtain up night. That is the only thing that I am massively fearful of. I am teaching myself all the drama breathing techniques and any other techniques that I can pick up to help with stage fright. I don't want to let any of the cast down and I definitely don't want to let my mentor down because she has done so much for me and getting it all right on the night is like my thank you for all the help I have been given.

Tuesday 16 April

What a day it's been today with all manner of feelings and senses of achievement. It was the first day that we actually did a complete run through of the whole play. The biggest scene for me is my monologue. I wanted to do so well with it and get it right without my script. The first part of it went really well but then it all started leaving my brain bit by bit and I had to start asking for a few prompts. I felt like I'd let myself down a bit. I so want to do the very best I can and do this part justice. To be honest, I'm going to be gutted once this play is over because I have made some great friends. I have also discovered an activity that I love to do and will try my best to carry on once I am out of here.

Wednesday 17 April

As the days go by I can't quite believe how fast each week is going and that by this time next week the first show is only five days away. The nerves and the adrenalin are starting to come through in a big way! We had a few run-throughs of a few of the scenes and it's always good to see how well the cast members are getting on with their lines. Watching each scene as it gets better and better with every practice makes me look forward to the show even more. The monologue is the only scene that I continually worry about and picture myself falling flat on my face with but I am teaching myself to get out of this self-defeating frame of mind by positive thinking, positive self-talk and repetitive scene reading. The more I do these things the better this important scene is going to be on show night.

Thursday 18 April

Today I was running over my monologue with one of the ladies that help out part-time. We worked on my actions, movements and how I have to say certain sentences. Are they in anger, scared or in a passive way? I have to be honest and say that I am absolutely shitting myself (sorry for the language) about doing this monologue and getting it spot on and doing my best without falling on my face or even forgetting my lines. There's definitely a nervous excitement among the lads and I feel that it's going to be a really good experience being on stage and acting for the public and friends and family of the students and lads. I don't know if my parents are going to be at the Thursday night show. I sincerely hope they are so they can see that I am using the time I am in here as best I can. I am always pushing myself to do the things that take me well out of my comfort zone. This play definitely has and I am going to write this up as a massive achievement. I'm determined to do it outside.

Friday 19 April

Today has been the first day that we did virtually no work on our scripts at all as this morning was taken up by the 'get in'. All the set, technical equipment, seating and, the best bit for me, all the cast's costumes! The thing that really stood out for me was how close to the stage all of the seats for the audience are. Seeing that has made it all the more acute and intensified – people are going to be so up close and personal. Next week is all about rehearse, rehearse, rehearse and things are getting very serious. I can't reiterate enough how scared I'm beginning to feel and as each day passes it gets a little worse than the day before. I seem to be using breathing exercises more and more every day whenever I feel a little strange or uptight. I am going to use these techniques to get me to the end!

Monday 22 April

We all tried on our costumes this morning and they are all really good and it makes each character very different. Some of the costumes people are wearing look so uncomfortable but I think that in those days the clothes were never made to be nicely fitted and comfy. This is definitely going to be an interesting week.

Tuesday 23 April

Now we're on our last ever week of rehearsals. All the work we do this week makes the five shows the best they can be. I didn't quite realise how much work comes with a task like this and I would usually steer clear of anything that would put me in the spotlight, so to speak, but over the last five to six years I have put myself forward to do more of these activities so I don't feel alienated from this kind of stuff. I want to do things like this outside of prison so I can meet new people, new friends and give me the big boost I need in steering away from crime, drugs and my old life. I believe this process has been a big help in my recovery and my new life. I really want to become involved in theatre on my release and I also want to become a lot more involved in music and singing as well. Because boredom has played a massive part in my past, it's activities such as this that will give me extra tools and hobbies I can use to fill time that I would usually spend going out committing various crimes and doing a variety of substances that I no longer need around me or in my life anymore. Whenever I put my mind to it and do my best at things I know I can do well and when I have done well it gives me even more of an inner confidence boost to try other things that I never normally do. Although I cannot wait for the shows next week I am going to be so gutted that this has to come to an end.

Wednesday 24 April

I am slowly becoming more positive and comfortable doing my difficult scenes. Some of the cast are trying to stay with their scripts as big comfort blankets and that's not good at all.

The one thing that's getting to me is scene six, act two. I seem to be finding this one scene a real struggle and what is even more annoying is the fact that it's not anywhere near my most challenging scene but I am still forgetting four or five lines and I am getting very frustrated by this. Even if I use breathing exercises I am finding it hard to do. Well, tomorrow is a new day and I am going to sleep on it and start again tomorrow.

Thursday 25 April

This week has been very eventful and quite nerve-wracking to say the least. I don't know why but I have been a little off the boil and I've had a bit of bother with scene six of act two and also a bit of trouble with my monologue and it makes me a bit annoyed. The thing that gets to me the most is that I know all my lines well and I'm still getting a bit muddled. I'm not going to begin worrying just yet because I still have four days to read, read and read through my script and drill all my lines into my head.

Today is my 36th birthday and what made it all the more special is that I found out today that my mum and dad are going to be there for the very last show on the Thursday evening and this performance is going to mean more than anything to me.

Friday 26 April

Today has been a very strange day and I have been a bit pissed off because I can't seem to get scene bloody six right and the more times I get it wrong the more and more annoyed it makes me and I shouldn't be feeling like that. Breathing techniques and other exercises give me the time to settle myself and calm my nerves but I had a really bad day today and it has made me very frustrated. The last two or three days have been a little bit hit and miss for me and I can't understand why because I have put everything into this. I refuse to let one scene get the better of me and beat me.

When we rehearse it on Monday everyone will see that I have worked on nothing but my script all my weekend.

Monday 29 April

Today has been absolutely unbelievable. I am so pleased with myself and the work that I put into this over the weekend. When it came to my monologue I was in the zone and I completely smashed through it word for word. Then it came to scene six of act two and again I tore through it word for word and I proper kicked arse. At the end I walked off feeling on top of the world.

Now that the first live show is upon us my insides are churning over and over and I am trying to replace the feeling in my stomach with excitement and not nerves or fear. Surprisingly, when I have been using the breathing and nerve-calming techniques over the last day or two they have been working an absolute treat helping my nervousness and keeping me calm. I believe and hope that after tomorrow night has finished most of us are going to be well used to the inner thoughts and feelings of failure and we can all beat them in the most positive way possible.

I have told a few of the team that on our last day together I have written a poem that I intend to read out to everyone before we all go our separate ways and go back to our daily lives.[3] The last day will be an emotional time – probably for some of us lads as well. I hope we all come together and do our absolute best.

Tuesday 30 April

OMG is all I can say about the first show. That was truly unbelievable and one of, if not *the*, best nights of my life. The feeling I had on the inside was the best buzz I have genuinely had and I could easily swap my old drug using life for that any day of the week no problem at all.

When 6 p.m. eventually came my insides were churning so badly I honestly thought that I would be sick but there was no going back. When we got to the end I felt better than I have ever felt in my life. All the cast were on such a high. I felt like I had achieved something massive and so did everyone else and it was beyond amazing.

We all had a few minutes with the audience and a lot of young ladies approached me telling me that my Harry character was compelling to watch and they asked how long I had been acting for. When I told them it was the first time and I wasn't a student, I was an inmate, they were so shocked. They told me that I should definitely take up acting.

I am going to join the ex-prisoner drama group at the university as soon as I can because I have seriously got the bug for it and I have learnt so much. I can't truly get out on paper the exact way I am feeling inside this very moment. The thing is, feelings on paper are very hard to express and, as hard as I try, I cannot think of the words to express my inner deep feeling of excitement at the next two and a half days to come and how I am actually going to be feeling on the last night. My parents are going to be there, so I am holding a little bit inside so I can put 100% and all that I have left inside me to make our last performance the most spectacular of them all.

I have faith in the team, the cast and all the hard work and passion that each of us has shown over the last nine weeks. Boy, this has definitely been the most special journey of my life so far and I am glad I did it with all the people that have been involved in it.

Wednesday 1 May

Another successful day of acting which I have enjoyed to the max. Both of today's shows were brilliant. I can't believe how much the audience was responding to tonight's show. It really made the night so much more special. The sense and feeling of achievement we all get at the end is so humbling. A few members of the audience came up to me at the end and told me how much they enjoyed it. Not only that, but three very pretty girls also said to me that they were moved by the 'Harry Brewer sees the dead' scene and how amazing it was to watch me take on the role and do it so well. I felt like I was on top of the world. I also felt a little big headed being told by three very good-looking ladies that they actually enjoyed watching me act; it definitely made me feel human again, and not just a prison con and number. Today I completely forgot that I was in prison and it was unbelievable. It felt like we had had a day out and that properly made me feel good.

A big thing that has come out of this process is the typical stereotyping of inmates within this environment; that we all sit around doing sod all except play play-stations and sleep all day. The amazing success of this production will maybe help people see that some of us lads in here do take stuff seriously and are willing to do our absolute best, especially when we see that others are willing to give up their time and make an effort to get out of us the potential that most of us choose to keep hidden away because nobody believes that anyone who commits crime has any kind of talent like this.

Annie has sparked something off in me that I never thought I would be able to do in a million years. When I finally get released I am definitely going to sign up to the university ex-offenders' theatre group as I have genuinely found a hidden talent that I never realised existed inside of me and I refuse to waste that.

Thursday 2 May

What can I say about today's two shows? Firstly, this may sound a little bit ungrateful but, the show to the inmates, I'm sorry to say, I couldn't wait for it to be over. Once it was over I was so relieved that I could refocus my thoughts to the very last show. My nerves, adrenaline and stomach were very much raring to go and get started. Before our last focus game I had to read my poem out to everyone. I couldn't wait to see and hear the team's reaction to what I had written about everyone. I asked to give a copy to everyone that wanted one and even some of the guys wanted a copy of it. It was nice to know it wasn't all that bad really.

Just before the show started my insides felt like they were going to burst through my chest. Before I knew what was going on the audience started to pour through the door and we were all, 'Hats on and let's go!'

Just before the first scene started, me and Duckling were both looking for where our parents were sitting so that we knew where they were. My mum and dad were both sitting at the corner of down stage left where Harry loses the plot and falls down in the 'Science of Hanging' scene in act two. So, 'That's exciting', was my very first thought. When I did my monologue, 'Harry Brewer sees the dead', my mum and dad were sitting directly in front of me, so that made it very special to me.

The last show sadly came to an end and we had about fifteen minutes at the end to talk to our parents and families. It was nice to meet the families of some of the students. Their praise and enjoyment of the show made the journey over nine weeks all the more special and important. Mum and dad were extremely proud. I felt so good that, even though I am where I am, I could feel good about something that I have done instead of making them feel let down and disappointed in me all the time.

Now I am back in my cell feeling really good and very sad all at the same time. The only thing that is left is for the equipment to be packed away and go back to the university and that is so sad.

I feel privileged to have taken part in something so brilliant and the friends I have made and the achievement of it all has been the biggest privilege of my life. I can't stress enough how grateful I am to have been the character I was. I just hope what I have done has entertained people and that I played Harry Brewer as best I could.

Friday 3 May

Today has been the saddest day I have ever had in prison as it felt today like we had to say goodbye to friends and that was the hardest of pills to swallow. None of us lads in the prison are allowed to stay in contact with any of the students we made friends with. A large team of adults that have all worked hard together for two months and have created something very special and come together to create a piece of art have had a decision taken away from us that we are all quite capable of making. Are we untrustworthy inmates or are we human beings? All the time we were doing this theatre production us lads were just normal lads and now it's all over we are just untrusted criminals again. This may sound like a rant or that I am having a go but I am just being honest about how I feel. The play is over and all us inmates are just a load of criminals and it's all gone a bit retrograde.

I understand that all the students that took part have studies to do etc. but are the students being told no contact because of that or is it purely because we (prisoners) committed crimes and the staff think that we would do something as disrespectful as lead them astray?[4] I sincerely hope it isn't for any of the reasons I suggested because if the chance came up to do this again, as brilliant, humbling and unbelievably exciting as I found this to be, sadly, I wouldn't do it again.

I am going to look into acting when I am released though because of how amazing it has made me feel. The only thing left to say is that I am so proud of my involvement in this fantastic production and all I can say is the most immense thank you to everyone. I hope when I get out I will get into this again through the Playing for Time Theatre Company and Winchester University!

***

Six months after the project had ended, whilst editing his entries, Scott explained what motivated him to write his diary:

'I wasn't going to do it. It's not a usual thing for men, is it? Girls like to keep diaries. But once I started, I ended up writing more and more. I said to other lads that weren't writing anything, "You're not really into this, are you?" But I thought, sod it, I'm gonna give this a go. It was part of the project and I think you might as well do everything. I'd have my tea and then write about what I did that day. When I read it, I see good days and bad days but, even on the bad days, I learnt something. Now I think, I did that well so why don't I do that again? It's a written photograph. I can look back on it in 30 years as a snapshot of a past life.'

Then he paused, thought for a moment, and added:

'You asked me to do it, so I did it'.

* * *

Notes

1 Poor dental health is a growing problem in the prison environment and Scott's experience of debilitating toothache is far from unusual. As a report into *Oral Healthcare in Prisons and Secure Settings* by the British Dental Association states:

> The demand for dental care in secure settings is rising in conjunction with a steady rise in the overall prison population. The prisoner profile is a familiar one across the UK; mainly young men from deprived backgrounds with low literacy and educational attainment, often with a history of drug-taking and alcohol abuse, underlying poor nutrition and heavy smoking. Overall maintaining good oral health is a challenge.

Equally difficult for prisoners such as Scott is gaining access to timely and consistent care, as the BDA further states:

> The nature of the prison environment makes the delivery of care as equally challenging as the oral health of the patients. The population present with incredibly high needs and there is a high number of emergency and urgent cases, however, access or following through with care as a prisoner isn't always easy. [...] Prison patient records are notorious for getting lost in the ether meaning the next dentist is back at square one. Accessing services even when in a facility can be difficult with the problems of moving and treating patients securely in an over stretched system. (British Dental Association [2014], *Oral Healthcare in Prisons and Secure Settings*, https://www.bda.org/dentists/policy-campaigns/research/patient-care/prisons. Accessed 8 July 2015.)

2 Scott is most likely referring to a reporter from the publication *Inside Time*, a monthly national newspaper for prisoners and detainees. The Ministry of Justice places heavy restrictions on other, external publicity for projects of this type in other media, such as local and national press. In 2008, the then Justice Minister Jack Straw responded to reports of a workshop being run by the Comedy School of London in HMP Whitemoor by instructing it be cancelled, saying, '[p]risons should be places of punishment and reform, and providing educational, training and constructive pursuits is an essential part of this. But the types of courses available – and the manner in which they are delivered – must be appropriate in every prison' (Straw 2008). This led to the National Offender Management Service confirming that governors of prisons would be briefed on the need to 'take account of the public acceptability test [in relation to prison classes]' (Tibbetts 2008).
3 See Appendix 1.
4 The rules of the prison, and therefore the project, stipulate that the student volunteers must have no contact with the prisoners once the project has finished, either whilst they are still in prison or after release. Any contravention of this would constitute a serious breach of security and prevent the students from working in the prison again, something that they are made aware of before the project begins. However, the students are allowed to work with the on-campus drama group; prison security staff know about this group and the professional context it operates within.

Appendix 1

Best Wishes and Hopes – a poem by Scott

I wish this production did not have to end,
I hope amongst you guys, I've made some good friends.
I wish you all well in the future to come,
I hope you're all proud of the work that we've done.
I wish the students the best in their exams and degrees,
I hope you'll pass with flying colours in these.
Marianne, your direction was great, and sometimes a pain –
but I hope that it made the lads feel human again.
Annie, you're a legend, you're second to none –
thank you for the opportunity, and all that you've done.
Steve, you're the man, and your coffees were great –
they kept me awake and in a right lively state!
Kass, you've been brilliant, a great member of staff –
my portfolio will help steer me along the right path.
All other staff, you've been ace to the last,
doing this has helped me turn my back on my past.
To the mentors, good luck in all that you do,

most of us couldn't have done this if it wasn't for you.
On a personal note, I have more things to say
before the end of this last final day.
Mollee, what a star you've been –
a rock that helped me through.
You've given me drive, presence, belief I'd be good at whatever I do.
Thank you for your patience and guidance to the end,
I couldn't have done this without you and now you've made a good friend.
Thanks to all the West Hill lads, and the Hearn ones too.
Good luck with all your future goals – I hope they're successful for you.
Thank you all for the experience,
I wish you all well for future success.
Regards to all, take care, be good,
But most of all God bless.

References

Straw, J. (2008), 'Straw condemns prisoners' stand- up comedy course', *The Guardian*, 21 November.

Tibbetts, G. (2008), 'Al-Qaeda terrorist taught stand-up comedy at top-security prison', *The Telegraph*, 21 November.

Chapter 12

Over the Wall Theatre Company

Fiona Mackie with members of the Company

Desistance is […] 'more than just an absence of crime. Desistance is the maintenance of crime free behaviour and is […] an active process in itself […] it involves the pursuit of a positive life'.

(Maruna, in Bilby, Caulfield and Ridley 2013: 5)

T his final chapter offers an insight into the ways in which taking part in a campus-based drama group has impacted on people who are working to overcome disadvantage in their lives.

Background

The group was set up in 2009 by a company of third year undergraduate drama students who had taken part in Playing for Time Theatre Company productions in HMP Winchester. The aim was to continue the Playing for Time project beyond the prison walls and to help combat recidivism through providing structure and a supportive environment for the participants after their release. In that first year, a company of six men successfully toured a devised show about substance abuse to Young Offender Institutions and to a centre for young people Not in Education, Employment or Training (NEET). In addition, each individual completed a locally accredited NCFE Level 1 Award called Taking Part, which sought to credit their creative collaboration and team skills. From a desistance perspective, the most significant marker of the project's success was the participants' desire to continue for a second year. The original students had graduated and moved on with their lives and it was left to Annie McKean as the Artistic Director of Playing for Time to bring the group fully under the Playing for Time umbrella and give it a sustainable footing. As part of my work for Hampshire Learning, I had collaborated with the original student group to create the Level 1 Award. Annie Mckean was subsequently able to secure the continuation of the group with a Community Learning grant from Hampshire County Council. The grant allowed for the creative performance work to be led by a new group of students each year whilst a paid tutor provided continuity and educational support alongside. Continuity was essential; the tutor was able to hold weekly sessions beyond the academic year, which provided vital structure for the participants, especially those in recovery from substance abuse who needed to look forward to a regular and absorbing activity. The grant also funded transport so that the group could meet at the university where they could use the specialist performing arts studios on campus.

The initial group was recruited through workshops held in a hostel for ex-offenders near Winchester (with the majority of participants being new to Playing for Time and new to drama). In the project's second and subsequent years, further outreach workshops were delivered in a number of hostels and homeless centres in the area, opening the group to anyone experiencing disadvantage, including women, and not just those who had served prison sentences.

By 2012, there were eight regular members who had made a strong commitment to the future of the group and had started to express ideas and theatrical ambitions for themselves. To meet this growing confidence and desire for more challenge, Deborah Gearing, an experienced theatre professional and established playwright, was engaged to take the group forward. Fiona Mackie continued to provide educational support whilst students joined the group in a volunteer capacity to maintain the important link to campus life. As a consequence, the group was relaunched as Over the Wall Theatre Company and a fresh and ambitious programme developed to reflect this appetite for new experiences, understanding and self-determination. Over the Wall's subsequent achievements included performances of two adaptations of local mummers' plays, an adaptation of Buchner's *Woyzeck* at the Theatre Royal in Winchester, as well as making *SPENT*, their first film. The group also worked on a project as part of Hampshire's contribution to the First World War commemorations. As an illustration of the group's growing sense of agency and desire to make their voices heard, each member wrote a letter as part of the *14–18 Now 'Letters to an Unknown Soldier'* project and joined the 21,439 people who gave words to this memorial.

Climbing the wall

Taking part in Over the Wall has given the participants, whatever their background, the opportunity to connect with others in a new and different context. To be able to use the specialist performing arts studios and to perform in the professional theatre spaces on the campus has the additional benefit of making participants feel valued and welcomed at the university. In the dialogue that follows, they discuss the impact on their work and sense of self when they interact with the undergraduates who join them each year to support and facilitate work. The experience of walking around the university campus, having a tea or coffee in one of the cafes and meeting a variety of different people gives them a sense of connectedness to the wider world.

The offer of a season of free tickets to attend performances at the Theatre Royal in Winchester (and later Forest Forge and the Nuffield Theatre) has had a significantly positive impact on the group, not just in widening their experience of live performance, but in contributing to a growing sense of belonging to the creative life of the local community.

The invitation to perform *Woyzeck* at the Theatre Royal sent an even stronger message of acceptance, providing support for the emergence of new identities that reflect a growing confidence and positive outlook on life. All this is important to support the 'pursuit of a positive life' (Maruna in Bilby, Caulfield and Ridley 2013: 5) against the continued challenges of daily life during a time of austerity measures, which have impacted on those requiring welfare support or facing prejudice and discrimination in the labour market.

Whilst Over the Wall is certainly not a self-help group, focused on people's past and present difficulties, the sharing of personal experiences forms a natural part of the creative process and preparation of a role. Aspects of life experiences are reflected through the choice of themes for workshops, play scripts and devised performances. Plays like *Woyzeck*, *Hamlet* and *Mother Courage*, as well as more contemporary plays, such as Jez Butterworth's *Jerusalem*, Willy Russell's *Blood Brothers* and *Bouncers* by John Godber, have provided inspiring creative spaces to explore themes that chime on a personal or group level. Similarly, theatre has provided a forum to share ideas about social inequality and injustice and for these issues to be debated with audiences in post-performance discussions.

Additionally, it has been important that participants develop more sophisticated acting and theatre skills, and opportunities to test these skills in performances with increasing demands, widening the group's understanding of the language and conventions of performance. Thus, traditional forms like pantomime and mummers' plays, as well as ritual and epic theatre, have informed the development of skills and offered inspiration to the devised work.

What follows is a dialogue that has been arrived at through a number of means that have formed part of Over the Wall's evolved working method (respond, improvise, devise, discuss, script, revise and script again). It is an edited conversation put together by Deborah and Fiona from several recorded conversations with the whole group and with individual group members. Every opinion expressed by each individual began as a verbatim comment, with contributors expressing personal thoughts in their own voices, but have been edited by the speaker as part of the writing process. It was very important that everyone taking part in this conversation had as much agency to approve/disapprove their words as any other contributor to this book; they are no longer the subject, but have true autonomy. They own this chapter, having become, over time, the true masters of their own voices.

Dialogue with the group

FIONA: As you know, we are writing a chapter about Over the Wall Theatre Company to conclude the book Annie is putting together...

ANNIE: It seems right to me to end the book with a glimpse into the ways in which engaging in drama and theatre can support people who are focused on overcoming difficulties in their lives. Over the Wall has always been about imagining a future, whatever your past has been. The book is about the theatre projects which have taken place in HMP Winchester; Over the Wall Theatre

Company came out of this work. As you know, this campus based drama group has been an inclusive group which has enabled people to take part who have experienced different challenges – from coming out of prison to coping with addiction, homelessness and mental health issues. Everyone involved with the group has been delighted with your successes over the years – not just as performers, but in the way you have rebuilt your lives through volunteering, training, employment, abstaining, offering friendship and support and making a commitment to each other and the work.

FIONA: The theme for the chapter is something called desistance …. Can I ask does that word mean anything to anyone?

VINCENT: Is it about stopping something?

FIONA: That's right Vinnie … and in the context of the book it's about the process of stopping offending behaviour and how a person might start to see themselves differently, reimagining themselves, if you like, so they can adopt a crime free lifestyle. It would be good to talk now about how Over the Wall may have supported any of you to make that sort of change – whether you have served a prison sentence or not.

BAZ: It started personal for me, how to deal with what was going on in my head just leaving prison, coming off drugs.

FIONA: You were a founder member.

BAZ: Yeah, when it was a student project … and being with students helped get it clear in my head. Acting … it was a public statement to myself, a commitment – you wanted them, the students, to trust you. The play was about drugs and I had to act out being high – an acid flashback. I had experience, I knew *how* to do it, but I did not want to do it again.

FIONA: And did taking part in that performance help you make a change?

BAZ: It helps you commit to it, not to relapse. I didn't… I didn't want to let anyone down, wanted to prove I could get back on the straight and narrow. Acting out means you don't have to go through it in life.

FIONA: So, it is like a public statement to live up to?

CAZ: It's like you are holding on to the students' belief in yourself.

NIGEL: Seeing the younger students [the young offenders in the audience of the toured show] concentrating and enjoying the performances made me feel good. I'm enjoying it, they're enjoying it, and it makes me feel better about myself. We are reflecting back enjoyment. It also opened my eyes a bit to what drugs can do to people.

BAZ: Yes. The beginning for me was when we performed for the young offenders. (COMPOSING HIS THOUGHTS) To try to help someone else not to make the same mistakes

NIGEL: There was a discussion after the play – I was buzzing with the feeling 'if we could change just one person!'

BAZ:	And if a couple of young people did change their opinions because of what we did. If you can do that … change someone else, stop them going through it, then it's worth it.
FIONA:	Are you saying that creating and performing the play has made you feel good about yourself when perhaps you did not hold yourself in very high regard?
NIGEL:	It helped me to express myself and speak out sometimes. People used to use me, now I have got more confidence, and through other group member's encouragement, to show I was not to be messed with. I can trust people here.
BAZ:	And I have gained real self-esteem from working with others … a core group to share all the work we have done and develop together. That's been really important.
JAMES:	Over the Wall has given me more confidence. It's helped me meet people who have turned their own life round and they help me with mine.
CAZ:	It's given me space and time dedicated to me and my needs, dedicated to making me think and choose. I have found choosing so difficult but I am learning.
FIONA:	Has the change been significant enough for you to see it – can you see yourself as a before and after?
NIGEL:	I look back on the plays I have done and think: 'I could never have done this five years ago'. It's showed me what I can do. Before, I wouldn't engage with people. I do now.
JULIA:	Yeah. I was so shy. I sat on the side for about a year, said I wanted to help out, that's all. One day I was asked if I wanted to join in with a game and I just thought: 'Get involved – it's the only way you're going to get any good at it'.
DEBORAH:	You took a big leap of faith!
JULIA:	(BEAMING) I did. Yes. Now I am better able to chat to people. Helps with outside life, it does. Walk into any situation outside of here now. Much better.
JAMES:	(TRIUMPHANT) What I think is, none of us are in prison. None of us are in a court case, so we are a success.
FIONA:	James has prompted me to ask a difficult question. Do you think of yourselves as living a crime-free life?
CAZ:	(LAUGHING) I believe I am less criminal than our political leaders! GROUP LAUGHTER, FOLLOWED BY A THOUGHTFUL PAUSE
BAZ:	Yes, I do think I am living a crime-free life. And why? Err … self-discipline – abstaining from drugs, err … not socialising with old associates, not craving illegal drugs, avoiding situations involving drugs. I obey the law and I have a good woman keeping me toed to the line. Over the Wall has given me something to think about and do each week.
FIONA:	Crime-free, Vinnie?

VINCENT: (THOUGHTFUL PAUSE) Well, all my offending was related to drugs as well. I had entered prison as an addict and it took me so much effort to get myself clean, almost a year, and I had started to realise that the next time would be harder. But I'd not decided on a future life of abstinence at that point; I think I held onto an idea I could take drugs every now and again. So yeah, in that respect I was still holding on to my old identity when I started drama.

FIONA: So to what extent was your involvement with Playing for Time in prison a step to finding a new identity?

VINCENT: Well, I was only 10 months clean when I first got involved with the prison play. I didn't approach the project thinking it would benefit me by helping me change my behaviour but I saw it as an opportunity to learn something and get involved in something which is the opposite as to where drugs had taken me, you know … withdrawal, isolation and detachment. I was still feeling empty and I saw it as an opportunity to reconnect with the environment. That's what I was interested in.

FIONA: And did it help you?

VINCENT: Yes.

FIONA: Can you say how?

VINCENT: I was like Baz, after the first successful performance I could see what this was about. I think that's where I started making changes. The person before was a drug addict person, and after, a person who doesn't do drugs. The important thing is that things have come from me, not a drug addicted me. If I can't do certain things then I should be able to accept my limitations, not retreat behind the artificial comfort of drugs.

FIONA: So what do you think Over the Wall has contributed towards your onward journey away from the life of an addict and offender?

VINCENT: I think actually it's been about participation and participation is about learning to acknowledge your failures as well as successes. It's taken all year for me to see that – a year to change and acknowledge difficult things – you know, to put myself in a position where I can fail. Success is doing something you couldn't do a year ago, that's moved you on. For anything to be successful it has got to be hard work; you've worked for it, you have gained integrity for yourself. Not present a play and then go back and stick a needle in your arm every night.

FIONA: Is it anything to do with the praise? You have had so much applause and positive feedback from your audiences.

VINCENT: No. If I can't play an 80-year-old man successfully (HE SHRUGS) I'll accept that too and not be bitter about it. Acceptance is the key.

CAZ: You're telling me! Praise is hard. If people complimented me before I thought they were, you know, blowing smoke up my arse.

FIONA: Why?

CAZ:	Thinking nice things about myself was an alien concept. In the past, stealing was okay because I had nothing … I hated myself so I hated everyone else. Drugs helped a lot, so did the booze.
FIONA:	So what do you think Over the Wall has changed for you?
CAZ:	Doing drama [SHORT PAUSE] has given me a *skill* I can use. I have done lots of training – five courses and also the Freedom Programme but, in the end, it is all theory and none of it has made it into my life! At 48, I am still not as confident and assertive as I'd like to be … but I can play a role now when I am working, I can be enough of myself and enough of someone else to get what I want.
FIONA:	Do you mean in everyday life?
CAZ:	Yeah, keep the customer happy and it works for me. It's not me – all the messed up stuff. It's me playing a role. I've got this calm persona now.
FIONA:	It sounds like you learned how to use an element of performance to cope?
CAZ:	It's like I have taken things apart, seen things I just don't want to do anymore, I don't want to be the damaged little girl anymore; I can't cope with her and the world can't cope with her … she still there, she's still me, but I am doing something different now.
FIONA:	And can you handle the praise now?
CAZ:	(BIG HEARTY LAUGH) I am LOVING it!
FIONA:	Vinnie?
VINCENT:	If I can do it I'll accept the praise.
DEBORAH:	What about the plays? We've done some demanding and difficult work that's asked a lot of all of us. I'd like to know if anything in the plays themselves touched anyone.
CAZ:	*Woyzeck* had a profound effect on me. Don't really know why. Perhaps it was playing a proper grown up lady, one who loved, had sex, got murdered!
FIONA:	Deborah challenged you by casting you against the type of role you are used to playing.
CAZ:	That's right. I really don't see myself like that, it was hard. To get these men vying for her. Killing for her.
DEBORAH:	You captured her life force.
CAZ:	Yeah. She had passion and it's so totally away from what I am. It was so powerful.
ANNIE:	I think it's always been really important for you as a group to feel you are moving forwards with each new project. You performed *Woyzeck* in a public venue, the Theatre Royal Winchester, which was a big step.
DEBORAH:	That goes for me as well … the group has unlocked some plays for me that I wouldn't have approached by myself … panto and mummers' plays for instance – we look at the history and give things a context as I think that's important too.

CAZ:	The mummers' plays were a revelation! Something really chimed there ... the outsiders coming in to entertain ... Lords of Misrule and all that.
BAZ:	We were able to put a few social comments and topical jokes into the mummers' play and the panto too, which was fun.
ANNIE:	Having a playwright lead this group has been important for the development of Over the Wall – it has opened up a rich seam of material for you all to explore that has been really exciting.
DEBORAH:	We've certainly looked at a wide variety of play texts as I didn't ever want to impose on the group – I wanted to see what you would respond to, as well as give us all a slightly broader view of theatre. We might start with a scene from *Mother Courage*, for instance, and then use it as a starting point to explore something that has come out of the scene ... it might be about acting or theatrical style to start with, but the themes will always trigger something too and then we go with that. Some of you will stay with the script and others respond in your own words.
JAMES:	We've written a lot of our own words.
CAZ:	Deborah made us the translation of *Woyzeck* and the mummers' plays ... it gave us wiggle room.
JAMES:	We perform better when we express ourselves in our own words. But we were allowed our freedom.
FIONA:	And what about the students? They are absent from our gathering tonight – as term has finished and they have left the campus – but they are such a significant part of the Over the Wall experience ... I wonder if they contribute something unique to the desistance process?
VINCENT:	At first you look at the students and see them acting and playing around in ways that you can't imagine. Maybe you get a bit jealous or feel a bit like this is something I could never do, but they put you at ease and assure you that we go at a pace acceptable to us and compatible with our capabilities. It is humbling having to accept that there are people half your age that have developed a skill and that you have to learn from them.
BAZ:	Yeah, we learn from them and they learn from us – through our age and our experience. It's been an honour, I think, to be involved with the students.
JAMES:	It's a two-way thing.
NIGEL:	And when they first came to the hostel, the students were nervous.
VINCENT:	That's true. You don't realise how nervous they may be feeling as well.
NIGEL:	It's hard to get things going at the hostel, there's nothing to do so you are down all the time, there's the temptation to get sucked into bad behaviour if there's drugs or money around. So the students were pleased because some of us joined in.
CAZ:	It's a valuable exchange of cultural and social understanding for everyone – I think it teaches each of us to express ourselves to people we perceive as 'not

like us' which enhances our social confidence away from the group. And I think it breaks down the 'posh' barriers that many of us adults will have experienced and demonstrates to the older members that our ideas will be appreciated by others, regardless of our educational or fiscal background. For the students – it helps them find their feet in an adult, non-student, non-peer-based environment.

FIONA: Because you are outside the education system?

CAZ: Yeah, and it enables them to develop the skills that they will need to negotiate with other adults in life. And they are coming into a group ethos, and they have to work with that. They have to collaborate.

VINCENT: What worked was the dynamics of differences in generations and differences in cultures at play – and fortunately the working towards the end goal ensured a constructive interaction.

FIONA: Baz mentioned the importance of being part of a group. There is always some tension in group work. How has that been?

CAZ: To start, I was nervous about keeping it all in. After work when you are tired is tough, but sometimes we need to get it out there, have a look at it all round – see how you are going to deal with it.

BAZ: And it's never personal. We all respect we are all different characters in a way. It is good we are all different characters ... we can pool it all together, that's what makes it good.

CAZ: It's good because we have to respect, in the end, that everyone's got an opinion.

JAMES: We have disagreements but we are all back next week.

CAZ   That's right, James, we are all grown-ups. There's tolerance. We can't be firing off all the time ... we'd never get anything done and it wouldn't be a pleasant experience and that's why we come.

BAZ: (WITH A FLOURISH) The show must go on!

FIONA: With everyone going through a process of quite considerable and positive changes in your lives, it seems like a good time to end the discussion with a thought about where you see yourself now, what you see as your achievements, how you have redefined who you are?

CAZ: I saw the world as us and them but now I see myself more as part of wider society and I can own my culture and heritage too. I will say who I am and be damned.

JULIA: I have the confidence to mix in large groups now and take on any role in drama and not be afraid.

NIGEL: I can express myself better.

JAMES: We've started something that gives us confidence – to express ourselves in a controlled manner. We can all imagine the words as 'gobbledegook' – but we can use our imaginations to find what the 'gobbledegook' means.

BAZ: I enjoy the freedom of the whole process. I know what's going on with me. Some people might think I don't. But now it doesn't bother me they think I don't.

CAZ: In drama we can actually be anything. That opens you up to the concept you might be more than you have been.

Conclusion

Caz may have summed up in a few words what this chapter has sought to define: that drama can help the process towards desistance because it allows you not just to stand in the shoes of someone else but walk, run, dance and even sing! To stand in another's shoes is to imagine yourself making their choices, experiencing their power, sharing their suffering, hearing their words coming from your own mouth. In many ways Over the Wall has been all about the finding of voice, the giving of words and the freedom to communicate.

At the point when the group started its new chapter with Deborah at the helm, individual members of the group were starting to find some stability in their personal lives, with relationships and other networks such as the church, Alcoholics Anonymous (AA), Narcotics Anonymous (NA) and other agencies providing support, and progress being made with volunteering. It seemed timely to consider a new identity for the group and for this to be expressed in a logo. The phrase over 'Over the Wall' suggests an escape and indeed the logo could be read as such – a figure atop the wall, ready to make a triumphant getaway. With escape in mind, we offered the group a chance to uncouple completely from Playing for Time, thinking that in the spirit of fresh starts they may wish to end any clear link to the prison. The group declined, voting overwhelmingly in favour of full acknowledgement that the journey had started with Playing for Time in HMP Winchester. Far from wanting to put distance between themselves and their past, members expressed an intense loyalty to the group's roots, including those who had never been in prison. Everyone agreed with the idea that they were each emerging from a confinement of sorts, whether from isolation, serious mental illness, long-term unemployment or addiction, and that prison was both a metaphor and a fact. Armed with that knowledge, you can see that the members of Over the Wall, like the figure in their logo, no longer consider a wall to be a barrier but see it as a launch pad.

It has demonstrated to Deborah and me how the opportunity to contribute to and help shape an activity, and to experience the results of decisions made as part of the creative process, is one way in which a drama group like Over the Wall can support the progress towards desistance. The positive repercussions are many; taking part in performance demands commitment, the taking of responsibility and a substantial personal risk – it demands bravery. And with that comes rewards: the applause and praise, personal achievement, but more importantly the opportunity, as Caz so wisely says, to be able to see yourself in a new light.

Postscript

Since the retirement of Annie McKean, Over the Wall has come to an end, but the group continue to meet informally, to receive free tickets (through Deborah's network) and to be invited to participate in community events. Most group members have settled into full-time employment and others have found stability in other ways…. There has been a gentle transition into life without Over the Wall.

The final word goes to Vincent:

> There's no doubt that involvement in the Playing for Time and Over the Wall projects contributed to the change in direction in my life and I can't thank you enough for having faith, belief and a priceless insight into human behaviour (a person's ability to change), when they have lost belief and hope in themselves.
>
> (personal correspondence, 2017)

Contributors to this chapter: James, Nigel, Barry E., Julia, Vincent, Caz Nash, Fiona Mackie, Deborah Gearing and Annie McKean.

References

Bilby, C., Caulfield, L. and Ridley, R. (2013), *Re-Imagining Futures: Exploring Arts Interventions and the Process of Desistance*, London: Arts Alliance, http://artsevidence.org.uk/media/uploads/re-imagining-futures-research-report-final.pdf. Accessed 16 February 2017.

Vincent (2017), email to Annie McKean, 17 February.

Postscript

Annie McKean

In July 2018, just as this book was in the final phase of publication, I received an email from Richie, who played the lead in the 2010 production of *The Government Inspector*. He wrote to ask for another copy of the DVD of the play, as his son had used his copy as a frisbee and broken it! An extract from his email, below (shared with his permission), serves as a small but powerful example of how the impact of these projects can still be felt years later. Often we do not get to hear these stories, so it is a privilege to have heard from Richie and learnt some of what his involvement with Playing for Time meant to him.

> […] Please could I have another copy of the play? I've treasured mine for many years. Now when I feel a little low I pop it on and give myself a boost of confidence and success. […I am now] running my own building company; it takes a lot of time and attention but I've done very well with it, providing a good life for my loved ones. […] I put a lot of it down to my experiences in Winchester. Yourself, Bethan and Kate helped me with broadening my horizons and making me see that you can accomplish anything with time and hard work so I thank you for that – it's put me in good stead since I got out. […] I'm more than happy for you to include me in the book in any way shape or form – it's given me a bit of a spring in my step if I'm honest.

Notes on Contributors

Kass Boucher is a writer and teacher. She has taught in both further and higher education and currently teaches creative writing at the University of Winchester. Kass worked in the Education Department of HMP Winchester between 2012 and 2014 during which time she taught creative writing, English and functional skills classes. In 2013 and 2014, she also worked with Playing for Time Theatre Company to stage theatrical productions in the prison. In May 2015, her paper on creative writing in prison was presented at the 6th Global Inter-Disciplinary.net Conference in Croatia as part of the Experiencing Prison Project.

Deborah Gearing is a playwright, director, writing teacher and Royal Literary Fund Fellow. Her first play, *BURN*, was produced at the National Theatre and since then she has written for theatres and diverse groups around the United Kingdom. Together with Fiona Mackie she founded The Fuse, a project that focuses on collaborative writing and site-specific work.

Ann Henry is associate lecturer at the Open University (OU, since 1993). She tutors a number of Undergraduate (UG) and postgraduate (PG) psychology and Social Science modules and is one of the co-authors for a new OU PG module in Forensic Psychology. Having completed her Ph.D in 1997 at the University of Southampton (on self-discrepancy theory and adolescent self-concept) she has worked as a senior lecturer and research fellow at various UK Universities. In 2008, she completed an MA (Social Sciences, OU) and in 2009, she completed an MSc in Forensic Psychology at the University of Portsmouth. She has worked in an NHS low secure unit with offenders with mental health problems. She has facilitated University of Winchester level 3 UG students undertaking drama workshops at an NHS low secure unit. She has been an external examiner for B.Sc. (Hons) psychology degrees in the United Kingdom and also an external examiner for two mental health programmes in Ghana (www.thekintampoproject.org). Her research interests are varied and have also included ADHD, Dementia and phenomenological perspectives on inclusive education.

Fiona Mackie has been a professional playwright since 2004 and has written for BBC Radio 4, the Nuffield Theatre Southampton, and Musica Secreta. In 2011, she was commissioned by conflict resolution specialists Radio for Peace Building to write a radio series for Age Concern's Older Offenders Project (ACOOP) to help men of pensionable age who have served long-term prison sentences prepare for their release. In addition to playwriting, Fiona is a qualified teacher, was arts and media specialist for Hampshire County Council's Adult and Community Learning Department until December 2015, and is now a freelance Adult Arts Education and Learning consultant.

Annie McKean worked as a senior fellow in Knowledge Exchange at the University of Winchester and was artistic director of Playing for Time Theatre Company. She developed a portfolio of work on the BA (Hons) Drama degree writing and teaching modules in the areas of Applied and Community Theatre and Drama and Theatre in Education. She also taught on the 4-year BA (Hons) Education (B.Ed.) teacher training degree. Prior to this she taught on the B.Ed. and PGCE degrees at Reading University. She was external examiner on the BA (Hons) Theatre, Education and Deaf Studies at the University of Reading. Her teaching in higher education was preceded by several decades of work in mainstream education including advisory work for the Inner London Education Authority and Hampshire Local Education Authority and running drama departments in two inner London schools and one rural comprehensive. She is an alumna of the University of Kent with an MA in Women's Studies. In 2009, Playing for Time Theatre Company was awarded The MacJannet Prize for Global Citizenship (third prize) for undergraduate engagement in exceptional community initiatives. This prize was established by the Talloires Network which aims to recognise and promote community engagement and service in the university sector world-wide. In 2010 Annie was awarded an MBE in the Queen's New Year's Honours list for services to higher education.

Kate Massey-Chase is an AHRC-funded Ph.D. student at the University of Exeter, researching how Applied Theatre could support young people in the transition between Child & Adolescent and Adult Mental Health Services. She is an alumna of the University of Winchester (BA English & Drama) and the Royal Central School of Speech and Drama (MA Applied Theatre). She is a visiting lecturer at RCSSD on the MA Applied Theatre, and previously ran the 'Theatre for Change' module at St Mary's University, Twickenham, for their BA Drama and Applied Theatre, and worked as a research consultant for University of Wales, Trinity St David. Kate is also a freelance creative arts practitioner, across a range of educational and community settings. Her experience includes delivering theatre-based and creative writing projects with young migrants, recovering addicts, and mental health service users. She also delivers sex and relationship education and workshops on intercultural dialogue in schools.

Scott took part in the 2013 production of *Our Country's Good* by Timberlake Wertenbaker, directed by Marianne Sharp. He played Midshipman Harry Brewer. Scott's diary was awarded a Bronze Award for Nonfiction Writing by the Koestler Trust in 2014. The Koestler Trust Awards is an annual competition for the creative work of the securely detained. Scott is now working and has a fiancée and two small sons who are the light of his life. He has told Annie that taking part in *Our Country's Good* is something he will never forget and that the experience allowed him to remain positive until he was released from prison in 2014. He said that taking part in the play and achieving what he did made him realise that things he had previously thought he was not good enough to do were now all achievable. He has used the experience of the play as a stepping stone back into 'normal' life. He said 'mad as it is, I still do those breathing exercises when I get stressed!' He is delighted that he is now a published author with his diary and photographs appearing in this book. He is now thinking of writing his autobiography.

Marianne Sharp is a director, performer and teacher of theatre practice, currently based at the University of Winchester. After studying at Central School of Speech and Drama, she worked as an actor primarily in touring theatre in the United Kingdom and continental Europe, and as a director of youth and applied theatre projects (including several years creating theatre with young people at Theatre Royal Winchester; drama advocacy work with Winchester social services, and directing plays in Feltham Young Offenders Institution and Winchester prison). She holds a practice-based Ph.D. from Royal Holloway College, University of London, and following that (2011–15) trained regularly in Los Angeles with Rachel Rosenthal and her improvisation company: Extreme Theatre Ensemble. Arts Council England-funded projects include directorial/dramaturgical collaboration with Anna Fenemore/Pigeon Theatre, on *The Twice-Removed* (2010) and devising/performing *Nora and I* (2014), an autobiographical show in dialogue with Ibsen's *A Doll's House*.

Other performances include: *Memory is a Strange Thing* (2012, with Doug Hammett at ESPACE DbD, Los Angeles) and *Shift*, by Doug Hammett (2013, at Nye+Brown gallery, Los Angeles).

Pat Thompson worked in the state education sector as a teacher of primary school pupils for several decades before moving into higher education and working on programmes of teacher training and undergraduate and postgraduate history degree courses. Her specialist areas of research were women's history and Victorian social history. This included aspects of crime and punishment in the nineteenth century. She is currently working on the history of the hulks in which convicts were incarcerated between 1832 and 1868. Her research on women convicts undertaken in the National Archives in London underpinned the research which led to the writing of the play *Refuge* by Dawn Garrigan, 2003. She has published a number of books in areas of primary school history teaching including Tudor warships. She has had articles published in history teaching journals including *The Historical Association Journal* and local history journals including *The Portsmouth Papers* and the Hampshire Field and Archaeological Society.

Brian Woolland worked as a senior lecturer in theatre at the University of Reading, before developing a freelance career as a playwright, novelist and theatre director. His academic interests include early modern theatre and educational drama. Publications include *Ben Jonson and Theatre* (Routledge, 1999) and *Jonsonians* (Ashgate, 2003). He has led theatre workshops throughout the United Kingdom, Europe, the Middle East and Australia. For Playing for Time he wrote and directed *Stand or Fall* in 2008 (playtext published by Oxford University Press, 2014), adapted Gogol's *The Government Inspector* in 2010 and directed *The Fight in the Dog* by Rib Davis in 2014. He was awarded Arts Council England grants to write plays based on *The Iliad* (*This Flesh Is Mine*) and *The Odyssey* (*When Nobody Returns*), both co-produced by London-based Border Crossings and Ashtar Theatre of Ramallah, Palestine, and published by Oberon Books (2014). *This Flesh Is Mine* was previewed in Ramallah in May 2014, before a short run in London later that year. *When Nobody Returns* was first produced in London in October/November 2016.

Index

transportation, 154–155, 164
Trounstine, Jean, 12, 64

U
Ubu the King, 45–48

V
volunteering, 127, 129, 177, 230, 236
voyeurism, 49, 70, 130

W
Wertenbaker, Timberlake, 10, 29, 41, 47, 148,
151, 155, 158, 161, 165
Woyzeck, 228, 229, 233, 234

Z
Zedner, Lucia, 80